# MARK TWAIN'S

# & HOMES & LITERARY TOURISM

MARK TWAIN AND HIS CIRCLE SERIES

*Tom Quirk, Editor*

# Mark Twain's Homes & Literary Tourism

Hilary Iris Lowe

University of Missouri Press
Columbia and London

University of Missouri Press, Columbia, Missouri 65201
Printed and bound in the United States of America
5  4  3  2  1    16  15  14  13  12

Cataloging-in-Publication data available from the Library of Congress.
ISBN 978-0-8262-1976-3

∞™ This paper meets the requirements of the
American National Standard for Permanence of Paper
for Printed Library Materials, Z39.48, 1984.

Jacket design: Susan Ferber
Text design and composition: FoleyDesign
Printing and binding: Thomson-Shore, Inc.
Typefaces: American Typewriter Condensed Light and Bembo

Americans are obsessed with houses—their own and everyone else's.

—DELL UPTON
(*ARCHITECTURE IN THE UNITED STATES*, 1998)

There is a trick about an American house that is like the deep-lying untranslatable idioms of a foreign language—a trick uncatchable by the stranger, a trick incommunicable and indescribable; and that elusive trick, that intangible something, whatever it is, is the something that gives the home look and the home feeling to an American house and makes it the most satisfying refuge yet invented by men— and women, mainly by women.

—MARK TWAIN
(*MARK TWAIN'S AUTOBIOGRAPHY*, VOLUME I, 1892)

# Contents

*Preface*

When I began this study, I hoped that in understanding the history of literary house museums, I might discover exactly *why people go to them*. I thought there might be a simple answer, or at least a set of answers that explained what visitors—in all their varieties—were seeking when they went to a literary house museum. After thinking about these questions for several years, watching tourists, and reading scholarly accounts of tourists and their motives, I fear I have less of a sense of why people go to these literary museums now than when I started. In the meantime, however, I have become fascinated with how and why these literary places come to exist in the first place, and how they come to tell the stories that they do about American literature.

My decision to focus on Samuel Langhorne Clemens's houses was a practical and a fortuitous one. Sam Clemens may still be the most famous American writer.[1] If you are going to study American literary sites, it makes sense to study the sites associated with an iconic American. These are places where the experience of American literary tourism is heightened and where layers of interpretation are the richest because so many people have a stake in Twain. William Faulkner asserted that "Mark Twain was the first true American writer, and all of us since are his heirs."[2] He was so popular in his own time that there were numerous imposters who tried to make a living off his name and image.[3] His movements, thoughts on every subject, and remarks were covered in the press, and his houses were reviewed just like his books. Clemens's status as the "first true American writer" has resonance in his houses. As a result, the commemoration of Clemens through his houses has been both an ideological and a commercial enterprise.[4] There is money to be made by claiming, "Mark Twain slept here." Because Sam Clemens has been configured as the ultimate American writer and as "*the* American," the proliferation of his houses, and, as a result, the house museums devoted to him is in itself a cultural phenomenon worthy of study.[5] These sites provide a multiplicity of potential interpretations of Clemens, and they provide a way to understand the work of literary house museums seen comparatively through a single literary figure. His houses show how Clemens has been meaningful to vastly different communities over time.

Studying Clemens's houses was also practical because there are four houses today that are devoted to commemorating Clemens, and they provide an excellent sampling of the kinds of literary house museums that exist in the United States. However, it was fortuitous because spending time in Sam Clemens's houses was more rewarding than I could have imagined. Clemens's houses could not be more different. One is barely a cabin, one is a middle-class home, one is so grand that visitors have a hard time imagining Mark Twain living there, and one is so comfortable that no one wants to leave. Aside from their physical differences, these houses present four very different case studies. His birthplace belongs to the State of Missouri; his boyhood home belongs to the City of Hannibal, Missouri, but it could be argued that the boyhood home has always belonged to Tom Sawyer. Clemens's Hartford house is owned and operated by a nonprofit organization devoted to its preservation. Clemens's summerhouse—really his sister-in-law's home—Quarry Farm is the property of Elmira College and is part of the Center for Mark Twain Studies. These houses each celebrate the memory of Mark Twain, despite their disparate origins, management, and architecture. At each site, individuals and communities have sought and largely found ways to connect their place with the biography and literary production of Sam Clemens.

During my research on house museums and literary memory, I read a great deal of travel literature describing not just Sam Clemens's houses but literary haunts of all kinds. This study is not a meditation on elite letters and travelogues, but an account of how the people who founded and managed these places over the years have constructed interpretations of Sam Clemens through the places where he lived. Literary tourism and tourists are the subject of this study, but so are the resulting literary destinations. I wanted to understand how these places came to be and how they came to tell the stories that they tell. I wanted insight into their interpretive choices. When I speak of interpretation at these houses, I mean exactly how museums convey their meaning. I wanted to know how the sites and their managers have—with exhibits, signage, restoration, interior decoration, expansion, museum designs, narrative construction, and all the other tiny choices that add up to what visitors see when they arrive at the doorstep of a literary house—crafted a story about literature, writers, and the places where they have lived.[6] I looked for models of literary house museum histories, and it ends up that few such histories have been written. As scholars, myself included, struggle to understand why people go to these places, it is useful to think about why these places exist for them to visit.

What follows, then, are origin stories, and origins matter in the United States. Each of these historic house museums is bound, as Patricia West has argued about other historic house museums, by the particular exigencies of its origin.[7] As Faulkner's statement about Clemens reveals, writers, scholars, historians, tourists, and others have been obsessed with American origins. If all "American" writers come from Clemens—if he is their origin—then the sites that celebrate him are important. Perhaps because the United States is such a young country, the origin of American writers, historic figures, and events are particularly important. Understanding Clemens's origins is a way of understanding something larger about the historical narrative of American history and literature. Exploring the origins of house museums devoted to Clemens, then, is a way to understand the need for origins stories and how this need is played out in place and in literature—specifically at historic sites.

Since beginning this project, I have moved twice—once across country away from my own place of origin. The changes in my life that have most affected my thinking about house museums have been: becoming a home owner—being committed to *one* place—and volunteering at a house museum that I adore—the Rosenbach Museum and Library. As I have written the last chapters of this study, the thousands of tiny and large changes we are making in our own house have surrounded me. Our house is not a museum; it will never be open to the public. But it, like any house or house museum, is the culmination of decisions. And those decisions have helped remind me that each museum manager and preservationist, no matter his or her interpretive agenda, is working within a practical set of conditions. The question of which to repair first, the roof or the awful exhibit in the visitor's center, is akin to our own everyday decisions about wiring, paint colors, and drywall. I understand the limitations to which any person who works within an existing house is subject.

My time at the Rosenbach Museum and Library in Philadelphia as a volunteer has not only grounded me in my new home city, but it has made me a more thoughtful writer of these histories. The little house museum, where twice a month I volunteer and occasionally give tours, is so full of wonder to me that I have begun to understand tour guides who love the objects of their house so much that their history becomes hagiography. No tour guide knows all the answers to the questions that visitors ask, they often don't understand why the museum is the way that it is, and my tours, like most tour guides', are always biased toward my favorite objects. At the Rosenbach I've overwhelmed people with

Marianne Moore's reconstructed living room, Herman Melville's book-case, and William Blake's watercolor—no matter what they might come to the Rosenbach to see. But most of all, I see how each visit to a house museum is a layered performance: volunteer performing guide, visitor performing tourist, and house museum performing a particular version of "home."

I have found myself during the writing of these histories swinging from one end of the preservationist scale to the other. I often catch myself thinking, "why do we need another house museum?" Frankly, I don't think we do. House museums are not places that we need. They are places that people have constructed because of personal, financial, famil-ial, nationalist, and sometimes spiritual reasons. I often take John Ruskin's side in this argument and find myself wondering why we have not been able to let these places fall to ruin, why we cannot allow them to get old and run down, or to live the natural life of a house. Ruskin was horrified by the "restoration" of ancient buildings in France and Italy. He begged his readers:

> Do not let us talk then of restoration. The thing is a Lie from begin-ning to end. You may make a model of a building as you may of a corpse, and your model will have the shell of the old walls within it as your cast might have the skeleton.[8]

Like Ruskin, when I am in a restored house I crave to forget that I am in a museum, but the fact of its restoration often gets in the way. I wonder what these houses would be like if they could have been frozen at the moment of authorial abandonment. Dusty for sure, but that desire to see things in their natural state—to see things come to ruin—is in me when I'm visiting historic sites. But I also see the need for historic house muse-ums and preserved historic buildings. There is a historical understanding that can only be imparted through the lived spaces of the past. Narrative histories provide accounts of the past, but history can be mapped and understood differently through spaces.

For example, across the street from my house in Philadelphia is a house so old that it *makes* me think about the history of where I live. It is no Petrarch's home, but by American standards, Cresheim Cottage is a very old house. Built in 1700, the house just became a gourmet Mexican restaurant. Places like the Creshiem Cottage catch me up, because I am a person who requires places to make historical connections. When I walk by it, I still wonder what the area would have been like before our street of row homes was built up in the 1920s, before train service, and before cars sped by on Germantown Avenue. Such historic structures can provide a glimpse of the way things might have worked in the past. They do not transport us back in time, they are not time machines, but they can help us to think spatially about the events and social conditions of the past. They give us something to hang our history on. The building, because it was preserved but not restored by the Colonial Dames of the Commonwealth of Pennsylvania and put on the national register, will stay roughly the same despite its new function. The little historic house helps me understand not just my neighborhood's past, but also its present.

Full restorations often tell us as much about the moment of their restoration as they do about the past. They remake the past for today—and this is why they are so fascinating and so offensive to Ruskin. The whitewash is always fresh, the windows always clean, the silver always polished, the brick pointed. Restorations cannot hide their own history. Three of Clemens's houses that are open to the public have been restored to some degree, and some have tried to disguise their restoration and some have put the restoration itself on display as an attraction to visitors. John Ruskin had sharp words on the need for restoration:

> But, it is said, there may come a necessity for restoration! Granted. Look the necessity full in the face, and understand it on its own terms. It is a necessity for destruction. Accept it as such, pull the building down, throw its stones into neglected corners, make ballast of them, or mortar, if you will; but do it honestly, and do not set up a Lie in their place.[9]

Ruskin points out that all acts of restoration are destructions; they actually remove pieces of the old house—the house where the writer once lived and breathed—and replace it with the new masquerading as the old. They are always a lie. But they are a lie in service of a need that builds new interpretative structures in place of the old. What I hope to do with these four histories is to get at the necessity of restoration, preservation, and interpretation—to understand why and how these places came about and what purposes they have served over the years to the people who visit Clemens's houses and to the people who maintain them.

## Acknowledgments

hen I began this study as graduate student, I had no idea how many thoughtful, kind, and helpful people I would meet—people who have spent their lives studying and preserving Mark Twain. In uncovering the histories of these four houses, I found their preservation had much to do with these same people and the personal reasons why we choose to read, remember, and celebrate Sam Clemens.

Many Mark Twain experts have contributed to this study through their scholarship, but nearly two dozen of them contributed directly to the project by talking with me about their own involvement in the histories of these houses. Among them Susan K. Harris, Alan Gribben, Shelley Fisher Fishkin, and the late Michael Kiskis were especially gracious. Ralph Gregory, John Huffman, Stan Fast, Regina Faden, Henry Sweets, Wilson Faude, Patti Philippon, Mark Woodhouse, Gretchen Sharlow, and Barbara Snedecor were generous with their time, institutional knowledge, and collections. John Cunning, Bryan Reddick, Karen Ernhout, Gayle Earley, Tim Morgan, Jeff Mainville, Terrell Dempsey, and Jay Rounds all consented to formal interviews or long detailed conversations from which I drew much knowledge. Irene Langdon was not only charitable with conversation and lunch, but twice invited me to attend services with her at Park Church.

Kerry Driscoll, Susan Pennybacker, Tom Registad, Mike Briggs, Ranjit Arab, Scott R. Nelson, Bruce Michelson, Karen Sanchez-Eppler, Brock Clarke, Anne Trubek, Mary Jenkins, and Laurence Buell all shared their insights on my study in its earliest stages. Bryant Simon kindly made sure I had library access and employment at Temple University. Heather Rudy, cultural resource preservationist for the Missouri Department of Natural Resources, helped me wade my way through the records at the archives in Jefferson City, Missouri, and Elizabeth Giard, collections manager at the Harriet Beecher Stowe Center, pointed me to Katharine Seymour

Day's early correspondence about saving the Mark Twain house in Hartford, Connecticut. Many other libraries tried to meet my ever-increasing need for ephemera on the celebration of Mark Twain and literary tourism. Among them the Missouri Valley Collections of the Kansas City Public Library; the Western Historical Manuscript Collection at the University of Missouri, Kansas City; the State Historical Society of Missouri; the Gannett-Tripp Library at Elmira College; the New York Historical Society; the Special Collections of the Philadelphia Free Public Library; Drexel University Library; and the Rosenbach Museum and Library were particularly helpful.

I am especially grateful for my time in Elmira, thanks to a Quarry Farm Fellowship at the Elmira College Center for Mark Twain Studies and a research fellowship from the Office of Graduate Studies at University of Kansas that allowed me to travel to Hartford to complete my primary research. At the Press, Tom Quirk and Clair Willcox provided guidance and support. Avery Dame provided editorial support.

I was lucky enough to spend my second trip to Hannibal, Missouri, with Susan K. Harris and the graduate students in her Mark Twain class. Her insights into Mark Twain's world, enthusiasm for the project, and kindness have been a great support. Ann Schofield kept my eyes focused on women's history and material culture and made me laugh with her own stories of literary tourism. John Pultz and Susan Earle have been the best kind of friends and advisors, providing support, friendship, and scholarly expertise. Cheryl Lester has provided exceptional mentorship and friendship as I moved further and further away from her company and advice. She tracked me down and held fast when it mattered most.

Friends and family reminded me there was much outside the sometimes-confining walls of Twain's houses. Anne Dotter, Lucy Folwer Glasson, Kate Hargis Haas, Jennifer Harris, Jenny Heller, and Noel Rasor have been supportive readers, editors, and friends. My in-laws, Debby and Charles Bruggeman, have provided encouragement in all my projects—big and small. My parents, Marilyn and Kevin Watley, first introduced me to the literary landscape by encouraging that I read about the place where we lived and the places we visited. Moreover, my mother's love for houses no doubt inspired my own love and obsession with them.

I took my first trip to a Mark Twain house with my closest friend and favorite literary tourist, Seth Bruggeman, and I can never thank him enough for his companionship and support throughout the long travels of this life. Our daughter, June, started her days as a literary tourist with us in the womb, and I can't wait to get back on the road with them both.

# Mark Twain's Homes & Literary Tourism

# Introduction

## Literary Homes in the United States

An account of Mark Twain in his various homes would be a
theme rich enough for a whole volume of absorbing interest. It
would be a miniature panorama of American scenery, cities, and
communities, North and South, East and West, at one extreme
pioneering and frontier life, at the other the most cultivated society in America: a comprehensive exhibit of American character,
life, manners, and customs, such as no American author but Mark
Twain possibly has known.

—CHARLES TILDEN SEMPERS (*NEW YORK TIMES,* 1901)

In 1901, Charles Tilden Sempers, a poet and literary critic, thought
an account of Mark Twain in his various homes would make for a
"rich volume" providing a panorama of the American scene. This is
not that volume. Rather, this is an account of what has happened to Sam
Clemens's "various homes" since his occupancy as they became museums.[1] However, the histories of these literary house museums do provide a panoramic view of the processes that make literary historic sites.
They also provide evidence of how our understanding of Sam Clemens is
mediated by his houses and how our understanding of writers can change
because of historic preservation and interpretation.

During his life, Clemens's houses were reviewed like his literary works
in the press, and the sites of his childhood were already tourist destinations. Three of the houses in this study are now open to the public. The
first of his houses to be preserved was his boyhood home in Hannibal,
Missouri. It was dedicated and opened to the public in 1912, only two
years after Clemens's death. His birthplace was opened to sightseers by

an enterprising man in Florida, Missouri, in 1915 and became part of the Mark Twain State Park in 1930. His adult home in Hartford, Connecticut, was saved from urban redevelopment in 1929 by the grandniece of Harriet Beecher Stowe and opened to the public shortly thereafter. Additionally, Quarry Farm, Clemens's summer retreat at his sister-in-law's house in Elmira, New York, escaped tourist development but was made part of the Center for Mark Twain Studies at Elmira College in 1983. Quarry Farm, open only to Twain scholars, is not formally a museum, but commemorates Twain nonetheless. Each place presents a version of Clemens's biography and his literary works through a house he inhabited. Managers at each house have struggled over the years to create interpretive exhibits and details that connect visitors to Clemens and his literature. These sites celebrate Mark Twain and contribute to the perpetuation of his mythic persona as much as they preserve his historic environments, and they promote very different interpretations of Sam Clemens.

Whatever the individual reasons that people seek out and visit literary sites in Hannibal, Florida, Hartford, and Elmira, these are places where visitors consume history. When visitors go to literary sites, they consume a writer's history and biography and the history of the place where he or she lived. Museums produce this history through a variety of interpretive techniques that connect the writer to the house and place and, in turn, connect the house and place to the writer's own literary production. It seems a simple exchange. Tourists demand history, and museums provide it. But it is never that simple an exchange. Each tourist goes to a site for his or her own reason, and some may not know why they go. The stories that literary sites interpret for literary tourists—whether the stories are literary, biographical, or historical—have to resonate, inform, and entertain for the site to remain relevant and open.

My goal for this study is to take a step toward creating a contemporary history of American literary house museums and tourism through the study of the houses devoted to Mark Twain. These places take part in creating and satiating Americans' varied needs for historical connections to the past. "American literary tourism" sounds grand, like something akin to the European "Grand Tour" of previous centuries, but in reality, I think most visitors to literary sites in the United States engage in touristic behavior not entirely unlike the kind that goes on at other historic and heritage sites. These sites narrate where important American stories begin. Over the years that I have worked on this project, I toured a number of noteworthy historic sites that communicate a similar need for historic origins, including Monticello, Mount Vernon, Kenmore (the estate of George Washington's sister, Betty Washington Lewis), George Washington's birthplace, Ben Franklin's house, and William Bartram's house and gardens. All of these museum-estates are nineteenth- and early-twentieth-century monuments to "great" white men and articulate the origin of the nation overtly. Even when such sites are in some ways monuments to women (as at Kenmore), they are more about men than the women who make them sites of interest.[2]

At Mount Vernon, for example, visitors hear stories about George Washington, but they will also hear the same stories that tour guides tell at every house museum in the United States, like the origins of the saying "sleep tight, don't let the bed bugs bite" and explanations of why kitchens used to be a building separate from the main house.[3] While Mount Vernon and other history sites inspire us to imagine how hard and dangerous it was to cook over an open fire, they often erase the labor of the enslaved and indentured people who did so.[4] In a sense, although Mount Vernon is a remarkable version of the historic house museum, it does many of the same things that any historic house does.[5] "Original" pieces—George Washington's bed, his office chair, his desk, his globe, and other items— are pointed out and revered. Both the tour guides and the visitors seem interested in getting as close as possible to the sanctified furniture.

But compare the Mark Twain Boyhood Home and Museum to Mount Vernon and you see a very different version of the house museum. Curators acknowledge that the Clemens family held and sold slaves. Visitors are told that Twain joined and deserted a local militia that supported the Confederacy. Perhaps most important, Hannibal area residents are pointed out as the inspiration for many of Twain's characters. At many sites, slavery is given short shrift. Not so at this literary site, which acknowledges the town's past, including the sites where slaves were auctioned. Today, the Mark Twain Boyhood Home and Museum uses Clemens's fiction to supplement this history.

Historic house museums describe how much better off "we" are today, because we do not have to tighten the ropes on our beds, cook over open fires, or split rails for our own fences. These museums create nostalgia for an indistinct past when average people appreciated the decorative arts, worked as a family, and led simple lives, uncomplicated by modernity. Historians of nostalgia, like Susan Matt, see Americans' interest in history museums of all kinds as an exercise in longing for a past that they know is out of reach.[6] With the literary past, perhaps it is not. *Literary sites can do something different.* Literary houses evoke for tourists moments of human inspiration. The interpretive stories that they narrate can speak to not just the birthplace or residence of a great man, but they can speak to origins of ideas, characters, and fictions that are meaningful to readers. They work to reveal the *genius loci*—the spirit of the place— that contributes to the moment when the literary idea is created. Visiting a literary site is not entirely unlike reading a book since the site itself can function as a text is to be read. It, like any place, is read anew each time a visitor encounters it. These sites are constantly changing as a result of each tourist's encounter. The literary house museum that I visited last week can be a very different experience from season to season or tourist to tourist. In this light, it is ironic that in a nation where critics constantly claim that literacy is on the wane, the United States has an ever-growing number of tourist sites devoted to authors and tourists devoted to seeing where writers lived and wrote.[7]

## Literary House Museums

It is possible that we need a separate model for the study of literary sites because they can function differently from other historic house museums. Literary sites can differ from historic sites in three primary ways. First, literary site managers can choose to interpret literature rather than history, or in addition to history. For instance, at the Edgar Allen Poe National Historic Site in Philadelphia, guides take visitors on a tour of the three-story brick home while explaining how Poe and his family used the house in the past. In the basement, however, visitors are most often treated with a stirring reading of Poe's short story "The Black Cat." The setting is perfect for the tale of a madman's murder of his beloved pet and wife. In the story, the narrator bricks up his wife's corpse in a false chimney in the basement of their house. Just such a chimney can be found in the basement of this national historic site. While there is no reason to believe that Poe's story is based on any historical occurrence in the house, the park has chosen to encourage its interpreters to introduce visitors to Poe's terrifying stories through the house itself. It makes a great finale to the tour, and it connects Poe's writing directly to the historic house. But importantly, the telling of the story of the basement moves visitors beyond Poe's biography and into his writing. They might not have read Poe before they visit the house, but by the time they leave they have a sense of how gripping and suspenseful his short stories can be.

This is the second way that literary sites are different from historic sites. Because site managers can choose to interpret literature, they can engage visitors in different ways than their peers at historic sites. Aside from scaring the pants off visitors with scary stories in basements, literary house museums can be used as sites of inspiration. One of Robert Frost's houses, owned by Middlebury College, is often used as part of the college's well-known Bread Loaf Writers' Conference as a site for current literary production. Other literary sites have engaged in similar outreach. These sites move beyond their historical period to connect with writers and visitors today in ways that are not necessarily available to other historic sites.

However, because literary sites can interpret literature they are not necessarily held to the same standard of historical authenticity as history sites. This third difference creates the tension I find most interesting at literary sites. Where historic sites are criticized by stakeholders for leaving out important details, literary sites can sidestep historical accuracy in the name of connecting to literature. Guides at the Turner-Ingersoll Mansion, more commonly known as the House of the Seven Gables in Salem, Massachusetts, for years led visitors through the house as though the events of Hawthorne's novel were not fiction at all, but rather the actual history of the house and Salem. The owner of the house, Caroline Emmerton, even went so far as to make a number of physical changes to the historic structure to make it match the house in the novel. Hawthorne's birthplace, along with four other historic structures, was moved from its historic location so that it could serve as a historic backdrop for the fictional tale told at the house. In this case, Emmerton overlooked the real history of the Turner-Ingersoll Mansion while she created a fictional literary Salem. Because Emmerton was not interpreting history, but rather a novel, her critics could hardly fault her for saving these historic structures. Tourists loved it. Many keenly remember climbing the hidden passageway that Emmerton had installed behind the fireplace to match the novel.[8]

Though literary sites may take liberties with the past, I do not mean to imply that historic house museums are infallible. Every historic house's board and staff have to make choices about what stories to interpret and how to instruct guides and staff about which stories are important to tell. But historians and visitors can point out interpretive problems and petition for changes, as they have over the years at many sites of national interest. Historic house museums can teach visitors about social environments in ways that books and documentaries cannot. At a historic structure like Monticello, visitors can see the lovely house and grounds but also the panoptic view that Jefferson created to oversee his plantation. Visitors can now tour slave cabins and compare the living conditions there with Jefferson's lavish home. These places can provide a physical map—evidence—of historical social relations. In a site that chooses to interpret fiction rather than, or in addition to, mapping the social relations of a particular period, there can be little room for historical criticism. After all, the House of the Seven Gables never sought to portray the living conditions of the Ingersoll or Turner families.[9] Criticism of the house's use of "history" could only lie within how realistically its managers had mapped the novel onto the house and whether they got details like the fireplace passageway and gardens "right." The expectation that sites of literary interest can provide both historical interpretation and literary interpretation creates particular conditions that are the exploration of this study.

## Literary Tourists in the United States

Literary tourism in the United States is by no means a new phenomenon. Rather, it has been picking up speed since tourists first saw fit to visit Concord, Massachusetts, to be close to the likes of Ralph Waldo Emerson and Henry David Thoreau.[10] Literary tourism is a booming industry in this country. In the last ten years alone, dozens of guides have been written to assist the literary tourist.[11] They include volumes such as *The Mystery Reader's Guide to Washington, D.C.* and *Stephen King Country: The Illustrated Guide to the Sites That Inspired the Modern Master of Horror.* Scholars have become similarly interested in literary tourism. Shelley Fisher Fishkin, a Mark Twain scholar, visited sites associated with Mark Twain and recounts her travels in her travelogue and history, *Lighting Out for the Territory: Reflections on Mark Twain and American Culture* (1997). Diana Fuss turned her touristic excursions into *The Sense of an Interior: Four Writers and the Rooms That Shaped Them* (2004). Most recently, Anne Trubek turned her cynicism about literary house museums into the contrary guidebook, *A Skeptic's Guide to Writers' Houses* (2011). Sometimes literary tourist guides map the important places that mark an author's landscape of inspiration (as with the Stephen King guide) and sometimes they map the "real" locations visited by fictive characters, like the slew of tourist guides inspired by Robert James Waller's *The Bridges of Madison County.* But each of these books and guides implies that there is something to be gained for the reader and tourist in visiting these sites.

Literary tourism has become a subject of serious scholarly research within literary studies and tourism studies and has recently been defined by Nicola Watson as "the practice of visiting places associated with particular books in order to savour text, place and their interrelations."[12] But during my site visits to literary house museums, I have not seen many visitors "savoring" texts. In my view, literary tourism is simply the practice of visiting places associated with literary figures or celebrities, whether these places are associated with the life of the author or associated with his or her fictional creations. Literary tourism is a multilayered phenomenon and the houses in this study have been carefully designed by museum professionals to *teach* tourists about writers and their worlds. I interpret the idea of literary tourism rather broadly to include any interest in authors' lives, worlds, and homes that require either a physical or imaginary "visit" to a place associated with writers. Even those scholars who "visit" the world of the author through historical investigation embrace a kind of historical and extra-literary tourism.

The study of tourism, of all the secondary literature on literary sites, has the most useful and frustrating insights for this project. Tourism studies gives almost no consideration to the literary interpretive work that sites do. The field of tourism studies is split between two camps. One is rooted in market research, management studies, and the desire to "improve" the tourists' experiences. The other is scholarly, primarily sociological, and responds to Dean MacCannell's *The Tourist: A New Theory of the Leisure Class* (1976). Neither camp focuses directly on American literary sites, but a few studies at sites in Great Britain have provided hints of what literary tourists might be after. Some of these studies have defined "literary pilgrims" as a distinct group of tourists who visit literary historic sites. Tourism studies analyst David Herbert sees true "literary pilgrims . . . [as] well educated tourists, versed in the classics and with the cultural capital to appreciate and understand this form of heritage." They are just the right kind of people to "savor" the text at these historic places as Watson describes. Herbert observes that these "literary pilgrims" visit sites because they want to see where a writer lived or where a novel took place. All other visitors to literary sites who are not "versed in the classics," he labels "users"—there for only entertainment and recreation, as though literary interest and entertainment were easily separable desires.[13]

In 2001, Herbert found that of the visitors to Dylan Thomas's home in Laugharne who saw his "writing shed," most "found it of interest, and about one-fifth expressed a sense of wonder." Meanwhile, at Chawton, Jane Austen's home, visitors sometimes questioned the authenticity of the objects on display.[14] These results *seem* to indicate that the average tourist visits literary sites with a critical eye and that many tourists visit to commune with authors—to find "a sense of wonder" in the places where authors have lived and worked. But such industry tourism studies are limited by their survey methods. Herbert's surveys were brief—check-the-box-if-you-felt-a-sense-of-wonder surveys. There is no way to find out what tourists really meant by "sense of wonder." Herbert's studies, like many within his field, were funded by the sites themselves and such studies can be driven by the concerns of the industry.[15]

A portion of the field is not as connected directly to the tourism industry but instead follows in the wake of Dean MacCannell's work. These scholars have attempted to theorize why it is that tourists visit sites. MacCannell posited that modern tourists seek out authentic experiences because they perceive their day-to-day lives as inauthentic. Their lives are mired in the postmodern world of "simulations," where they see little that connects with the real and authentic. MacCannell argued that the authentic experience is almost always already out of reach, because destinations and cultures that are the sites of tourism present a commodified version of themselves to tourists. But as studies of tourism have developed, other definitions of authentic touristic experience have emerged. Discussions about the material or object authenticity of places, cultures, and souvenirs—such as MacCannell's—have been supplemented by discussion of the tourist's authentic experience. Today there is a great focus on existential authenticity found in the experience of the tourist. Both the material and existential authenticities are important for understanding Clemens's houses and they have changed over time. The staff at the Clemens sites have tried to meet the needs of tourists who seek both an authentic experience with material culture—through the historical arrangement of interiors at the houses—and an existentially authentic experience—through new experiential methods of visitor engagement, like the interactive exhibits at the Mark Twain Museum in Hannibal, which allow visitors to jump on a stagecoach and ride west, as Clemens did in *Roughing It*.

According to scholars like Ning Wang, it is in the experience that tourists can transcend their everyday lives and find the selves that are missing in the postmodern world. This argument might speak to the important ways that individuals work to define themselves through tourism, as more and more people visit museums and historic sites each year. Museum professionals and managers have seized this idea that tourists do "identity work" to define themselves in museums.[16] In this model, museum goers visit museums to test their identities in a structured environment. Museums are safe places to test the limits of self because they present a structured and often chronological narrative into which tourists can place their own experiences or question what their responses to a historical period or event would be. But what identity work do tourists do at literary house museums and does object authenticity still matter to them? It seems that many literary tourists, at least at Twain sites, care about both and see object authenticity as distinctly connected to their own experiences at museums and have done so for some time.

Historians, like others who study tourism as a phenomenon, have made meaningful contributions to the analysis of historic sites and history museums. They have attempted to answer the question of why and how Americans are interested in history and why they become history tourists. They found that Americans are particularly interested in their own history—the history of their families, specifically genealogy. In essence, Americans are interested in origins—their own and their country's. They see themselves and their family histories as part of a larger historical narrative. Roy Rosenzweig and David Thelen's study, *The Presence of the Past: Popular Uses of History in American Life,* explored the ways that Americans consume and produce histories in their daily lives, and found that nearly half of all Americans visit a historic site or history museum every twelve months. They uncovered through extensive surveying that "Americans put more trust in history museums and historic sites than in any other sources for exploring the past." Unlike the survey methods employed by Herbert, Rosenzweig and Thelen's study encouraged detailed responses about experiences with history. The authors found that Americans trust history museums and historic sites more than family members, high-school history teachers, documentaries, and nonfiction books.[17] This trust has renewed historians' efforts to study and critique historic sites and museums. If these are the sources that Americans most trust, then it is more important than ever that sites present histories that are worthy of this trust.

Additionally, Rosenzweig and Thelen revealed through their survey that Americans may trust museums so much because of the objects that they see displayed there. Their respondents believed that in visiting museums they were able to approach "artifacts and sites on their own terms" and "could cut through all the intervening stories, step around all the agendas that had been advanced in the meantime, and felt that they were experiencing a moment from the past almost as it had originally been experienced—and with none of the overwhelming distortions that they associated with movies and television, the other purveyors" of history.[18] This belief in the truth-telling ability of objects and artifacts as they are displayed at historic sites has meaningful translation to literary house museums, especially at sites like the Hartford house. Their research disputes the idea that tourists disregard material or object authenticity or see artifacts at museums as merely part of a fractured and multilayered postmodern presentation of the past. Some of Rosenzweig and Thelen's conclusions indicate that the fictive elements at literary houses are worthy of careful consideration.

In 1989, the literary scholar Lawrence Buell issued a call for the study of the ways that authors become canonized outside the academy—specifically at sites associated with their lives and work. His article, "The Thoreauvian Pilgrimage: The Structure of an American Cult," looked at the tourist phenomena that surround Henry David Thoreau and Concord, Massachusetts. Buell argued that literary pilgrimages like the ones that tourists take to Walden Pond to commune with nature and the "spirit" of Thoreau are a part of the "ritual process" of canonization. Buell described the rites and rituals associated with visiting Walden

Pond: stacking stones upon the cairn at the shore, walking along Walden Pond's edge, and attempting to imagine the locale sans tourists, just as Thoreau might have. Tourists to Walden Pond seek the place—the origin or *genius loci* that inspired Thoreau to write *Walden*. Buell also pointed to changes at the site over time and how pilgrims' rituals changed accordingly. He made a convincing argument that Thoreau is a special case; because Thoreau's *Walden* is about the act of spending time in a reclusive state in the woods, the tourist who visits Walden Pond is in fact reenacting Thoreau's deeds.[19]

But Buell's call for more in-depth studies of how authors become canonized by commemorative acts has largely gone unanswered. Little research has been done that looks at how tourists contribute to the canonization of an author by seeking out where they live. This kind of popular canonization—what happens when readers try to gain access to a writer's personal life—is still little documented.[20] Buell's article remains one of the only serious scholarly treatments of an authorial residence. Much of the other literary scholarship on authors' houses is more akin to travel writing than literary criticism or history.[21]

In October 2006, literary scholar Anne Trubek published a short piece in *The Believer* on the melancholy of writers' houses. She argued that "going to a writer's house is a fool's errand." She believed that "we will never find our favorite characters or admired techniques within these houses; we can't join Huck on the raft or experience Faulkner's stream of consciousness." Instead, "we can only walk through empty rooms full of pitchers and paintings and stoves."[22] But if Rosenzweig and Thelen's study is right, it seems likely that many tourists find the display of pitchers, paintings, and stoves and perhaps the historic structures themselves the very things—the authentic objects—that most connect them to the literary past and the origin stories that they seek.

Literary scholars, and maybe the highly literate "literary pilgrims" that Herbert and Watson describe, go to literary historic houses to seek a clear connection to the author they admire and the origin works that they study and love. This particular variety of literary tourist is the subject of my chapter on Quarry Farm—where scholars and self-described Twainiacs are the primary visitors. Both Quarry Farm and the Mark Twain House and Museum in Hartford, Connecticut, have had a significant effect on how literary scholars, and their students, understand Clemens. House museums and the decisions of their managers affect our understanding of literary figures and deserve critical attention and analysis like any other primary or secondary source of information on an author.

It is likely that some tourists visit literary sites to get close to literary figures they admire and to find the origins of settings of the books they have read—as in the case of literary scholars' travel narratives. They travel to interact with the authentic objects displayed there, and to do so "on their own terms," as Rosenzweig and Thelen have described. And literary tourists of all stripes likely seek out both authentic and inauthentic connections to literature and the past, and go to these places to test and maintain their identities, as tourism scholars have argued. However, most literary scholars, historians, and even tourism scholars have not been concerned with the history of these places, who created them and why, how these places interpret literature and history and how this interpretation has changed over time, or how the sites come to affect our understanding of American literary figures.

## Understanding Literary Sites in Person

To understand these places, I found it was necessary to visit them, to take tours alongside other tourists, and to think through each space as a place that tries to tell a story about Sam Clemens and about its own essential role in who he was. When I visited the sites, I went through each first as a "regular" tourist, paying my entrance fee, and making my way through the historic sites, visitors' centers, and museums. I toured Sam Clemens's birthplace—peering through the windows and doors of the little cabin like a peeping Tom all alone. I went through Hannibal's Mark Twain Boyhood Home and Museum with my husband, and we followed the designated route for the self-guided tour—through the Interpretive Center, Huck Finn House, Boyhood Home, the Becky Thatcher House, John Marshall Clemens's Law Office, Grant's Drug Store, and finally the Mark Twain Museum. I went to Hartford and took the guided tour of the elaborate house and the special "servants' wing" tour. My visit to Quarry Farm is a separate story, because it is not a site where you can visit as an "average" tourist. There, if you are an average tourist you can only drive by the house and look at it from your car.

At each place, I scrutinized how people moved through these spaces, how they interacted with the houses themselves, the artifacts, and the staff. Regrettably, at the birthplace, I was never there when other tourists were looking at the house. In Hannibal, I watched the careful order through which tourists encountered the collection of historic sites. I noticed most visitors seemed to have some familiarity with the characters Tom Sawyer and Huck Finn. Most visitors were white families, some were parents who attempted to recall plot details for the children with them. In Hartford, tourists were quiet on the guided tour, and I saw a tourist pick up and handle artifacts on display when the guide was not looking.

At these places, the existing studies of literary and history tourism did not always match what I found. Many people did not seem to be there to connect with Sam Clemens because they admired his literary output, and few seemed interested in uncovering the settings of the novels that they had read. Most did, however, seem interested in the objects on display. They pointed them out to each other, they handled them when the opportunity presented itself, and they leaned against doorways and touched the houses' walls, siding, bricks, moldings, displays, Plexiglas, and furnishings. They looked at their feet and scrubbed the toes of their shoes against the historic flooring. I could not necessarily see "identity work" going on, except perhaps through the interactions of families. Parents often recalled stories of their visits to these same sites when they were children. A great number of people commented on the furnishings to the effect of "isn't that a lovely dresser," or "is that a lady's hoop skirt?" Many people just quietly read the displays, listened to the guides, and looked at the interiors with little comment. Visiting literary sites tends to be a social enterprise: only a very few tourists visited the sites alone.

I attempted close readings of these houses and their visitors as if both were texts that might reveal how literary tourism works. My observations did not explain what was there on display, what the displays meant to the tourists, or how these displays came to be there. The houses and tourists did not reveal how the routes through the historic sites were plotted, how the exhibits that conveyed background information were written, or how the houses came to be furnished with the objects that inspired so much conjecture and handling. For these answers, I would have to look elsewhere—to the history of the museums themselves.

Unfortunately, no one had gone before me to sift through the board meeting minutes, newspaper clippings, handwritten correspondence, old brochures, bills, receipts, photographs, newsletters, and other detritus of these museums to create histories of these house museums. Administrative histories have become standard at national historic sites and at many state historic sites, but smaller museums—even ones devoted to the most famous of American authors—do not often have the staff or budgets to provide these meaningful documents that help explain a museum's origin. Many institutional histories are passed on orally from staff and board members, if they are passed along at all. Quite often current staff cannot tell you why it is that things are the way they are. They have merely always been that way. In most cases, staff members do not have the time to note their decision-making processes outside of the standard minutes for meetings. In uncovering these histories, each site proved to be its own archival challenge. Some were more forthcoming with records than others. Some meeting minutes were detailed and included quotes from board members, some did not even list who attended. The process of reconstructing a museum's past through its documents is neither easy nor exact. In the resulting histories that follow, many details are omitted. Even shifts in policy, changes in staff, all of these cannot be noted or accounted for in one chapter.[23]

I have done my best to include details about events that were pivotal in the museums' histories—events that marked their growth and change—but I could only choose those pivotal events from what was left in the records. Notably, these records do not often include hints of what was going on outside the museum that might have motivated changes within. Hartford's archives do not mention the race riots in the city in 1969. Hannibal's archives do not mention the desegregation of its schools or the near riot at a nearby cement plant. The birthplace's archives were split among so many different branches of state oversight that huge gaps in their records remain. Only Quarry Farm presented no immediate obstacles because it has only been open to scholars since 1983, and Elmira College had the wonderful sense and means to hire an excellent archivist. Crucial to understanding the relationships between the documents I found, I also sought out other sources, from local histories of the towns where these sites are located to the actual people who had worked in the museums over the years.

My research also included interviews with staff, scholars, and community members. Most of these interviews do not appear in this book; however, they supplemented much of what I found in the archives at each site. At one site while reading the official meeting minutes, I noticed that the tenor of meetings shifted. The notes themselves, though still taken by the same note-taker, became formal and distant. Without an interview, I would not have known that discussions had gotten so heated that the board decided to meet fewer times during the year to avoid contact. In addition, a number of interviewees made comments about controversial decisions made at the sites only in confidence. Sometimes informants asked that I turn off the tape recorder and put down my pen. Individuals that seemed deeply adversarial in meeting notes often had only the nicest things to say about one another in interviews. As a result, these sources are just as subject to critical examination as any other, but made the process extraordinarily interesting.

My first interview was with Ralph Gregory, the then ninety-eight-year-old former founding curator at the Mark Twain Birthplace State Historic Site. I drove to Marthasville, Missouri, to his house and interrupted him walking his elderly dog. I had prepared pages of questions to ask Gregory about his time at the birthplace and about his research into its authenticity. I hoped to get him to admit that he knew the birthplace was a "fake." But Gregory wanted to talk more about his current research projects and his love for the semiotician Charles Pierce. We talked for four hours. I learned a lot in the interview about Gregory's investment in Mark Twain (and Pierce and Daniel Boone) and his experiences as a radioman in World War II, but I learned very little about the history of the birthplace and its function within the larger Missouri State Park System. As a result, early on, I found that I was interested in the origins and histories of these sites, but the people involved with them often wanted to talk about Mark Twain and the many other things that interested them.[24]

I asked each person I interviewed to describe the "average tourist" to his or her site and quite often this was a very difficult task. Some of these museums had done demographic exit surveys of visitors from time to time but no one felt that they could quite put their finger on who visited. I asked why he or she thought that people went to literary sites; why visitors made the trek to Hannibal; why they made their way to Florida, Missouri; what brought them to Hartford; and what led them to Quarry Farm. In each case, no one could give a definitive answer, because there is no one answer to why people come.

*The Chapters*

Each of the following chapters recounts the origin of a house devoted to Mark Twain and the moments of its development and growth that document important crises and changes in interpretation. When possible, the chapters recount early tourist encounters at these sites that predate the establishment of the house as officially open to the public. I reconstruct the crucial debates that have led the museums to their specific interpretations of Clemens's biography and uncover how their managers have constructed narratives that connect Clemens to these particular places over time. "The Many Birthplaces of Mark Twain," my first chapter, uncovers a history of the site that reveals how the State of Missouri came to claim that one cabin out of many contenders was the site of Sam Clemens's birth. The history of the birthplace is both very ordinary—a basic story of how state historic sites function—and extraordinary, in that the entire site may be spurious. American birthplace commemoration has a troubled history.[25] George Washington's birthplace was grandly "rebuilt," while nearly destroying the actual foundations of the modest building that was likely really where he was born. Abraham Lincoln's birthplace has also now been declared counterfeit, after years of speculation and research by the National Park Service. Questions about Mark Twain's birthplace have plagued the site at least since state recognition in 1924, and the cabin that the State of Missouri has preserved may well be *similar* to the cabin where Clemens was born, but no evidence clearly supports its authenticity. The history of Clemens's birthplace raises many questions, not the least of which is why do we need birthplaces so much that we may be willing to fabricate them?

Mark Twain's boyhood home in Hannibal, Missouri, is the most visited of any of the historic sites associated with him. In my second chapter, "Hannibal as Hometown: The Stories Started Here," I trace the long history of the site, which opened to the public a hundred years ago in 1912 as one of the first literary house museums in the United States. As the first public museum to commemorate Clemens and to claim his childhood, the site has successfully tied the origin of Clemens's literary production to Hannibal, Missouri. The boyhood home, although never at the center of any controversy about its authenticity, found itself at the center of the crisis of the historical representation of slavery. This is a common dilemma at historic sites in this country. Even the National Park Service has struggled, somewhat unsuccessfully, to make meaningful changes in the interpretation of slavery at many of its sites.[26] As a case study, the boyhood home offers an interesting literary supplement to the growing literature on slavery at historic sites. George Mahan, the museum's founder, was determined early on to interpret Twain's best-known novel, *The Adventures of Tom Sawyer,* at the historic site. *Tom Sawyer* coincidentally presented Hannibal in a positive and nostalgic light. As a result of Mahan's early efforts to mark the town as the origin of Clemens's tales, the museum there has only recently represented the Clemens family as slave owners after local criticism required it. The boyhood home is the one site in this study whose managers have consistently chosen to interpret Clemens's fiction. Because fiction had such a strong hold on the house museum and still has a place there today, the history of the site is fascinating. It shows how literary sites can benefit from the interpretive leeway that literature provides, but sometimes at the cost of local history. Because the museum has chosen to interpret Tom Sawyer's life as nearly identical to that of Clemens's, the town now has the difficult task of separating itself from fiction to create a realistic and more historically accurate portrayal of its own origin.

My third chapter, "The Right Stuff: Mark Twain, Material Culture, and the Gilded Age Museum," uncovers how Katharine Seymour Day, Harriet Beecher Stowe's grandniece, "saved" the Hartford Twain house and turned it into a library and then a museum and recounts the effort to restore the house to *exactly* as it was during the Mark Twain period. The house in Hartford is the grand author's house writ large with gold stenciling and Tiffany designs, and the house was painstakingly restored to this state between 1955 and 1974. The story of Clemens's house in Hartford and its meticulous restoration is a cautionary tale about the power of material culture and object authenticity. The museum staff's attention to the perfect arrangement of the house with exact artifacts sometimes left little room inside the home for the interpretation of why Clemens mattered and why his time in Hartford was important.

At Quarry Farm, the story of preservation is quite different. My fourth chapter, "Quarry Farm: Scholars as Tourists," is much shorter than the others in this book because the history of the site is still beginning. Founded more than seventy years after the first Mark Twain site was opened to the public, the house and the grounds at Quarry Farm have *not* been restored to the time when Clemens and his family summered there. Instead, they are semi-frozen in 1983, when the Elmira College received the farm as a gift. In the other house museums, a visitor may dream of spending time alone walking the halls and imagine actually living there, but at Quarry Farm, if you are a Twain scholar, you can actually spend the night.[27] Limited access to the site means the house is preserved less as a museum and more like a living archive for scholars who reside there for extended visits. At Quarry Farm, scholars can be the ultimate literary pilgrims, but even this historic site is interpreted for its particular tourists' needs. However, the limited-use arrangement and interpretation has created an incredibly loyal tourist base. As historic house museums across the country close their doors, this particular arrangement seems prescient. In many ways the story of Quarry Farm may be a common story of preservation in the future.

In conclusion, this study of Clemens's houses and their preservation points out that each site's moment of origin is particularly important. The conditions that create a historic site set its course—sometimes for decades—and it takes extraordinary work to change its interpretative narratives. As these literary sites evolved, they grew and faced challenges to their interpretations of Clemens. While I am not ultimately any more confident answering the question of why we celebrate authors through preserving their homes, why tourists visit them, and why it is that visitors want to touch the objects there on display, I have uncovered a critical tool for getting closer to these answers. By looking closely at the origins and changes at these sites over time, it is possible to discover a sense of what it is that tourists seek in the literary sites devoted to Clemens. They are looking for where his story and stories begin.

At each site, through careful review of managers' changes over time, you can begin to see how individuals tried to meet the demands of the tourists who visited. Not every site had the ability to meet those demands. The Mark Twain Birthplace State Historic Site, for example, never had the funding or support to make meaningful interpretive changes. But all the other sites have adapted to try to meet the needs of their visitors. We might not be able to determine why visitors have gone to these sites, but we find in the ways that managers made changes at these sites efforts to anticipate why. These sites present narratives that explain their place in relationship to Clemens and the origin of his genius. Visitors may well seek out literary houses that celebrate authors because they believe that houses are sites of origin, which carry the traces of the people who have lived in them. These histories are a good place from which to begin to see why there is a "necessity for restoration" and commemoration at literary destinations.

*Chapter One*

## The Many Birthplaces of Mark Twain

The house that we were born in is an inhabited house . . . over and beyond our memories, the house we were born in is physically inscribed in us. It is a group of organic habits.

—GASTON BACHELARD (*THE POETICS OF SPACE*, 1958)

S amuel Clemens's birthplace in Florida, Missouri, has changed a great deal since the author's birth in 1835. Florida was never a bustling metropolis. In Clemens's day it had a population of one hundred, but as of the 2010 census, its population was gone.[1] The town is now merely a crossing of three roads near the northern reaches of Mark Twain Lake—a place that is visited by more vacationers and speedboat fans than by Mark Twain devotees. Florida survived the 1984–1985 flooding of the Salt River Valley by the Army Corps of Engineers to make Mark Twain Lake, but only because what was left of the town sits on high ground. It is near this place that the state of Missouri has put forward one cabin, out of a multitude, which locals claimed to be the site of Samuel Clemens's birth. In 1960, the state's cabin was enclosed by a modern museum building that marks it as a shrine. However, the cabin that is kept there has always been the subject of controversy.

This is the story of this particular cabin and its claim to be Samuel Clemens's birthplace, and its history explains why the site's managers have not been able to create an interpretive narrative that successfully connects Clemens with the place of his origin. The history of this site reveals the same kind of questions that scholars have brought to bear on the fraught history of Abraham Lincoln's log-cabin birthplace, which like other historic sites, has recently been declared an "authentic replica," or in the National Park Service's most recent linguistic terminology, "symbolic birth cabin," rather than the *actual* birthplace of Lincoln.[2] In addition, I look at Clemens's own thoughts on the preservation of birthplaces, the troubled history of the commemoration of birthplaces in the United States and the story of Samuel Clemens's many purported birthplaces in Florida, Missouri. The Missouri state park, which commemorates his birth, has a complicated history of its own that evolved between 1915 and 1960, and then stood still until today.

Mark Twain's actual birthplace may be impossible to track down. It likely no longer exists. There are conflicting accounts of what happened to the building where he was born. Some say the house was carried away piece by piece by relic seekers and Mark Twain fans sometime before 1905. Others say the house was whittled down into mementos and canes and distributed at any number of World's Fairs. If this is the case, then the house circulates out there in shards and fragments. Missouri's Mark Twain Birthplace State Historic Site ignores all of these accounts. But the history of the site brings up important questions: Why do birthplaces need to be remembered? What is it that they reveal about the origin of American character? Is there a story that site managers can tell with inauthentic birthplaces and false relics? And most important, do we need sites of origin—birthplaces—so much that they have to be fabricated? Frederick Jackson Turner's frontier thesis and popular understandings of it have moved many, especially in the early twentieth century, to consider that there was a direct connection between place and character.[3] The American celebration of birthplaces at places like Florida, Missouri, reveals the necessity for a meaningful national origin story. This site's history reveals the need for just that connection between place of origin and writer.

## The Mark Twain Birthplace State Historic Site Today

If you visit the site of Mark Twain's birth in Florida, Missouri, you will find an empty field, a concrete pedestal that was once part of a monument, and a plaque put there by the Missouri Department of Natural Resources. The pedestal is missing a bronze bust of Mark Twain, removed in 1964, and looks peculiar addressing an empty field.[4] There is no building here. Although the plaque shows old photographs of Florida that reveal there once really was a town on this site, not much of that town remains.

There are a few buildings nearby, one a newly "restored" log-cabin structure on display about a hundred yards beyond the odd, bust-less Twain monument, and recent residences within sight.[5] Not much is left of the little hamlet of sixty white families and enslaved peoples that—

the plaque points out—lived here during the time when the Clemens family was here. Founded in 1831, Florida was established just ten years after the Missouri Compromise, allowing Missouri to enter the Union as a slave state. At that time, Missouri was the farthest western state where slaveholding families could relocate and bring with them the human property and way of life to which they had become accustomed. The Clemens and Lampton family, like many other white slaveholding families from Kentucky and Tennessee interested in new opportunities, immigrated to this area and set up new lives in Monroe County. Not long after Jane Lampton Clemens, Sam Clemens's mother, saw her favorite sister, Patsey Ann Lampton Quarles, immigrate to Missouri in 1934, the Clemens family followed.[6]

When the Clemenses arrived, Florida was a city as well positioned as others to be a new boomtown. Local and state agents were convinced that the Salt River could be made navigable and that before long, the western town would be as booming as Kansas City, St. Louis, or even Chicago. For the white families that relocated to Missouri, Florida was an ideal location. It was positioned along a decent waterway, had plenty of fertile land and woods, and recreated a familiar community. For the enslaved people who were moved with them, this area was a change from the highly agricultural work they might have done in Tennessee or Kentucky. In Missouri there were few large farms and little soil that was amenable for cultivating cotton or other monoculture crops, and, as a result, enslaved people in Missouri toiled on agriculturally diverse smaller farms and in households.[7] However, during the three years that the Clemens family lived in Florida, it quickly became clear that the Salt River would never be made navigable. Not long after, it became apparent that the major and minor train lines through the area, and both major east–west thoroughfares through Missouri, would miss the town by at least thirty miles.[8]

On my first visit in June 2007, the Mark Twain birthplace was hard to find. It took a good bit of effort to make my way to Florida, Missouri. I thought I had missed my exit twice because it was not marked. Eventually, I had to pull over and find a more detailed local map. Signs to it are not posted along State Highway 36 from Kansas City as I drove east toward the Mississippi River, but there are a number of *other* Missouri boyhood homes advertised.[9] You pass General John Pershing's, Walt Disney's, and J.C. Penney's childhood homes.[10] Although the state marked the place where Sam Clemens was born, the state has moved the cabin a few miles down the road to a museum. The exact spot of Sam Clemens's birth remains uncertain, as you will see in the story that follows. If you are seeking the site of Clemens's origin, you can visit the birthplace cabin inside a museum that resides on the easternmost tip of what is now

The Mark Twain Birthplace State Historic Site, near Florida, Missouri, formerly Mark Twain Memorial Shrine

Mark Twain State Park. On the official map of Mark Twain State Park, the birthplace is noted with just the words "Historic Site."[11]

Mark Twain State Park abuts Mark Twain Lake, an Army Corps of Engineers project that dates to planning efforts in the 1930s when the National Park Service in conjunction with the Civilian Conservation Corps (CCC) and the Missouri State Park Board drafted a master plan for the area that included strategically damming the Salt River and creating a lake for "flat water recreation" and local drinking water supply.[12] The 1930s were a boom for historic preservation. While the Great Depression crippled other fields, the New Deal was good to national and state parks. Historical architects and archeologists were hired for the first time by the federal government to document and preserve American historic structures. However, the Corps of Engineers did not officially begin the lake project until the 1980s, and the lake finally opened to the public in 1986. The area surrounding the historic site and museum is made up of 2,775 acres of state park land and a "55,000-acre land and water project" that makes up the Army Corps of Engineers lake.[13]

On your way into the state park, there is a sign that directs you down a road either to the "Historic Site" or to the "Park Office." The building that houses the birthplace cabin is modern in the extreme. It swoops up at you as you drive down Shrine Road. Made of local limestone, glass,

The birthplace cabin enclosed in the 1961 building, June 2007

The birthplace cabin, June 2007

Interior of the birthplace bedroom, complete with a cradle and a child's shoe, June 2007

and concrete, and its roof forms a "hyperbolic parabaloid."[14] A sign over the entrance reads, "Mark Twain Memorial Shrine." Nothing here tells visitors whether it is a birthplace, a historic site, or a museum. Visitors have to go inside or read a nearby plaque in order to determine what kind of Mark Twain shrine they have happened upon. Rarely are museums labeled shrines today as they were in 1959 when this building was designed and constructed. The sign above the door speaks to the fact that the act of preserving any historic site or building is itself always a literal act of enshrinement and marks the people who visit as pilgrims seeking the equivalent of authentic religious insight into Mark Twain.[15]

Inside the building to the left is a wing devoted to the birth cabin and to the right is a museum wing. Visitors pay a four-dollar fee and can look into the house and explore the museum. There are no tour guides to introduce or interpret either feature, though there is a short film on Mark Twain's life, which is recommended by the staff person on duty at the front desk in the hall that connects the two wings of the shrine building. In the wing where you find the house, you can look through the windows and doorways into the 1830s two-room home. One room is set up as a multipurpose kitchen with a fireplace filled with cast-iron cookware, a kitchen table, a bed and trundle made up with the requisite log-cabin quilt, child-sized chairs, and marbles scattered across the pine floor as though a child lives and plays here. The other room is recognizable as a bedroom with a large ornately carved bed with pineapple bedposts and an elaborate coverlet, a wardrobe, a trunk, a chamber pot, and a cradle. Oddly, both rooms contain life-like stuffed sleeping cats, perhaps because Sam Clemens was known to love cats. If this is the house where Sam Clemens was born, it is likely that he would only have lived here as an infant for a few months, from his birth November 30, 1835, sometime early that same winter.

The house has three doors and three windows through which you can see the arrangement of historic objects. The staff has neatly whitewashed inside, and the house seems cozy with handwoven rugs in the two rooms and period decorations. Outside the cabin in the front is a wood-chopping block and woodpile, a hand-hewn bench made from a log, and a rattlesnake skin. The tableau is classic pioneer Missouri. It is common at other historic Missouri sites that commemorate western expansion before the Civil War, and not much stands out about this site except the few very nice pieces, like the carved bed, its coverlet, and the cats.[16] Nowhere in the house is there any evidence of the Clemens family. There is no evidence of Jennie, the enslaved woman whom the Clemens family brought with them from Tennessee, who no doubt lived with the Clemenses and their seven children.

At first glance, there is little to lead a visitor to understand that this is anything other than a classic example of a pioneer cabin. Surrounding the house are displays that speak to this same idea of pioneer Missouri. There is an exhibit about women's pioneer handcrafts like weaving and spinning. Two displays remind visitors that they are at a Clemens site. One is a display on Clemens's mother, Jane Lampton Clemens, and the other is a display about his connection to his Aunt Patsey and Uncle John Quarles's farm nearby. The Quarles farm exhibit includes a few archeological finds—some marbles that were found on the farm that Sam Clemens might have played with, two silver spoons that belonged to the Quarles family—and some quotations about the farm taken from Mark Twain's biography. Included is a note about Uncle Dan'l, an enslaved man owned by the Quarles family, who Clemens claimed at various times was a partial model for Jim in his novels *The Adventures of Tom Sawyer* and *Adventures of Huckleberry Finn*.

The display on Jane Clemens is curious. There is a scene set here—a rocking chair with a small table nearby with an oil lamp, a teacup and saucer, and a copy of *Adventures of Huckleberry Finn*. Also on the table is a transcription of Jane Clemens's description of her son's premature birth. A visitor can imagine Mrs. Clemens drinking tea, rocking in her rocking chair, while recalling her famous son's birth, and simultaneously reading his novel.[17] Next to this scene, the display's text reads: "Jane Clemens, 1803–1890: '. . . she had no career; but she had character, and it was a fine and striking sort.' —Mark Twain's Autobiography." Below these words are two images of her, one is a photocopy of a photograph in which she is wearing a broach that features the miniature photograph of a man, and one is a copy of a painted portrait. A caption explains that Jane Clemens served as the model for Aunt Polly in *Tom Sawyer* and *Huck Finn*.

Part of this display is an old clock, a panel about "button strings," where, according to the label, "In the 1800's [*sic*] young female collectors arranged buttons in lengths known as 'charm strings' or memory strings. . . A young woman began with a 'touch button' and the string grew as each friend and relative donated a special button." When she reached either ninety-nine or one hundred buttons, "her love would appear." What this gendered romantic tale has to do with Jane Clemens is unclear. Surely, a woman who had already married and had six living children by the time that Samuel Clemens was born did not spend her time collecting buttons as she pined for a husband. Also on display is an embroidery hoop framing red calico fabric with sloppy needlework in bright red, orange, and green. What this display says about who Jane Clemens was is so confusing that a visitor has to wonder. Did she have a charm string, is that how she met "her love?" Did she do needlework? Did she like clocks?[18]

In the other wing of the shrine building is a small museum.[19] Here items that belonged to Sam and Olivia Langdon Clemens are enshrined in simple displays. The museum includes their carriage, a comb used in Olivia Clemens's hair, a desk, a divan, and many other items that may have belonged to the family when they lived in Hartford, Connecticut, from 1873 to 1891.[20] These items are on display in no particular order and have little to do with Clemens's time in Missouri. Today nearly 15–20,000 people make the convoluted trek to visit these displays and look through the birthplace cabin each year.[21] What they find there does not tell them very much about Sam Clemens or about his connection to Florida. The fact that they continue to visit this place, despite its lackluster interpretation, indicates a desire to understand Clemens through his place of origin. Visitors have made this pilgrimage to Florida for over a hundred years.

### Early Pilgrims to Florida

The first guidebook written to aid sightseers looking to find "Mark Twain Country" was Clifton Johnson's 1906 *Highways and Byways of the Mississippi Valley*. His first-person travel narrative mimics Twain's use of regional dialect at times, as he makes his way first to Hannibal and then to Florida. Over several pages he describes his travels and the house he finds in Florida. He found that "the railroad doesn't go nearer than a half-dozen miles" and it was a "savage sort of highway that I travelled—a chaos of ruts and ridges, mud and pools." The roads looked as if they "had been ploughed by Satan and his imps to plague mankind" and the "low spots were a wild mixture of sticks and stones and liquid clay, and how a team could get along and keep right-side up was a mystery."[22]

Obviously, Johnson's journey to Florida was not easy. Nor was it easy for any literary pilgrim until the roads were paved and the house was moved in 1930 to Mark Twain State Park. In 1905, Johnson might not have found the birthplace without the help of a local woman, who may have led many other tourists to the Clemens houses in Florida. She "remembered distinctly when the Clemens family were [sic] residents of the place." He reported that John Marshall Clemens "built a log house to live in," and "while this log dwelling was being erected, the family occupied a little two-room frame house, and in the kitchen of that house Mark Twain was born, November 30, 1835." Johnson found that the "house still stands, though now vacant and tater ruinous," and that even the log cabin had "survived until recently, but during its later years no one lived in it and people got in the habit of taking away bits of it as Mark Twain relics."[23]

A Mark Twain birthplace cabin, no date, courtesy Library of Congress, Prints &
Photographs Division

"Why they tore the house pretty near to pieces!" said the old lady.
"They'd carry off brick-brickbats from the chimney and pieces of
glass from the windows and splinters of wood from the doors and
other parts, until they'd got everything but the logs."[24]

Johnson came too late to gather a relic from the log house, where Clemens
spent much of the first four years of his life. This fact alone points out that
he was not one of the earliest tourists to the area seeking a connection
to Clemens's place of origin. By this time, and in spite of the arduous
journey along muddy rural roads, most of the traces of the log house
were long gone. Yet, most of the framed birth house was intact, though
dilapidated. What Johnson does not tell his readers is that relic seekers
picked the log house apart because they believed *it* was Sam Clemens's
birthplace—the object of their quest.

As early as 1890, a local debate had arisen as to *where exactly* Clemens
was born. Some locals said he was born in the log house that was slowly
razed by memento seekers, others said he was born in the little framed

house that Johnson saw on his visit, in a two-story log cabin, in another framed cabin nearby, or at his Uncle John Quarles's house, and some said he was actually born one county over. Wherever Clemens was born, it was significant enough to Twain pilgrims that they often destroyed the physical structures of the cabins, which might have served as cradle for his genius, in their desire to hold on to a relic of him.

### Sam Clemens and Birthplaces

Although Clemens could not have known that his own boyhood home would be preserved for posterity, or that a few years later his birth-place would become a Missouri State historic site, that the house he built with Olivia Langdon Clemens would be opened to the public in 1932, or that eventually even his summer retreat would be preserved and open to scholars from around the world, he believed that the origin place of an individual was *sometimes* essential to who he or she would become. Even before Clemens's birthplace was commemorated, Clemens himself expressed an interest in historic birthplaces and occasionally championed historic preservation. Clemens's own interest in relics and historical preservation is an essential place from which to consider the proliferation of tourist sites associated with him. In a 1907 *New York Times* editorial, for example, he argued that the Abraham Lincoln Farm was a "birthplace worth saving."[25]

Of all the sites that Sam Clemens might have supported as places worth preserving, he chose only Lincoln's birthplace in Kentucky to endorse unreservedly. Lincoln's connection to that place was so central to who he would become, how his campaign would be marketed, and how his biography would fit within the larger national narrative that many people believed his birthplace deserved special attention.[26] In a broadside essay in support of the Lincoln Farm Association, Clemens wrote:

> Some people make pilgrimages to the town whose streets were once trodden by Shakespeare . . . But in most cases the connection between the great man or the great event and the relic we revere is accidental. Shakespeare might have lived in any town as well as in Stratford . . . But it was no accident that planted Lincoln on a Kentucky farm, half-way between the Lake and the Gulf. The association there had substance to it. Lincoln belonged just where he was put. If the Union was to be saved, it had to be a man of such an origin that should save it.[27]

In the case of Lincoln, the narrative was deterministic, and his birth-place was preordained like that of no other American figure, save George Washington. In the face of growing national interest in the commemoration of "historically significant" great men and the belief that American History was the result of these great men's actions, Clemens still understood that such places become monuments akin to religious shrines filled with "relics" for the people who visit them.[28] He even understood that a great number of people made pilgrimages to places where their reverence might be misplaced. Clemens supported the preservation of at least two other birthplaces, but at these, he seemed to dismiss a meaningful connection between the person and the place.

Clemens visited the most famous English literary birthplace, Stratford, and later even dedicated a birthplace in his home state in the memory of the St. Louis poet Eugene Field. He and Olivia made the trek to Shakespeare's birthplace as tourists in 1873.[29] Although Clemens had visited Stratford—the birthplace of Shakespeare—a year earlier on his own and had seen all the sites and even signed the register, he arranged a surprise visit for his wife.[30] He even endorsed an effort to build a memorial theater in Stratford shortly after this trip so that Shakespeare's works could be performed in his hometown. The Clemenses came home from Stratford with a Shakespeare relic of their own, a Mulberry sapling given to them by the Stratford mayor Charles E. Flower.[31]

The sapling, or "slip" as Clemens called it, was a descendant of the mulberry tree at Stratford rumored to have been planted by Shakespeare himself at his retirement home, "the New Place."[32] Not only were many relics said to have been made from this famous tree after it was felled, but numerous descendant trees were cultivated and sold as mementos to tourists.[33] Clemens was so taken with his relic tree that he wrote about it on at least two occasions and referred to it as "the Shakspeare mulberry."[34]

When a New Yorker offered in 1880 to plant a number of these Shakespeare mulberries in Central Park, a columnist in the *New York Evening Post* ventured that the trees might be stolen because of their value. In response, Clemens wrote a letter to the editor of the *Post* that recounted his experience with his relic sapling to reassure New Yorkers that these trees were not valuable:

> I prized it [the sapling] then, for its great lineage; I prize it yet—for other reasons . . . They tried her in a green house, but she wouldn't go; they tried her in the back yard; in the front yard; in the stable; in the cellar; on top of the house; in the kitchen; in bed—everywhere, dear, sir, but she was calm, she was indifferent, she gave no sign . . .
> When I got her she was seventeen inches high—now she is only

twelve inches. But what she has lost in longitude she has made up for in latitude, for her stem is twice as thick as it was at first. The nature of the Shakspeare [*sic*] mulberry is to grow downwards & sideways; you want to find that out early, & keep it in mind, & you will save yourself a good deal of trouble & the tree a good deal of annoyance.[35]

Although Clemens declared his initial interest in the tree came from its impressive literary lineage, by the time he finished his letter, he managed to challenge Shakespeare's immortal literary status, by indicating that the tree would likely outlive Shakespeare's reputation. Clemens's letter to the editor speaks to his distance from the relic industry at Stratford, his humorous take on the relic industry, his interest in it, and his realization that the authentic and inauthentic relics and mementos of a famous man may well outlive him.[36]

Many years later, Clemens visited and endorsed another birthplace in St. Louis, or so he thought. In 1902, during his last trip to Missouri he set aside time in a busy schedule, which included receiving an honorary doctorate and piloting a steamboat full of famous people up the Mississippi, to dedicate a plaque that commemorated the birthplace of fellow Missourian and poet Eugene Field. Field is largely forgotten today, but if remembered it is for his children's poems "Little Boy Blue" and "Wynken, Blynken, and Nod." Field died in 1895, and the literary elite in St. Louis held him in very high regard.[37] Clemens unveiled the plaque in front of a large crowd, which included international dignitaries who had come to St. Louis from France to prepare for the 1904 World's Fair.[38] He dedicated the plaque, saying, "My Friends—We are here with reverence and respect to commemorate and enshrine in memory the house where was born a man who, by his life, made bright the lives of all who knew him, and by his literary efforts cheered the thoughts of thousands who never knew him."[39] The shrine was short lived. Less than a week after its dedication, Roswell Field, the poet's brother, revealed that the historical commission and Clemens had enshrined the wrong building. Although a number of newspapers covered the mishap, at least one acknowledged that it was an easy mistake to make, because the family had lived in two houses during Field's very early childhood. Some coverage joked that Clemens would have to come back to Missouri just to remove and replace the plaque.[40]

When Albert Bigelow Paine, Clemens's biographer, made him aware of the mistake, Clemens replied, "never mind. It is of no real consequence whether it is his birthplace or not. A rose in any other garden will bloom as sweet."[41] Given Clemens's comments on Field's birthplace, his devotion to Lincoln's birthplace seems odd. It is ironic that historians then suspected and now recognize that the log cabin that the Lincoln Farm

Association secured as Lincoln's birthplace was counterfeit; the cabin was cobbled together from a number of local cabins.[42]

Clemens's statements in support of and ambivalence about birthplaces are confusing. He both champions the commemoration of writers' birthplaces through his personal effort to commemorate Lincoln and through his attempt to propagate the Shakespeare mulberry, but was unconcerned when Field's birthplace is revealed as misidentified. Sam Clemens's thoughts on birthplaces are a decent place to begin a discussion of his own. The story of his birthplace is equally confusing and perhaps fitting. But before the story of the cabin that is enshrined in Florida, it is important to briefly delve into the history of birthplace commemoration in the United States and England.

## Birthplace Commemoration

Birthplaces seem strange to us in a day and age when most are born in a hospital. Why do we remember birthplaces at all? Little has been written about remembering birthplaces in the United States until very recently, but a few themes seem to rise to the surface.[43] Birthplaces have been celebrated since at least ancient times in Greece and Rome. Bethlehem, Mecca, and Lumbini are among some of the first birthplaces that became the sites for religious pilgrimage. The celebration of birthplaces in the United States has had a decidedly shorter lifespan. The first birth to be formally celebrated in the "New World" under British rule was that of Virginia Dare. As the first white child born in North America to survive, Dare's birthplace on Roanoke Island was worth marking to English settlers.[44] Ultimately, the celebration of a birthplace makes the link between a historical figure and a place, between that place and the story of a nation, a religion, a region, or some other narrative to which a larger culture gives value.

Birthplace sites always assert a connection between personality and place, between local history and national history, and often between origins and genius. Birthplaces are essential in establishing national origins—and they are still the primary way that Americans qualify for the privileges of citizenship. A birth certificate would be unnecessary, if not for the need to confirm the link between rights and place. Birthplace museums often assert the *genius loci*'s influence on the celebrated personality. Literary birthplaces provide evidence of a connection between an author and an autobiographical link in his or her writing.

Birthplaces in the United States have troubled claims to authenticity because widespread interest in their preservation came about after the historical figures of the Revolutionary War and early republic had died, as had anyone who might have been present at their births. Commemorative efforts largely followed the Civil War, and sites were established as ways to heal the great national rift by embracing the country's early history. But these efforts were not necessarily concerned with issues of historical accuracy.[45] The 1931 "reconstruction" of George Washington's birthplace, for example, nearly destroyed the archeological foundations of the actual house. The log cabin designated as Abraham Lincoln's birthplace has been declared counterfeit after years of speculation and research by the National Park Service. Many other birthplace "replicas" have been constructed as shrines across the country. Theodore Roosevelt's, Andrew Johnson's, Davy Crockett's, and Millard Fillmore's "birthplaces" are merely replicas. There are plans in the works to build a birthplace replica for James Monroe.

Most often, birthplaces—real or replica—commemorate a famous man, but quite often, the people behind the early preservation of such historical sites were women. Women's volunteer organizations were the driving forces of efforts to commemorate historical figures following the Civil War and maintained an important presence in the preservation movement, even as historical preservation and commemoration became professionalized fields dominated by men. At Washington's birthplace, for example, the women of the Wakefield Association worked hard to make sure that a replica house was built to enshrine the birth of the first president because the original had long ago burned.[46] In the era that was still reeling from what Barbara Welter has called the "Cult of Domesticity," who could better establish birthplace shrines devoted to emblematic fathers of the nation than women, who, with their special domestic status, had exceptional insight into the kind of homeplace that gives rise to great men.[47] Even though women have often been involved in the preservation of birthplaces and many other types of house museums, the sites themselves rarely tell us much about mothers or women.

Mothers would seem an essential component of a birthplace, because they are the essential witness to any birth. A very few birthplaces have come to be interpreted through the lens of a mother.[48] Sam Clemens's birthplace celebrates Jane Lampton Clemens in the small display that conflates her life with that of the stereotypical pioneer woman. Jane Clemens herself tried to point interested fans in the direction of her son's birthplace during the last years of her life, because Sam Clemens remembered nothing about the place that he was born. Jane Clemens left Florida, Missouri, in 1839 but visited her sister there during the summer with Sam when he was little.

When the editors of the *Paris Mercury* were interested in determining where, exactly, Sam Clemens was born, Jane Clemens and Orion

Clemens, Sam Clemens's older brother, had a hard time pointing to the exact house. Their letter describing the birthplace was published in the newspaper in October 1890, but did not offer many details that helped solve the controversy. They explained that the birthplace was "a little white frame [house], one-story, with two small rooms or one room and a shed under the same roof" and that it was "too small for a baby to be born in."[49] Unfortunately, this described a number of cabins that claimed status as Clemens's birthplace. Sometimes even a mother cannot lead interested parties to an authentic birthplace.

## Literary Birthplaces and Childhood Homes

Are literary historic sites, like Sam Clemens's birthplace, any different from the places associated with and commemorated for other famous people? In the United States, like other historic sites, literary sites are most often dedicated to famous men. They frequently overlook the history of women, the history of enslaved peoples, and the history of a place before it was settled by Europeans.[50] What these sites might do differently is to incorporate the literary vision—or try to critically interpret the place as directly related to the authors' literary production as an origin point for inspiration—for the people they celebrate. As a result, their process of enshrinement can be distinctive, but is not necessarily so. Some literary sites emphasize the literary texts that authors have produced, but most focus on biography. These biographical sites often emphasize biographical connections at the place that led to the "greatness" of the author in just the same way that historic sites draw connections between the place and the "great" man that they usually celebrate. To understand Americans' interest in literary birthplaces it is useful to recount briefly the history of English literary tourism. Americans were some of the most enthusiastic visitors of English literary sites—including birthplaces—and many English guidebooks to literary places were written with American readers in mind.[51]

Though recent scholars have traced English literary tourism to the rise of Romanticism in English literature, the origin of English language literary birthplaces has long been traced to Stratford. Péter Dávidházi has argued that the celebration of Shakespeare's birthday in 1769 at the Stratford Jubilee, organized by actor David Garrick, was the origin of the "cult of Shakespeare" and the beginning of large-scale national attachment to literary personalities.[52] Nicola Watson has argued that Shakespeare's birthplace was the first celebrated literary birthplace.[53] Before Garrick's Jubilee, if someone had wished to commemorate Shakespeare, he or she would have wandered the streets of London where he lived and worked, or perhaps visited his graveside. Graveside literary tourism had been in practice since at least 1400 when Chaucer was buried in Westminster Abbey in what would become "poets corner" when William Blake, Charles Dickens, George Eliot, Samuel Johnson, and many others were buried there.[54]

The literary historian Aaron Santesso, in his article "The Birth of the Birthplace," argued that the replicated model of literary tourism came out of the development of Stratford as a tourist destination. This model of tourism "is based on the premise that by gazing at a literary site—particularly one connected to the origins of an author or work . . . allows us to understand it more fully than we would only by reading literary criticism."[55] In Santesso's Stafford model literary sites provide for tourists direct access to the *meaning* of a literary work, seemingly without the intervention of literary scholarship or historical interpretation. However, visitors are often unaware that the historic sites are the products of human intervention and that they have their own histories and interpretive take on the authors that they celebrate. Birthplaces seem particularly tricky, because the infant Shakespeare did not pen *Hamlet* any more than an infant Sam Clemens penned *A Connecticut Yankee in King Arthur's Court,* so access to birthplaces seems to provide dubious insight into some non-autobiographical texts. Indeed, often site managers and literary biographers have to construct the tenuous connections between birthplaces and adult writing. Anything that these sites can tell us about the author as a child must *directly* relate to the adult author we admire in order to make the place important enough to visit.

Sam Clemens's birthplace does not create these connections for its visitors. Removed as it is from its original site and with no real trace of Florida nearby, visitors cannot get a sense of the environment into which Clemens was born. As the shrine is currently set up, with the exception of the short film, there is no "critical text" offered as an interpretation of literary meaning at the site. What you can know from a visit to the current site is that Clemens was born in rural, rustic poverty that included manual labor—like chopping wood and spinning wool, that he grew up to be an important writer who wrote *Huck Finn* and *Tom Sawyer,* and that later in life he had a carriage, a wife, and many expensive pieces of furniture.

Santesso argues that Stratford and other sites like it exploit the literary expectations of visitors, create for them a world that panders to their visions of the writer's youth, *and* carefully construct a physical place that matches an expected historical experience. But evidence as to what tourists' actually think about a site and expect when they visit is hard to come by. If a literary historian were to track the interpretive changes at Shakespeare's birthplace over time, she might be able to eke out hints of visitors' expectations in how site managers have made changes.[56] Santesso juxtaposes the "Stratford model" with the less structured path of tourists to places like Hawthorne's Salem, where a visitor "envisions the site as an imaginative meeting place where the reader might engage with the author."[57] Specifically, Santesso, and many literary historians and critics, is interested in the kind of tourism that comes from a connection with place that creates a meeting of the minds between reader and writer, which happens largely outside structured tourist experiences. He cites Henry James's 1904 account of his experience tramping through Hawthorne's hometown (not visiting the House of the Seven Gables or Hawthorne's birthplace, as it exists today).[58] However, James himself elsewhere was very critical of literary tourism as a practice. His short story, "The Birthplace," ridicules and reviles the kind of people who would devote themselves to caring for Shakespeare's birthplace, and his novella, "The Aspern Papers," shows literary historians and biographers in an even more detestable light. Likewise, the literary critic Anne Trubek finds that literary sites do not create a connection between the author and the reader the way the simple act of reading does. She even advocates that we stop spending our time and money visiting and maintaining these sites and instead commemorate great writers through making their work available to more readers.[59]

Santesso sees John Milton's birthplace, and Salem, as the earliest models for a more sophisticated literary tourism. The London Bread Street location where Milton was born was not easy for literary pilgrims to transform into a simple symbolic story about Milton and the origins of his work. This is largely because Milton's work itself is not easily separated from the religious and political climate of his day.[60] Because Milton's work is harder for tourists to understand, his birthplace cannot tell a simple story of its relationship to place. Shakespeare's accessibility to the average reader, then, relegates his birthplace to tell a simple story. If this logic holds, Clemens's birthplace should be fated to tell a simple story as well. The story of many literary birthplaces and childhood homes like "Stratford . . . [are] a physical and occasionally architectural articulation of an argument about William Shakespeare: he was a humble man inspired by nature." It is very similar to the story that *might* be today at Sam Clemens's birthplace.[61]

Ultimately, Santesso argues for a more sophisticated tourist, one attracted to sites where he or she can seriously "commune" and "converse" with the creative spirit of an author. Childhood homes are rarely places where this might happen. The writer with whom the sincere literary tourist wants to commune did not exist yet at these sites. Perhaps this is why so many academic literary tourists are disappointed with what they experience at historic sites.[62]

## American Literary Birthplaces

Occasionally, the place where a writer grows up does figure prominently in his or her literary works, as in the case of the Mark Twain Boyhood Home in Hannibal, Missouri. However, the Clemens family only lived for a few months at the cabin that was Clemens's birthplace.[63] The commemoration of his birthplace is a bit of an anomaly in the United States. There are fewer historic sites devoted to the birthplaces of American authors than one might think. In her state-by-state guide, *American Author Houses, Museums, Memorials, and Libraries,* Shirley Hoover Bigger lists sites devoted to celebrating at least two hundred authors, and only twenty-three entries mention a birthplace as a primary or secondary point of interest. Most of the time, the place where an author is born is interpreted as less important than where he or she may have grown up, as childhood homes figure largely in the guidebook. According to *American Author Houses,* you can visit the birthplaces of Erskine Caldwell, Flannery O'Conner, Carl Sandburg, Ernest Hemingway, Ernie Pyle, James Whitcomb Riley, Robert Penn Warren, Arna Bontemps, Henry Wadsworth Longfellow, Emily Dickinson, William Cullen Bryan, John Greenleaf Whittier, Nathaniel Hawthorne, Sinclair Lewis, Eugene Field, Mark Twain, Joyce Kilmer, Walt Whitman, Will Rogers, Conrad Richter, Rachel Carson, Booker T. Washington, Pearl S. Buck, and Laura Ingalls Wilder.[64] These sites, unlike the Mark Twain Birthplace State Historic Site, do not emphasize a literary birthplace so much as they celebrate the site of a literary childhood. These sites may technically be the places where these authors were born, but importantly they make a connection between author and autobiographical literary text. As remote as Clemens's birthplace is, it is a stand-alone museum and shrine to a birth, akin to those devoted to figures of national history like Lincoln and Washington who similarly only resided in their birthplaces for a short period of their first three years.

At other literary birthplaces, the fact of the writer's birth is not the primary focus of the commemoration at the site. For instance, at the Homestead, Emily Dickinson's home for most of her life and where she was born, her birth is not the interpretative focus. Rather, curators have focused on Dickinson's seclusion at the house, her virginal white dresses, and, especially, the poetry that she wrote there as an adult while hidden away from the public eye. Nathaniel Hawthorne's birth house was moved to downtown Salem in 1958 to sit next to the House of the Seven Gables, a house he never lived in but where he set his famous novel. Carl Sandburg's birthplace sits across the street from his boyhood home, which is a popular tourist site, but the birthplace house is not open to the public. Sarah Orne Jewett's birthplace was saved for its historical associations with her ancestors in the Maine town where she grew up, and later the site was reinterpreted to honor her and her writing. Pearl S. Buck's birthplace was her grandmother's palatial plantation house in West Virginia, and the interpretation there has been slightly reworked to highlight Buck's literary efforts. Most of these birthplaces call upon the "Stratford model" in some way to connect the writer with the immediate environment to show the story began here and sometimes this is enough to keep the visitors coming.

A hope for a more sophisticated literary tourist might be doomed in the United States—as a place so intensely concerned with stories of its origins. Nonetheless, the recognition of birthplaces may be necessary because they claim points of entry into a national narrative, where important national biographies, like Washington, Lincoln, and Clemens's begin. Likewise, at the sites devoted to great men, this association is almost always presented as predestined. Lincoln was who he was because he was born on Sinking Spring Farm in Kentucky; Washington was who he was because he was born at Pope's Creek, Virginia; and Clemens was who he was because he was born in the kitchen of a small cabin in Florida, Missouri. The preservation of such places can be tied to the furor around Frederick Jackson Turner's thesis as well. With his assertion that the necessary conditions of the "American character" were disappearing with the growing population of the West, combined with the interest in celebrating American history after the Civil War and the Centennial, these places were all that was left to indicate the origins of "the American character."

### A Florida Shrine for Mark Twain

Each of these national birthplaces has been shaped by the conditions of their creation. Each interprets the connection between a great man and the place he was born. With Lincoln and Clemens, part of their biographical narrative appeal was the humble circumstance of their births. The humble circumstance of their births contributed to the fact that their birthplaces were likely destroyed or broken apart to be made into other humble vernacular structures long before they could be preserved. However, Lincoln, Washington, and Clemens were important enough—

to the people who decided to commemorate them, who made pilgrimages to their birthplaces, and who made a living of their popularity—to reconstruct.

## The State of Missouri's Birthplace Cabin

In 1890, it looked as if one of Clemens's birthplaces might be on the move. This was not uncommon.[65] The *Monroe County Appeal* reported that the Sam Clemens birthplace had been sold and was on its way to Chicago. The *Appeal* editors asserted that "Florida, one of the oldest settlements in Missouri, situated some 12 miles east of Paris, contains an old residence, a one-story, double frame house, with brick and stone chimneys at the end and the middle, built some 80 years ago, and known as Mark Twain's (Samuel Clemens) birthplace . . ." The cabin, it seemed, had "just been sold for world's Exhibition in Chicago in 1893, for the sum of $600." The new owners of the cabin pledged to have it moved overland "so that Mark's numerous admirers may behold the place of their hero's birth." The *Appeal* editors joked that Florida had "more old houses . . . which can be bought for half the price as this one—houses that Mark Twain looked at and played in."[66]

This article was followed a few weeks later by one in another local paper, which explained that the difficulties of moving the house were too great and that the house was to remain in Florida.[67] Just seven years later, in 1897, a notice appeared in the *Monroe County Appeal* making readers aware that a W. G. Roney had just purchased the Mark Twain birthplace and he had "received so many requests for souvenirs from the building that he has decided to work the oak and walnut portions of it into canes, brackets, pen holders, etc. which he will sell very cheap." The *Appeal* editors vouched for Mr. Roney, arguing that for "those who want a relic of the birthplace of the great humorist . . . he is one of the best men in the county and no one need have any fear of being humbugged."[68]

However many birthplaces there were, it is clear that people were interested in having a piece of Clemens's birthplace. By the time the next big American exposition was being planned, rumors again surfaced of the birthplace being moved to the site of the celebration, although this time the move was to be "in pieces." According to a 1934 account of the 1904 exposition in the *Paris Mercury*, "a frame house was cut up into canes, which were sold at the St. Louis World's Fair as having been made from the timber in the house where Mark Twain was born."[69]

Despite the accounts that reported the demise of Sam Clemens's birthplace as a result of memento seeking by Twain devotees and enterprising locals willing to piece apart the house for mementos, Florida resident Merritt Alexander "Dad" Violette argued that the building survived. The building he claimed was the author's birthplace was one that he purchased, preserved, and eventually gave to the state; it is now the primary attraction at the Mark Twain Birthplace State Historic Site. Dad Violette was born in 1849 in Florida, fourteen years after Sam Clemens. In Florida he found his fortunes lay entwined with those of Samuel Clemens. When Sam Clemens's biographer, Albert Bigelow Paine, visited while doing research on Clemens's early biography, he interviewed Violette's mother about the probable site of the birthplace. As Ralph Gregory notes in his biography of Violette, "Paine was informed, there were diverse beliefs in the town and state, and far beyond, in regard to which house in the town had been the birth house." According to Ralph Gregory, a local historian and the first site administrator at the Mark Twain Memorial Shrine, "Paine was convinced that house that Mrs. Eliza Damrell (Violette) Scott, Dad's mother, pointed out was the real one."[70] Paine inspiringly wrote:

> It is still standing and occupied when these lines are written, and it should be preserved as a shrine for the American people; for it was here that the foremost American-born author—the man most characteristically American in every thought and word and action of his life—drew his first breath, caught blinkingly the light of the world that in the years to come would rise up and in its wide realm of letters hail him as king.[71]

Paine's influence on the preservation of all things related to Sam Clemens in Florida and elsewhere cannot be overstated. In his effort to promote the notion that Clemens was the "man most characteristically American in every thought and word and action," Paine may have created the need to have a site that celebrated Clemens's birth.[72] It was not until Paine's urging that anyone nearby thought to preserve the Clemens houses in Florida. Dad Violette seems to have taken this sentiment to heart, and after Paine's visit, Violette became interested in the preservation of the cabin that his mother had identified.[73]

Paine's call for a "shrine" was answered. Although the cabin was occupied until 1910, suffered years of severe neglect, lost its windows and front porch, its fireplace or fireplaces, and perhaps its lean-to kitchen in the back, Violette was able to purchase it in 1915 and move it onto his property to restore. This was one of the earliest efforts in the United States to preserve a literary birthplace. According to a report in the *Hannibal Courier Post,*

> The humble little one story frame dwelling of three rooms has been purchased by M. A. Violette of Florida, and he will individually assume the responsibility of looking after the preservation of the landmark. . . . The roof was about gone and has been restored as it was, Mr. Violette, with due reverence to sentiment, having a number of Spanish oaks felled and the boards for the roof made with an old-fashioned frow . . . A platform is also to be built in front on which touring parties can have their pictures taken.[74]

Violette's work on the house showed that he intended to keep the house in working order and not dismantle it piece by piece. Even before restoring the house, Violette had built a number of campsites for tourists to the Florida area. The natural beauty of the Salt River Valley was a tourist draw for early twentieth-century Missouri campers. Violette eventually built cabins and a clubhouse and led tours of the cabin. In the 1910s, these facilities attracted Camp Fire Girls from nearby Missouri towns of Moberly, Mexico, and Santa Fe. Throughout the late 1910s and early 1920s, Violette ran the birthplace as its sole caretaker. There is no evidence that he ever charged for a tour of the house.[75] "Like Mark Twain," Ralph Gregory wrote of Violette, "he had a special tenderness and ideal respect for girls," and "they felt as highly and kindly toward him, they called him 'Dad.'"[76] The birthplace remained in his hands until one of the young female campers who visited and toured the house suggested to Violette that the birthplace be made into a state park.

### The Birthplace and the Origin of the Missouri State Park System

While camping there in 1922 as part of the Girl Reserves, a Christian girls camping club based in Moberly, Missouri, Ruth Lamson began a conversation with Dad Violette about the future of the cabin. She suggested that the cabin should belong to the state of Missouri. She was able to convince her father, Frank B. Lamson, to join her cause. As a result, the Lamson family spent the summer of 1923 in Florida staying in one of Violette's cabins, and Ruth Lamson helped run tours of the birthplace. Frank Lamson, secretary of the Moberly Chamber of Commerce, was already a Mark Twain admirer and became the treasurer and secretary of the newly formed Mark Twain Park Memorial Association.[77] He organized the association with H. J. Blanton, and together they raised endorsements, money, and support for a state park in Florida to memorialize Sam Clemens's birth.[78] Although the development of the park was Ruth Lamson's idea, the project shortly became the work of others—professional men—interested in the development of the area. In a document that he used to raise support for their cause, Frank Lamson explained that "Florida has but one claim to greatness and that is associated with the internationally great author, Mark Twain." He claimed that "the old Scotch Presbyterians of that section declare that Florida was foreordained to become his birthplace" and recited "the fact that Mark Twain made his home in many different cities and found the background of his stories in different sections of this and other lands, but only one place can lay claim to his birth and that is the little hamlet of Florida."[79]

The idea that the birthplace of Clemens was a site more deserving of commemoration than any other associated with the author's life certainly made it seem as though the association sought to compare the cabin with the Mark Twain Boyhood Home in Hannibal, Missouri, which by then had already been open to the public for more than a decade. The people in the area saw Florida as important in Sam Clemens's biography as the town of Hannibal and hoped to garner the same kind of tourist attention. According to Ruth Lamson, Violette had lamented that "he felt it [the birthplace] should be given more publicity as Hannibal seemed to receive all the attractions that Mark Twain brought."[80] After her inspiration to begin a park in Florida to commemorate Sam Clemens's birthplace, Ruth Lamson nearly slips from memory. Until 1994, there was no mention of her in the museum, no memory that she was the one to orchestrate the effort to get the interested parties together in the service of the state park project. In 1994, members of her family toured the birthplace and found no mention of her and brought her story to the attention of park officials. The site administrator John Huffman invited Ruth Lamson, now Ruth Lamson Armstrong, back to the park, and in 1995, she visited the birthplace. The park threw a party in her honor. A few months later, she died at her home in Kentucky.[81]

In preparing for the founding of the park, Frank Lamson and H. J. Blanton did most of the groundwork to convince Missouri governor Arthur M. Hyde that a Mark Twain Birthplace Memorial was a worthwhile project. They established the Mark Twain Memorial Park Association with E. E. Swain from Kirksville, W. C. Van Cleve and Frances Nise from Moberly, Omar D. Gray from Sturgeon, and Edgar White from Macon, Missouri, in 1923 at a meeting of the Northeastern Missouri Pressmen's Association.[82] The organization, made up largely of local bankers and "pressmen" interested in promoting Missouri's most famous newspaperman, Sam Clemens, were particularly proud that the author began his career as a typesetter and editor in northeastern Missouri.[83]

Lamson hoped that local pride and state interests would lead to the development of a Mark Twain State Park. He wrote in 1924 that "[i]f the plans of the Mark Twain Park Association . . . are realized, little Florida will become a literary shrine as famed as Stratford on Avon, England's Memorial to the immortal Shakespeare."[84] Of course, this was not quite the fate of the birthplace, for many reasons, not the least of which was geography. With Hannibal close by and already serving as an established tourist site and Florida virtually inaccessible to visitors, Florida residents had little chance to develop their site into a tourist destination the world would recognize.

The association, however, had raised enough money by 1924 to purchase most of the land needed to found the state park, and Ruth Lamson convinced Violette to donate the cabin to the association. The efforts of the association helped move the state closer to having a functional state park system. In 1924, their work was recognized in the proceedings of the *Missouri Historical Review*. The journal supported the association and urged its readers to do the same, asserting "perhaps the Mark Twain Memorial State Park will be the harbinger of a system of state parks for Missouri such as reflect so much credit on Eastern commonwealths" and "if so, again would the spirit of Mark Twain be pioneer."[85] The organization's goal was that the site of Sam Clemens's birth would inspire the birth of a state park system in Missouri that would celebrate all its native treasures, from Mark Twain to the Ozark Mountains. Until this time, although the Missouri State General Assembly had voted to appropriate 5 percent of all fish and game licensing funds to the development of State Parks and Lands in 1917 and in 1923 increased the percentage, no state park system had been established.[86]

In 1923, Missouri governor Arthur Hyde informed state residents of his intention to develop a state park system and even encouraged citizens to make suggestions to his office about landscapes in Missouri worth preserving.[87] The Mark Twain Memorial Park Association set out to answer Hyde's call with its charter. They proposed to acquire land for the park only in preparation to give it to the state. They planned a public park "that will be maintained for all time as a literary shrine for the nation, and as a fitting memorial to Samuel L. Clemens, better known as 'Mark Twain,' whose writings have made the world a better place in which to live." They wanted the park "to be a place to which people may resort, for reflection, diversion, recreation, and the enjoyment of such natural and artificial advantage, as the said park might afford." But most important, they hoped that a Mark Twain Memorial State Park would "advertise Missouri as the home of a people who appreciate genius, and a state in which the sciences, arts, literature, agricultural, and other activities peculiar to Christian civilization flourish on every hand under the inspiration of public appreciation, a state in which the humblest child, if possessed with talent, industry, character, and ambition may rise to the pinnacle of usefulness and fame, as did the one in whose name the Park is established."[88] Mark Twain was synonymous with Missouri, and celebrating his genius was a way to claim the origin of their own. Many of these ideals were nearly identical to those expressed by George A. Mahan in his 1912 dedication of the Mark Twain Boyhood Home in Hannibal. In 1924, Mark Twain State Park seemed poised to bring in a new state park system. And the state seemed to embrace the birthplace as the centerpiece of a state park that would be both a shrine to the author and a place where tourists could engage nature and reflect upon its connection to Missouri's most famous resident.

## The First Controversy at the Birthplace

With all the work from local businessmen to make the park happen, the almost universal support of people interested in history, nature, and literature across the state, all the funds raised to purchase the land to make the park, and Dad Violette's generous donation of the birthplace cabin, the birthplace seemed poised to be Missouri's first state park. However, questions about the birthplace's authenticity that had faced Albert Bigelow Paine in his search for the birthplace came up again. Although Paine had accepted Violette's mother's identification of the Clemens house, many others in the immediate community of Florida disputed this claim. It seems locals were willing enough to let Violette draw visitors to the area and to let the small community benefit from the modest tourist revenues that the Twain pilgrims brought with them, but when it came time for the birthplace to be officially sanctioned by the state, rumors began to surface that the cabin was *not* the birthplace. By 1925, the state had agreed to accept the gift of the land for the new park and began developing the area, but the birthplace cabin was not moved to its new location as planned. It stayed in Dad Violette's yard where he tended it every day, waiting for the state to accept his gift and relocate the birth cabin to the new state park.

In a 1927 letter to Frank Lamson, who had moved his family out of state by this time, Violette described the work that had taken place at the new park:

> The improvement on the Mark Twain State Park is going on slowly, they are going to make some more driveways in the Park and are going to build a house to enclose to [*sic*] Mark Twain birth house. I was in Paris the other day and saw Mr. Blanton[;] he is going to turn

the house over to the State when they make the proper arrangements to enclose it and I guess it will be done late this summer or early in the fall. The park looks very nice now and quite a number of visitors are coming every day. I have a man to look after the Mark Twain birth house and they have about filled the registration book that they had while you were here, it contains about 50,000 names of people from everywhere.[89]

Although the cabin was still receiving great numbers of visitors and the state had dedicated Mark Twain State Park in 1924 after garnering national attention to the area for its celebration, the park progressed without the birthplace cabin. The park association had secured a place to commemorate Sam Clemens and his relationship to Florida, Missouri, with a beautiful stretch of land that had little, if any, historical connection to Sam Clemens.[90] The park association chose the original one hundred acres for Mark Twain Memorial State Park because of its view of the Salt River Valley. Sam Clemens might have roamed the area when he visited his uncle and aunt on their farm, but there was no concrete connection between the place and Clemens. The view from the bluffs was lovely, and campers came to admire the scenery, but they did not find the birthplace cabin there. Without the house, the site was incomplete. Many made the hike from the state park to Violette's yard where there they could complete their pilgrimage. But why hadn't the birthplace cabin moved to the park as soon as it was established? Violette mentions the need for a structure to enclose and protect the birth house in the letter to Lamson, but there were other reasons. No one was sure if the house was really the place where Clemens was born.

A full two years later in 1929, local newspapers sought to investigate what they referred to as the "unfortunate question as to the authenticity of the old house owned by the Mark Twain Association."[91] In response to an article that appeared in slightly different versions in local newspapers, Violette and the editor of the *Monroe County Appeal* claimed that Clemens's father, John Marshall Clemens, had "built the present house the year after he settled in Florida," and it "was later saved from destruction by M. A. Violette, who bought it and, with rare vision for the future, preserved it for posterity."[92]

Published at the same time was a letter to the editor from M. A. Dad Violette that explained his claims about the cabin's authenticity. It deserves to be included in its entirety:

> In regard to the birth house of Mark Twain, I will state that I was born in Florida in 1849. My mother lived here for many years. She

was fourteen years of age at the time Mark Twain was born and remembered him to the time his family moved to Hannibal.

My grandmother, Mrs. Edmund Damrell, was a friend of the Clemens family while they lived here, and no doubt present when Mark Twain was born. My mother told me a number of years ago the present birth house of Mark Twain was where he was born, and some years after, I learned that the owners were going to tear down the Mark Twain birth house, as it was too old to repair, so I bought the old house and moved it across the street from the original place.

I could not buy the land it was on, and in due time gave it to the Mark Twain Park Association, which I hope they will move to the Mark Twain park, and place it where future generations can see it.

Bigelow Payne [*sic*] was here and decided that this was the Mark Twain birth house and the State Commissioner that erected the marker investigated the place where he was born and erected their marker accordingly.

I hope that you'll have the house moved to the Park and a substantial building erected over it to protect it for all time.

I am eighty years old now and would like to see the house removed while I live and have Madame Clara [Clemens] come back, as she promised to do and sing us a song.[93]

Violette's letter seems a desperate plea to have loose ends tied up before he died. Because the State of Missouri had already accepted the land and the cabin as gifts and authorized and opened the Mark Twain State Park, it was required to take responsibility for the cabin on Violette's property, whether it was really Sam Clemens's birthplace or not.

Finally, a year later, in June 1930, Violette got his wish. The house was moved and incorporated into Mark Twain State Park during his lifetime. Using one horse and a rig ordinarily used to pull stumps, workers jacked up the house, set it upon wheels, and transported it to a bluff overlooking the Salt River. Atop the house rode two boys, one dressed as Tom Sawyer and the other dressed as Huck Finn. Though some locals were likely still suspicious of the structure's authenticity, the boys atop the house certainly did their best to cloak the cabin in Twain's aura. Later that year a temporary shed was constructed around the birthplace to protect it from the elements and from curio seekers. The structure provided visitors with a view of the cabin through wire windows on four sides and was nothing more than a shed with a lock on it, sometimes opened to the public. Violette continued to walk up the road to the state park from his house on Sundays to open the birthplace for tourists when he could. He died on January 30, 1931.[94] The birthplace would stay in the shed enclosure until 1960 when the current museum building was constructed.

## Stunted Growth at the Park

Many state parks during the Great Depression found support in the relief programs of the New Deal and particularly in the widespread efforts of the Civilian Conservation Corps. The residents of Florida thwarted the development of Mark Twain State Park by opposing a "colored" unit of the CCC, and in doing so, it is likely that they not only sealed the fate of Florida, Missouri, but also devastated the development of their primary attraction. By the time the CCC got to Mark Twain State Park in 1939, many historic sites across the United States had benefited from the CCC's efforts in national, state, and even city parks. A number of factors, including Florida's remote location, the Great Depression, state budgets, and World War II, hampered the development of Mark Twain State Park. However, the single greatest obstacle to the park improvement was the surrounding population's opposition to the black enrollees of the CCC. Florida may have lost its greatest opportunity for economic development by banning African Americans from its village borders.

When news came to Florida that it was to receive CCC Company 1743, a "colored Junior Company," Florida residents argued that "a camp composed of white boys will fit into our economical and social life much better than colored boys."[95] In early October 1939, Charles Hamilton, owner of a general store in Florida, and resident John Massey delivered a petition to the State Park Department in Jefferson City with twenty-eight signatures that read:

> We the undersigned citizens of Florida, Missouri and Monroe County hereby certify that we do not desire to have a colored Civilian Conservation Corps Camp established in Florida, Missouri. We feel that situated as we are surrounded by thirteen (13) towns that have a negro population that it would be just a matter of time until this town and county would also have an excess population of negroes. The women folks of Florida, Missouri fear that the establishment of a colored Civilian Conservation Corps Camp in Florida, Missouri would be a menace to their safety and welfare. However, we are willing to cooperate in every way possible to establish a Junior White Civilian Conservation Corps Camp at Florida, Missouri, and will give our support and cooperate in helping to establish, and maintain this said Junior White Conservation Corps Camp, if an[d] when same is established.[96]

Among the signees of the petition were Dan P. Violette (Dad Violette's son) and his wife.[97] Although the park was a tourist site for the surrounding area and in much need of the kind of development that a CCC company could offer such as campsites, working roads, support buildings, and signage, Florida's commitment to its all-white status is clear; any "negro population" would be an excess.

The Missouri State Park Board and the National Park Service had devised a plan for Company 1743 at the Mark Twain Memorial State Park to span over six years. The company was set to construct a man-made lake and to build a lodge, cabins for visitors, new campgrounds, a marina and boat ramps, fishing facilities, roads, and trails. Most important to our story of the birthplace, the plan included "a museum dedicated to Mark Twain and removal of the author's birth cabin back to its original location in the village of Florida."[98] This plan would have given the residents the literary shrine that they had dreamed of since Ruth Lamon and her father first envisioned a state park that would be the American Stratford. It would have returned the cabin to its historical environment, ensuring the necessary connection between the environment, the cabin, and Clemens to create successful interpretation for tourists to site.

Despite the promise of the shrine, the people of Florida enlisted Missouri governor Lloyd Stark on their behalf to take their petition directly to the director of the CCC in Washington, D.C. Not long after the petition was delivered, I. T. Bode, the Missouri coordinator for the CCC, came to nearby Paris to talk to residents about their opposition to Company 1743. He let them know that he understood their objections and had looked into the conduct of the company. He reported that "the official information [is] very much in favor of the Negroes." The last town where the company had been stationed, "instead of wanting to get rid of the organization . . . the citizens [there] had protested against its removal." "Unfortunately," according to a *Monroe County Appeal* article recounting Bode's visit, "the state authorities had no control over the matter and [Bode] feared it might resolve itself into a choice between getting a big job done by well-behaved Negro workers or not getting it done at all."[99] Florida residents eventually rescinded their petition against the black workers' camp with some stipulations. The CCC was to "go right ahead with its plans for developing the Mark Twain State Park at Florida into a national literary shrine but [they would] not permit Negro enrollees who do the work to enter the village of Florida at any time for any purpose."[100] The ban may have been the death knell for the tiny hamlet.

The enrollees in Company 1743 were often men from the surrounding area with local connections and families. Many sent their paychecks home and spent their down time there as well. Eventually, after determining that the camp posed no threat and that Florida businesses were losing enrollee paycheck dollars, which went to other nearby communities like Perry and Paris, Florida residents allowed the black workers to enter.[101] One enrollee recounted his experience with the CCC in Florida in an interview with Missouri State Park officials in 1997. "When we came to Mark Twain, things were a little hard at first. We couldn't go into Florida or Stoutsville. . . . They thought a group of Colored boys was gonna be unruly but we were like everyone else, we came to do a job."[102] Many enrollees, like Ernest Dickerson, decided to never venture into Florida and got into the habit of spending time and even settled in areas nearby. As he recalled in an interview, "I was in Florida . . . not in Florida, Mark Twain State Park, Company 1743. We weren't allowed to go into Florida but that didn't bother me because I went home, Monroe City, just about every weekend."[103]

World War II cut the efforts of the men in Company 1743 short. In July 1942, Company 1743 was disbanded and many of the men transferred into active military duty. They had only just begun their work at the park but had been able to develop trails, campgrounds, and a park office building and to provide a working water system throughout. Little of what Company 1743 built at Mark Twain State Park still stands today. State park historian John Cumming uncovered the few of the buildings that remain, but many had already been razed. One old barn, now used for park maintenance and storage, is still standing; Cunning uncovered the names of the men who built it marked on the walls.[104] The birth cabin stayed put, enclosed in the shed.

### The Mark Twain Birthplace Shrine

After Company 1743 left the park, all park development halted until roughly 1959. No roads were built, no campsites developed, and most important for the birthplace, little was done to maintenance the cabin inside the shed. When visitors could get a tour inside, they would see the cabin outfitted as it had been since it was moved from Dad Violette's yard. In the wake of World War II and throughout the buildup to the Bicentennial in 1976, historical tourism in the United States boomed. In Missouri, this meant that historic sites began to be developed separately from other kinds of state parks that focused on natural resources. At Mark Twain State Park, this meant that the birthplace came to have a separate institutional identity from the rest of the park. It became a historic site within a larger state park. In 1959, the historic site was finally slated for development. During this same time, a local resident, Twain-fanatic, collector, and secretary of the Mark Twain Research Foundation, Chester Davis, saw his dream come true. Davis was the primary motivator for the foundation, and for many years, he was the editor of *The Twainian,* a part fan and collector magazine and part scholarly journal devoted to Clemens. Davis had a national audience with *The Twainian* to which he circulated stories about the dangers he saw facing the birthplace.[105]

Davis and other local enthusiasts had been collecting Twain memorabilia for decades. Most significantly, many of these local collectors had made a trip to Los Angeles to the April 10, 1951, auction held by Clara Clemens of her father's personal items. Members of the Mark Twain Research Foundation collected most of the objects in the museum side of the shrine building today. While the birthplace was semi-protected by the shed that the state had built around it, the shed was not outfitted for fire protection and could not keep vandals out. The foundation members lobbied their state congressional representatives arguing that the birthplace cabin needed better facilities and that they needed a museum devoted to their collection. By late 1958, the State of Missouri had decided to dedicate considerable energy and resources to providing a proper memorial and "shrine" building for the birthplace.[106]

Built of local stone, concrete, and glass, the modern building stood out in the state park where all the other structures had been built by the CCC in the 1930s. Designed to be the new home of the birthplace cabin, the little cabin was enclosed in a great hall with limestone walls and red industrial tile floors. The rest of the building serves as a repository for the Twain items on loan from the Mark Twain Research Foundation, including a carriage he had used, chairs, a desk, and a pipe that once belonged to Clemens. The building was not part of the rustic scenery of the Salt River Valley, nor was it in the style of the buildings that had been built by the CCC, but the controversial birthplace cabin now had a new home, and the objects collected by Chester Davis and others had a venue for appreciation. Although housed in a new building, the house was still largely the same. In 1959, the state hired a professional historical decorator to outfit the house with pioneer Missouri artifacts.[107] Period appropriate furniture and items for the house replaced the hodge-podge collection that had accumulated in the cabin. Photos taken at the birthplace cabin before and after the 1960 move show other changes as well. Images taken, but not used, for a 1944 *Life* magazine photo-essay showed the interior as spare and the walls as deteriorating. Inside, visitors would have seen pioneer-era items alongside portraits of Sam Clemens, first editions of his works, and various and sundry other mementos—much like the boyhood home in Hannibal's displays from the 1920s and 1930s.

In the new museum space, the spinning wheel and organ that had been strangely crowded into the little house moved outside. The cabin was now so packed with "new" historic objects that there was almost no room to imagine its ten occupants. Despite the move and the new arrangement inside the house, the interpretation of the birthplace did not change. The house did not and does not tell visitors much about Clemens, other than this is where he was born. Today, it does not even clearly indicate that Mark Twain Lake is a new addition to the "historic" landscape. It certainly does not point out that if there was connection between the area and Sam Clemens, most of that historic landscape is now underwater. This fact alone hinders the site's ability to make a direct environmental determinist argument about Clemens's origins at the birthplace.

Although most of the displays have stayed the same at the birthplace from 1960 until today, in the mid-1990s, the site briefly introduced poster-board exhibits on its own history. Staff members at the Mark Twain Birthplace State Historic Site tracked down and interviewed the last remaining local members of Company 1743, as part of the Missouri Department of Natural Resources assessment of CCC activities in the state. This effort was in part to ensure that the CCC-constructed buildings could themselves be historically preserved and protected.[108] Some outtakes of interviews were transcribed; these are still held at the Mark Twain Birthplace State Historic Site archives in Florida. As part of a staff effort to celebrate Black History Month, edited portions of the outtakes made their way briefly into a poster-board display about the work of Company 1743 and the difficulties they faced. In the display, the site staff made sure not to include the names of any of the signees of the petition, nor did they include the portion of the petition that referenced the "menace" that the CCC troops posed to white women. The small exhibit was carefully edited to suggest that the local population was racist in its stand against Company 1743, but not the extent to which residents participated. These events were still too recent in local memory to include the names of the people who sought to keep Florida white.[109] The exhibit was destroyed soon after Black History Month to make room for a new exhibit. After Ruth Lamson's visit, the poster board and other materials were repurposed for an exhibit on her contribution to the state park that was meant to be temporary.

The Lamson display replaced the Company 1743 exhibit, in honor of a Women's History Month over a decade ago. This display still stands next to the front desk and includes snapshots of Lamson at the party the park staff threw in her honor in 1995.[110] Other than the now semipermanent Lamson exhibit, all of the interpretation at the museums remains the same as it was in 1960. Many times since, new interpretative master plans were drawn up (1961, 1979, and 1985), but never implemented. The largest change has been the inclusion of a slide show and later a short film about Sam Clemens's life.[111] It is possible that these interpretive delays, like the building of the museum itself, were caused and even canceled because of state budget concerns. It is also possible that the State Park Board, and then the Department of Natural Resources that subsumed it, decided against implementing new interpretive plans because of lingering suspicions that the birthplace cabin was not actually where Clemens was born. Throughout the park's existence, interested tourists have occasionally brought in picture postcards of other buildings that claimed to be the *real* birthplace and challenged park staff about the cabin's authenticity.[112] The persistent question about the site's authenticity has meant that the state has never given the site the kind of financial and intellectual backing that would help it develop into a major tourist destination. Despite recurring complaints, even from high-ranking officials in the Department of Natural Resources, basic signage at the birthplace still barely exists.[113]

## A Park Unsure of Its Origin

The museum's first curator, Ralph Gregory, hired in 1960 with the advent of the new museum building, is still convinced the house the state has enshrined really is Sam Clemens's birthplace.[114] Gregory spent a great deal of his time as curator, as the wealth of handwritten notes in the site's archive testify, trying to prove the cabin's absolute authenticity. As late as 1980, Gregory was still publishing short research pieces on the birthplace, each one supposedly the last word on the cabin's authenticity.[115] When I interviewed the ninety-eight-year-old Gregory in 2008, he nearly convinced me with the evidence he has collected, though all of it ultimately came from the same source—Dad Violette.

However, the state park system has never been entirely convinced. As recently as 1983, then site administrator Stan Fast set about studying the cabin for evidence of its age and history. His report did not "vindicate" the cabin:

> For some time we've been interested in trying to establish both the authenticity and the number of structural changes the cabin has undergone since its completion in the 1830's—in other words, its history. Very likely these questions will never be answered to everyone's satisfaction. . . . As for the authenticity of the cabin . . . this museum holds no incontrovertible documents. A few long time local residents have an oral tradition that the real birthplace either burned

down or fell down before the state got possession. In the absence of proof to the contrary such traditions die hard . . . . The most discouraging bit of news is that the cabin does not vindicate itself.[116]

Fast, a trained architectural historian, found—through an extensive analysis of nail types, saw cuts, and structural clues that remained hidden under the cabin's sided exterior—that Dad Violette's claim that the cabin was 80 percent "original" to the time of Clemens's birth was seriously flawed. Most of the nails, boards, shingles, siding planks, and even the door and window frames were newer than the period in which the Clemens family would have lived there.[117] Whether Violette's restoration was the cause of most of these changes is unclear.

Fast discovered evidence that the cabin was cobbled together from a number of sources. Although this would not have been uncommon in a settlement where lumber was in high demand and residents were impoverished, much of the cobbling looked to Fast as though it would have happened long after the dates of the Clemenses' residence. Fast concluded that the state should "be very cautious when drawing conclusions about either authenticity or the extent of structural change to the cabin over the years" and believed that the "question of authenticity remains unanswered." He recommended further research into the structure and the cabin's history because, as he asserted, the "museum's major artifact is important enough to warrant close examination. *The site's visitors are entitled to know, is this the cabin faithfully though amateurly* [sic] *restored or is it Violette's replica made from material that once may have been part of the birthplace cabin of Samuel Langhorne Clemens?*"[118] Although the site's visitors and the state taxpayers might be entitled to know whether the cabin is the birthplace of Sam Clemens, it is likely that they never will.

Fast's report has had no impact on the way that the state continues to present the birthplace. Although every few years someone raises a question about the cabin's authenticity, we may never see the state admit that the cabin is a fabrication. Despite his research, even Fast still argues, "I think I could say that I was pretty convinced that that cabin had a direct association with Mark Twain of some kind. I don't believe that I could say that there was any physical evidence so much that pointed to that. But the more I looked at Dad Violette, the more I kind of saw him and his character as such that I don't believe he would have tried to perpetrate a hoax on people just simply for the few dimes and nickels that he might be getting by just showing that cabin . . ."[119] Of course, all the evidence Fast and others have about the character of "Dad" Violette has come primarily through the research and writing of Ralph Gregory. The recently retired site administrator John Huffman believes that the evidence that was amassed by Gregory "proves" the house is authentic.[120] All of the claims of authenticity at the site come down to whether you can believe Violette's account above all evidence to the contrary. The site never acknowledges the rift between oral history and the physical evidence the house provides.

Ultimately, like many other historic sites, this site's claim of authenticity may not matter as much as the stories that a place tells or enables us to tell about Missouri history. Today, the birthplace presents a simple, generic, and partial story of one pioneer family, which gave birth to Mark Twain. A pioneer site in Missouri that promotes a famous Missourian is enough to keep interested tourists coming in the doors. But the site does not tell the story of Florida, Missouri. In essence, it cannot do so because there is so little left of the town to interpret for visitors. The history of Florida has not been directly tied to the history of Clemens at the state site. The story of the Clemens family's meager means, and those of their neighbors and other early Missouri settlers could be told with a replica cabin. The cabin could help visitors understand how a family of nine people and at least one slave lived. But the interpretation at the site has not effectively connected the place to the man.

The Mark Twain Birthplace State Historic Site attempts to interpret a version of Clemens's story that matches the "Stratford model" that Santesso outlined, and it fails to do what that simple model requires—to make a connection between the place and the genius born there. This failure might not matter much to the average tourist—who finds the site by accident, but to the literary pilgrim who has found his or her way to the site, the cabin does not illuminate the origin of the writer. As a result, even though the cabin sits in a museum, the story that the site tells about Clemens has stayed essentially the same since Dad Violette's time: *This is the place where the great man was born.* Nothing more and nothing less. The 1960s museum exhibits do not connect Clemens's literary work with his first four years in Florida, nor do they connect with the world of scholarly research into Clemens and his world.

The state park and Mark Twain Lake are lovely. On my second trip to do research at the birthplace, during a very hot week in August, I was tempted to go for a swim and call it research. But, Sam Clemens never swam here, because the lake did not exist. He certainly may have gone for a dip in swimming holes along the Salt River, but those spots are at the bottom of the lake now. Everything that you see outside the museum has drastically changed from the time of Clemens's birth. However, ironically, it may be that lake that will keep this particular historic site afloat. The museum is well located for tourists to the area who are seeking "flatwater recreation." It gleams in the sunlight from across the lake. Half of the people who come into the museum today come in to ask directions to somewhere else. Upon finding they are at the Mark Twain Birthplace State Historic Site they think "back [and say,] 'oh, my goodness, this is one of America's, if not the most famous, author we've ever produced; we'd better spend a little time here.'" Visitors, according to former site administrator Stan Fast, "would come in and spend between half an hour, maybe, and forty-five minutes and learn a little bit about Mark Twain," and have "this really neat cultural resource experience in the middle of what had started out to be simply a site-seeing trip or an effort to enjoy some flat-water recreation or something of that sort."[121]

Visitor numbers at the Mark Twain Birthplace State Historic Site have fluctuated between 100,000 and 13,000 visitors a year since 1999. More visitors come to this state historic site than to any other associated with a single Missouri personality except Harry Truman. The birthplace saw ten times as many visitors as the Thomas Hart Benton house and the Nathaniel Boone home in 2008.[122] Perhaps with these visitation numbers, Clemens would laugh off the conflicted history of his birthplace and venture, as he did with Eugene Field, "never mind. It is of no real consequence whether it is [my] birthplace or not. A rose in any other garden will bloom as sweet." But for scholars of Samuel Clemens and historians invested in the effort that state historic sites do their best to make a meaningful contribution to educating the public and presenting local history accurately, this site leaves much undeveloped.

The State of Missouri might make a meaningful interpretive shift, follow the lead of Lincoln's birthplace, and reveal the "replica" status of the cabin, while making a concerted effort to tell the real history of Florida and its demise. The story of the development of the park—Ruth Lamson, the community's resistance to African American CCC workers, the tacit cover-up of the legitimacy concerns surrounding the cabin, and the largely un-mined history of the building of the lake—are more interesting than the story told at the "birthplace" today and might say a good deal more about Missouri history in the meantime. If only we could convince Missouri that it did not have to tell the story of Sam Clemens with a "real" historic house.

Stagnation at small sites like this one is not uncommon, and all across the country historic house museums face the same problems. With no budget or institutional prerogative, there is little reason for these sites to change. One of the most troubling findings in my research on the site was that the State of Missouri had invested in three different plans that would have updated the museum in the 1980s and 1990s. Most of these changes would have required little funds. But the state's decision to not publicly acknowledge what Stan Fast's research into the cabin reveals—

that the cabin cannot be considered the authentic birthplace of Sam Clemens—has prevented the site from making an interpretation that engages Clemens's origin and his very real connection to Missouri.

The Lincoln "symbolic birthplace cabin," George Washington's birthplace "memorial house," Laura Ingalls Wilder's birthplace admit that they are replicas, symbolic structures, or "memorials." Not all of these sites have worked out the kinks of embracing their "fakeness." Lincoln's house invites visitors to celebrate and learn about the other "authentic" elements nearby and points visitors to the nearby boyhood home of Lincoln while ignoring that gigantic marble mausoleum that encloses the symbolic birthplace at the park—the most fascinating relic of Lincoln commemoration the site offers visitors. The George Washington Birthplace National Monument does not even mention that it has a fake birthplace on its Web site, despite the fact that the house is the primary building that any tourist would see upon visiting the site.

Replica status does not keep tourists away from "historic" sites. In fact, as discussed earlier, while tourists are interested in "authenticity" at heritage sites, that authenticity can come in many forms. Tourists are savvier than many think and are used to, and may even enjoy, finding out that things are not what they seem. Perhaps if these symbolic birthplaces could band together, they could work on an engaging interpretative story that explains how these places came to be, and, in the process, speak meaningfully about the commemorative impulse in the United States that has led to the perpetuation of these birthplace "replicas." Their histories might remind us that birthplaces and origins matter and that they may matter most when we cannot find them.

# Chapter Two

# Hannibal as Hometown

## The Stories Started Here

Somewhere in the geography of the American mind lay an image—a literary icon—of a small-town boy named Sam Clemens and his great muddy god the Mississippi. Even now, after we've transplanted hearts and left junk on the moon, the legends of Huck and Tom and Nigger Jim and Injun Joe won't go away. All summer long, like Canterbury pilgrims, tourists come in their Winnebagos and Airstreams and station wagons, to this rangy, ragtag, but somehow endearing river town 100 miles upstream from St. Louis. Some cannot even say why they are here.

—Paul Hendrickson (*Washington Post*, 1978)

Samuel Clemens lived long enough to see the places associated with his early life, including his boyhood home, become tourist destinations. Clemens visited his boyhood home for the last time in 1902 and had his photo taken in front of the house, just as a tourist might. The image is famous today, in part, because the museum at Clemens's boyhood home has embraced it as a touchstone for interpretation at the museum. However, the site's popularity over the years has made the house almost as synonymous with Tom Sawyer as it is with Clemens. Several editions of *The Adventures of Tom Sawyer* use Clemens's boyhood home in Hannibal, Missouri, as the direct model for illustrations of Sawyer's home with Aunt Polly. Even in the original 1876 illustrations for the book, the house looks strikingly similar. The house, in effect, is as tied to the fiction

Clemens at the boyhood home, 1902, courtesy of the Mark Twain Boyhood Home and Museum

of Mark Twain as much as it is to the life of the young Sam Clemens. The history of the Mark Twain Boyhood Home and Museum is perhaps the most important case study in this collection because the boyhood home is one of the literary historic sites where the interpretation of literature has thrived.

It has thrived because visitors to Hannibal have always looked for Clemens's characters there. A less renowned contemporary of Clemens, Clifton Johnson, devoted an entire chapter of his own book, *Highways and Byways of the Mississippi Valley* (1906) to "Mark Twain Country." Johnson was not only interested in the author's boyhood home and birthplace. He also visited other houses and sites in Hannibal associated with the

TOM AT HOME.

Detail of illustration from the first American edition of *The Adventures of Tom Sawyer,* 1876. Courtesy Mark Twain Archive, Elmira College

characters in Clemens's fiction. Johnson tracked down and visited, for example, what was left of the "Huck Finn" house, a dilapidated structure said to have been inhabited by the Blankenship family during the time that Clemens lived in Hannibal. Clemens had many times named Tom Blankenship as one of the models for Huckleberry Finn.[1]

Although Johnson was ostensibly in Hannibal to write about Clemens's home, he seemed more interested in the surrounding countryside. He described the great change in Hannibal since Clemens's childhood, when "the Mississippi was far more interesting than anything else to the inhabitants, and the big steamboats arriv[ed] daily out of the mysterious unknown." "The world lay whence they came and whither they went," wrote Johnson.[2] In 1906, Hannibal was still riding the wave of its lumber fortunes. Some residents made their living by shipping lumber down the Mississippi, and several lumber barons made Hannibal their home. In fact, during Clemens's last visit to Hannibal, he addressed a crowd from the front steps of a mansion built by a lumber tycoon.[3]

Within years, however, the lumber industry would yield to a new industrial order where the railroads exported goods manufactured along the Mississippi River. Despite the changes in the landscape, Johnson still considered Twain's home a link to the past: "The house the humorist lived in still stands and is much the same as it always was—a stumpy, two story, clapboarded dwelling close to the sidewalk."[4] The Clemens family lived in downtown Hannibal, which by the time of Johnson's visit had become a bustling city. The Clemens house was firmly located in the middle of the bustle, just three blocks from the steamboat landing and the rail hub. The house was "snugged" in among others and had a small back yard in which residents might grow vegetables and hang laundry. Houses abutted both sides of the boyhood home, which faced more homes and businesses across the street. Unlike the other places he visited in Hannibal, Johnson, did not stay long at the boyhood home, perhaps because he did not have to. Although it was still then a private residence, everyone already knew that the house was special. Postcards of Clemens in front of the house on his 1902 trip were sold all over town, and many readers had already come to see the house as the literary home of Tom Sawyer through the illustrations of "his" abode in the novel. In the popular imagination, the house could be the home for *both* Clemens and Sawyer.[5]

First opened to tourists in 1912, the house is now part of a museum, interpretive center, and collection of other historic houses that tell the story of Samuel Clemens and his creations. In fact, the Mark Twain Boyhood Home and Museum's motto is: "The Stories Started Here." Visitors "discover how a young boy growing up in the small village of Hannibal became one of the world's most beloved authors."[6] The overarching story that the museum relates to its visitors is that everything that Sam Clemens ever needed to become the author of *Tom Sawyer* and *Huckleberry Finn* came from the time he spent growing up in Hannibal.

The tour begins in at the interpretive center where visitors learn the basic history of Sam Clemens's life in Missouri—that he was born in Florida, Missouri; that his shopkeeper father died young; that the Clemens family occasionally owned and leased slaves; and that many of Hannibal's real characters inspired Clemens's fictional characters. Once inside the house, visitors look through Plexiglas windows into rooms that depict a typical middle-class Missouri home from the 1850s and 1860s. None of the original furnishings still exists, but the house looks cozy and lived in. It has terra-cotta-colored walls in most rooms and antique beds covered with pioneer quilts. Little details like a pair of reading glasses placed next to a Bible and marbles and slingshots scattered throughout a child's room suggest recent activity. The boyhood home is typical of most house museums in that its various period rooms indicate the way people once lived.

Highly atypical are the life-sized snow-white plaster Mark Twain mannequins arrayed throughout the house. The ghostly white figures seem out of place in this otherwise traditional historic house museum. After all, the childhood home was, as its name suggests, home to Sam Clemens the boy, not the man. Throughout the house, the white plaster Twains together with the other displays fill each room with Clemens's reflections and physical presence. In the dining room and the boys' bedroom, other interpretive exhibits evoke Clemens as he reflects back on his life and on the characters he imagined in St. Petersburg, Hannibal's fictional counterpart.[7] The white figures and historic markers pointing to Tom Sawyer's fence and Becky Thatcher's house indicate that this is no run-of-the-mill historic district. Fact and fiction mingle here and have done so, as we will find out, since the museum's first days. The effects of this mingling have largely been good for Hannibal. But the town has now interpreted Tom Sawyer's past in Hannibal for so long that it has had a very difficult time making room for an exploration of its own past.

### Early Tourists to Hannibal

Even before there was a Mark Twain museum in Hannibal, visitors wanted to know where Huck Finn and Becky Thatcher lived, where Tom Sawyer's cave was, and whether sites mentioned in Clemens's fiction were "real." Hannibal residents promoted the idea that all of Sam Clemens's characters from the Tom Sawyer and Huck Finn books were based on actual historical residents of Hannibal, Missouri. Clemens himself did not dissuade readers of this idea.[8] When Clifton Johnson visited Hannibal, he spent more time at Huck Finn's house than anywhere else; he devoted six pages to his interaction with the black family that lived in "Huck's house."[9] As he describes it, the house was in a ruinous state. Johnson set the scene with language that readers would have recognized as regional dialect, not unlike the dialect Clemens used in his own writing, but this time deployed to authenticate the travel experience through local color narrative for the reader. The author asked, "this is the Huckleberry Finn house, isn't it?" A woman seated out in front of the house replied, "it sholy is, an' las' year Huckleberry Finn and Mark Twain both was hyar to see it. Dey come togedder in a two-horse coach, an' dey each one give me a quarter." When a man's voice from inside the house cautioned that Huck Finn had "daid long ago," the woman replied, "[h]e was a little dried up ole man and he had whiskers an' look some like Santa Claus. You seen Santa Clause picture, ain't you, mister?" Although Johnson did not reply, the exchange angered the other man

Nellie Smith in front of the Huck Finn house, 1903, courtesy Hannibal Free Public Library, Steve Chou, hannibal.lib.mo.us

who "began swearing and stamping about and finally slammed the door." The woman explained to Johnson that "my man git plumb crazy over his own mistakes. He doan' know he wrong when I tell him so, an' when de neighbors tell him so, too. I gwine go away to St. Louis an' jine a show if it ain't nothin' but de hoochy-koochy!"[10] Johnson dwells at length on this exchange, portraying the woman as though she herself was a character from one of Clemens's stories.

Although we cannot be certain, it is possible that Johnson's new acquaintence was the notorious Nellie Smith, or as locals referred to her, "Cocaine Nell." Smith lived at the Huck Finn house from 1880 until at least 1903, when the back portion of the house was destroyed in a fire. According to her *Hannibal Courier Post* obituary, she was often arrested for public drunkenness and disturbing the peace. Everyone in Hannibal knew her, in part, because she lived in the Huck Finn house, located right downtown. She "was seldom ever seen on the streets without a basket on her arm." Many assumed she carried a pistol in her basket.[11]

In a photograph taken before the back portion of the house burned, you can just make out Nellie Smith in front, waiting to show tourists to the house that once belonged to Huck Finn.[12] That Clifton Johnson included Nellie Smith in his guidebook suggests that he considered her a part of the authentic scenery of "Mark Twain Country."

Despite the conversation he recounts with Smith, Johnson retells the local myth about the relationship between the real Tom Blankenship and the fictional Huck Finn. He explains that when Huck Finn "left town it was to go to the penitentiary," where he died.[13] He dismisses the woman's story of Huck Finn and Mark Twain's visit to her house. However, in 1902, Sam Clemens and another childhood friend did indeed tour Hannibal together, revisiting places that Clemens had known as a child.[14] That Johnson spends so much time at this house instead of the home where Sam Clemens actually lived indicates that he thought his readers would be particularly interested in this encounter. Part of the appeal of the Tom Sawyer and Huckleberry Finn stories to readers was their setting in St. Petersburg, Missouri, and their depiction of small-town life in the South during slavery. As a former slave who just happened to be living in Huck Finn's house, Nellie Smith was a living artifact of that way of life—a person who represented Hannibal's tour-able authenticity. Johnson did not present her as an expert on Clemens or even Huck Finn, but rather as a bona fide artifact of the literary past. Despite Johnson's interest (and presumably that of his readers) in the Huck Finn house, the people of Hannibal razed the house in 1911. Not so with Clemens's and Tom's house.

## Creating the Literary Past in Hannibal

In 1911, when the boyhood home's demolition was rumored, the local chamber of commerce rallied to save it but could not raise enough money. Chamber member George A. Mahan and his wife, Ida Dulany Mahan, saved the day by purchasing the house, repairing it, and then donating it to the City of Hannibal. Although the house became city property, held in trust and open to the public at no cost, the Mahans and their descendants stayed actively involved in its protection and management until 1978. During the dedication of the boyhood home on May 15, 1912, George Mahan gave the house to the city, saying, "I take pleasure in presenting the home of Mark Twain to the city and to the people of Hannibal with the hope and in the full belief that it will be maintained and used, as to be an inspiration to them, to the people of Missouri and the world as well." Mahan strongly believed that "Mark Twain's life teaches that poverty is an incentive rather than a bar, and that any boy, however humble his birth and surroundings, may by honesty and industry accomplish great things."[15] Mahan wanted the house museum to tell a story of financial and moral uplift, not unlike the Horatio Alger stories that were best sellers at the time and that sometimes even held shelf space right alongside the likes of *The Adventures of Tom Sawyer*. To that end, the City of Hannibal elected to create a local committee, the Mark Twain Home Municipal Board, to make the day-to-day decisions about the running of the house museum; Mahan, of course, was a member of the board.

A devoted Twain fan, Mahan was also a state senator and had a strong sense of how he wanted the city of Hannibal to develop and market the memory of Mark Twain. Mahan wanted to commemorate the boyhood home of Samuel Clemens as representative of the Hannibal he remembered from his own youth. However, he also wanted the commemoration to serve his image of the New South, a vision in which he expected Hannibal's future to be rooted. The idea of a New South embraced by Mahan was popularized by the Georgia orator and journalist Henry Woodfin Grady, who sought to steer the South away from a plantation economy and toward a modern industrial economy following the American Civil War. Mahan's involvement in relocating eastern organizations like the Atlas Portland Cement Company into the area was dependent upon the idea that Hannibal was an ideal place for industry. And, in many ways, Hannibal was. The collapse of the lumber industry together with access to the Mississippi River meant that new industries found workers and a wealth of natural resources to exploit.

Hannibal's connection to Mark Twain meant that it had a ready-made myth to improve upon its history. As historians of the New South have demonstrated, Mahan's brand of myth-making was not unique, but his literary focus was. As perhaps the first southern booster to use literature to advertise and inspire industry and tourism, Mahan participated in the kind of the myth-making that was typical in places like Birmingham and Atlanta where industrialists—often from the North—made the post–Civil War economy palatable by draping it in a contrived southern heritage. Mahan combined literature and historical preservation to sentimentalize and market Hannibal, and Tom Sawyer's history supplanted Sam Clemens's and Hannibal's histories.[16]

The labor historian Gregg Andrews argued that Mahan's investment in Sam Clemens did not come entirely from an unmitigated interest in Clemens's literary efforts. Mahan served as the corporate attorney for the Atlas Portland Cement Company located just outside of Hannibal in the tiny company town of Ilasco, Missouri. Ilasco was part of a New South industrial campaign that Mahan and other local businessmen wanted to see thrive in the area.[17] The history of the Atlas Company in Missouri was not always a peaceful one. In 1910, not long after Clemens's death, Hungarian-American machinists in Ilasco went on strike, causing fears that an ethnic riot might erupt. The governor called out the Missouri National Guard, thereby alerting the national press.[18] Mahan and others may have seen their devotion to the boyhood home as a way to booster Hannibal, but it also served to support their investments in developing industries. The development of Clemens's boyhood might draw in industry while also instructing both visitors and immigrant laborers about the particular place that Hannibal held in the American literary historical imagination.[19] Mahan's work at Atlas and on the boyhood home linked the New South Hannibal of the future with his interpretation of the Old South Hannibal and its history.

Mahan did have a sincere affection for Clemens and admired him even though many of the literary elite disapproved of Clemens's work and commemoration.[20] Sam Clemens's literary reputation in the years following his death was significantly different from what it is today. Many still merely saw Clemens as a rough southerner. As one critic put it, "'Mark Twain' lacks the education absolutely necessary to a great writer; he lacks the refinement which would render it impossible for him to create such coarse characters as Huckleberry Finn; furthermore, he is absolutely unconscious of almost all canons of literary art." Even worse than his coarseness, Clemens "wrote for the uncritical masses." Even Missouri's literati mocked Clemens in the publications of the State Historical Society of Missouri, the society to which Mahan was appointed as an officer for decades and where he served as president for eleven years.[21] Albert Bigelow Paine's 1912 four-volume biography boosted interest in Sam Clemens, although he was still largely seen by critics and fans alike as a children's author and humorist. Van Wyck Brooks's *The Ordeal of Mark Twain* (1920) was the first serious critical work on Clemens to reach a popular audience, but his assessment in many ways matched those of Clemens's harshest critics.[22]

Beyond preserving the home, Mahan set out to mold the entire town into the image of the fictional St. Petersburg through a series of other commemorative acts. In his own way, he was an enterprising pioneer in developing literary tourism, and he used Hannibal's literary sites to inspire community renewal. In 1926, he commissioned a sculpture of Tom and Huck to sit at the base of "Cardiff Hill," which Tom and Huck explored together in Clemens's novels. The sculpture at the base of "Cardiff Hill" may well be the first memorial sculpture dedicated to literary characters in the United States. When providing feedback to sculptor Frederick Hibbard, "Mr. Mahan had a very definite idea of what he wanted."[23]

Map of Hannibal/St. Petersburg illustrated by Everett Henry, 1954, courtesy of the Harris Corporation

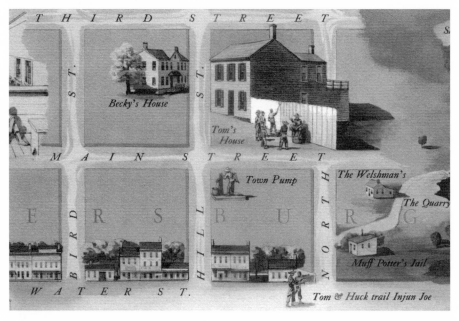

Map detail

Boyhood home with "Tom Sawyer's Fence" sign, November 2006, courtesy
Seth C. Bruggeman

He wanted to make sure the "boys" looked out toward the Mississippi
River and that they appeared impoverished. Mahan specified that Huck's
clothing be tattered and torn, but that Tom's be patched because he had
his Aunt Polly to care for him. Mahan's interest in depicting the boys as
impoverished matched his desire that they serve to remind Missourians
that birth and poverty are not barriers to individual accomplishments.
Mahan proclaimed at the unveiling of Tom and Huck that "Mark Twain is
a man who invested lavishly in humanity's stock and made the dividends
payable to the world."[24]

Mahan also spent considerable money and effort erecting plaques on
behalf of the State Historical Society of Missouri around town at the
"historic" sites associated with Clemens and his fiction. Most of these
plaques can still be seen in Hannibal today. The one directly in front of the
boyhood home and its famous, although completely fictional, fence reads:
"TOM SAWYER'S FENCE: Here stood the board fence which Tom
Sawyer persuaded his gang to pay him for the privilege of whitewashing.
Tom sat by and saw that it was well done." The sign confuses history with

a plot point in Clemens's novel and has stood asserting Tom Sawyer's real presence in Hannibal as historic fact since 1934.[25] Mahan made permanent the local tradition of interpreting Hannibal's history through the "historic" lens of Tom Sawyer. These signs merely made material the literary critical technique of understanding an author's work through his or her biography, performing Mahan's own version of literary criticism. They asserted that these places had a fictional history as important or perhaps more important than their actual history. This assertion mattered. The hill on which the sculpture of Tom and Huck was placed was originally called Holiday Hill after residents that lived atop it. In 1934, the hill, already home to the sculpture of Tom and Huck, was outfitted with a sign designating it "Cardiff Hill," and it has since come to be known by most residents as Cardiff Hill. Each sign argued that Clemens's inspiration was Hannibal; that each place, character, and episode had a biographical basis and real locale; and that these cognates were "mapable "on Hannibal's landscape. Eventually, maps were made that reinforced Mahan's interpretation. This interpretation made Clemens's fictional characters even more appealing to tourists—because they could go to their houses. It certainly made Hannibal's history more appealing, too, because life in St. Petersburg, Missouri—Hannibal's fictional correlative—came to be romanticized as ideal life in small-town America.

Not all of Mahan's signs still stand. A sign that once pointed to Mark Twain Cave also noted where "Huckleberry Finn and Niggar Jim stopped for a few days on their way down the Mississippi." This sign conflated the historical and the fictional, while also using a racial epithet. It was not until 1987 that the city removed "Niggar" by grinding the word off the otherwise unchanged sign. This attempt to assuage complaints did not solve the problem, especially since it was still evident what word was missing from the sign. Sometime over the next few years, the city removed the sign without fanfare and stored it away.[26] That the sign existed at all demonstrates how Mahan's conflation of fiction and reality figured the history of slavery and racism within the same interpretive schema that presented Hannibal as romanticized small-town America. In Mahan's version of Hannibal's history, slave owners were loving characters like Miss Watson and Aunt Polly who enslaved people like the innocent and kindhearted Jim.[27] It was likely that this idea of a kinder version of slavery was popular among Hannibal's white residents as it flourished at historic sites throughout the South.[28] In this light, it bears repeating that the sign stood unaltered until the late eighties.

During Mahan's time, using the word "Nigger" to describe Jim was commonplace among even the leading white citizens in Hannibal.[29] At the 1935 Mark Twain Centennial dinner, "Nigger Jim Coffee" was served

Mahan sign from 1934, now lost, courtesy Hannibal Free Public Library, Steve Chou, hannibal.lib.mo.us

alongside "Huckleberry Finn Cocktails," "Gilded Age Pie with Roughing It Cream," and the bizarre "Pudd'nhead Sawyer of Arc Salad."[30]
Mahan was instrumental in planning the event and served as chairman
of the Mark Twain Centennial Committee alongside the likes of local
men such as Dan Violette.[31] Although Violette and Mahan strove to keep
the memory of Sam Clemens alive, they both wanted to construct that
memory by rewriting and idealizing the past—to make it more palatable
to Hannibal's white residents and tourists.

Mahan was such an influential figure in Missouri that one month
after his death in December 1936, the Missouri State Assembly rose
for a moment of silence in his memory. Missouri governor Lloyd Stark
addressed the congressional assembly. Mahan was, according to Stark,
"what a highminded, public-spirited citizen should be." He remarked
that "[o]ne cannot visit the City of Hannibal without recognizing, on
every hand, memorials to Mark Twain, and nearly every one of these is
also a memorial to George A. Mahan."[32] In preserving Sam Clemens's
childhood home, George Mahan and the City of Hannibal managed
to assert a very particular vision of the Missouri past—one that whitewashed much of Hannibal's real history. Their ability to overlook, ignore,
and omit those realities from both local history and their biographical
interpretation of Clemens's novels created an environment where Hannibal visitors for years to come could see everything in Hannibal, including
the black population, landscape, and history as literary artifacts.

## The Boyhood Home as Museum

From the time Mahan founded the boyhood house museum until
today, the museum was open to visitors seven days a week and every day
of the year but Christmas.[33] When the museum opened, there was no
charge for touring the house, and the city employed a caretaker to live
upstairs. There is little documentation of the activities at the museum
during the teens and twenties, but a few visitor accounts survive. In one,
a 1925 review, the pastor at the Park Methodist Church in Hannibal,
Franklin Poage, recounted his visit to the boyhood home. He found
Clemens's favorite chair and the "the type-writer used by Mark Twain"
of particular interest. However out of place in the boyhood home, the
typewriter that Clemens used as an adult writer was a sanctified instru-
ment of his craft and genius. Poage's interest in Clemens's relics matched
his response to the holy house itself. He raved that "in providing this old
home, and preserving it for the world to visit, the donor and the City of
Hannibal perform a sort of spiritual ministry; . . . it is a shrine, indeed."

For Poage the house was a religious site. He even implied that it was sacrilegious to stand in the house "with [an] uncovered head." He believed
that Hannibal had performed a sacred duty in preserving and opening the
shrine to visitors, and he was not alone in his belief.[34]

Other non-Missourians were also on the "trail" of Tom Sawyer, Huck
Finn, and Jim. In a 1929 travelogue published in the *New York Times*, artist Donald McKay reported on his visit to Hannibal as part of an effort
to illustrate a new edition of *The Adventures of Tom Sawyer*. While he
was there he reported, like Clifton Johnson before him, that much had
changed in Hannibal since Clemens's youth, not the least of which was
tourism to the boyhood home. He reported that "the old Clemens house
[which] stands on Hill Street . . . is a modest frame house, and *quite obviously* the scene of Tom Sawyer's eventful residence." He got up early to
sketch the house before tourists arrived on the scene, "but visitors were
all over the place, even in the morning." He described the caretaker, as
a "woman somewhat harassed by the concurrence of her duties and her
cooking, ran back and forth, answering questions and trying to prevent
the beans from burning."[35] George Mahan was not alone in his conflation of Clemens and his fiction; McKay was just as likely to see Clemens's
residence as Tom Sawyer's as well. The crowd already gathered at the
boyhood home was large enough to interrupt McKay's sketching and
prevent the caretaker from her cooking, but apparently not enough to
deter her from cooking beans during hours the museum was open.

On the ground floor, visitors like McKay would have seen the collection of "original" artifacts that George Mahan and others had put
together to give visitors a sense of Sam Clemens's life and works. McKay
noticed, "Mark Twain's favorite chair was in the living room," but points
out that "it had been hoisted half way to the ceiling, so that visitors
could not try sitting in the seat of greatness." In the chair, "an American
flag was draped slantwise across the seat."[36] McKay, like Pastor Poage,
sensed that Clemens's personal items were authentic religious relics, and
that these items aroused in visitors the desire to touch and use them.
That the chair was hoisted into the air indicates that draping an America
flag across the seat was not enough to deter visitors from wanting to
sit where Clemens sat. The setting was similar to the kind of hodge-
podge display of authors' curiosities that occurred at other literary sites.
It does not seem as if there had been an attempt on the part of the
museum board to display a historical scene in the house as it was when
the Clemens family lived there. The house was furnished with relics,
photographs of Clemens, and old furniture of roughly the same period
as Clemens's residence. Though McKay was disappointed that he could
not sketch the house in the morning because of early rising crowds, he

did spend some time in the upper portion of the house, which was usually off limits to tourists. Because McKay was set to illustrate a character's home based on the *real* home of Sam Clemens, the caretaker provided him an insider's tour into her private quarters. Peeking around the caretaker's personal belongings, McKay elatedly described the house. He recalled here was "the room Tom shared with his brother; here, probably, was the room where Aunt Polly slept, where Tom crept in, planning to leave the sycamore scroll telling her that he and Huck and Joe were not really drowned."[37]

What McKay was most interested in, however, was the authentic Hannibal that Clemens would have known. He searched high and low for these traces of Clemens. He particularly searched for Hannibal's black population because, "Mark Twain ascribed part of the *charm* of Hannibal to the fact that it was a slave town, with leisurely traditions." But McKay had a hard time finding what he was looking for at first, and bemoaned that "[t]here are comparatively few negroes there now," although "[a] good many of them live along the river." He found that of the population of 22,000 in Hannibal, only 800 were black. Nevertheless, he did find a small group he could observe, "placid" "negroes fishing along the banks" of the Mississippi River. McKay wanted to find "real" examples of the fictional black characters responsible for St. Petersburg's "charm."[38] He, like Clifton Johnson more than twenty years before him, was intensely interested in representing authentic black culture to the readers of his travelogue. Black residents in Hannibal became a conduit for McKay to relay his understanding of the literary past that he encountered while illustrating Clemens's novel. His account does not similarly connect Hannibal's current white residents with the past. In Hannibal for some tourists, black residents became an essential component of looking for St. Petersburg and the traces of Mark Twain.[39]

McKay and other illustrators, including Norman Rockwell who visited in 1935 to sketch Hannibal for his very popular edition of *The Adventures of Tom Sawyer,* created the visual representations that thousands of readers would come to know as St. Petersburg, Missouri.[40] Postcards showing Clemens on the sidewalk in front of the house during his 1902 trip conspired alongside McKay's and Rockwell's illustrations, with the fictional historical markers that Mahan added to the town's landscape, to conflate the boyhood home of Sam Clemens for all time with the boyhood home of Tom Sawyer. The house was perhaps more recognizable as the home of Tom Sawyer than as the Clemens house, because these illustrated editions found their way into so many children's hands. Visitors having read or even flipped through these editions would find the house *exactly* as it had been in the book. It was as though Sam

Norman Rockwell's Tom as he goes out the upstairs window, based on the rear window and downspout at the boyhood home, 1935. Reproduction courtesy of MBI, Inc. and thanks to the Mark Twain Boyhood Home and Museum; copyright MBI, Inc.

Front room at the boyhood home, circa 1937, courtesy Library of Congress, Prints & Photographs Division, HABS

Clemens had written the house on Hill Street into existence, or McKay and Rockwell had drawn Tom into the house so effectively that there was hardly any room for Sam Clemens.

## The 1930s and Expansion of the Boyhood Home and Museum

This confusion over whose house it was—Clemens's or Sawyer's, may have been exactly as the city of Hannibal wanted it. Samuel Clemens and Tom Sawyer were big business for Hannibal in the 1930s. Though the city suffered from the effects of the Great Depression and the agricultural recession that preceded it, Hannibal found interest in Mark Twain could raise spirits. The numbers of tourists interested in the literary origins of Clemens's characters eventually led to a massive expansion of the properties owned by the city that were deployed to celebrate Clemens's fiction. Eventually, federal interest through New Deal programs like the Civilian

Conservation Corps came to Hannibal to help preserve the boyhood home, through projects like the construction of a protective firewall and preservation work on the boyhood home itself.

In fact, unlike the efforts at the Florida birthplace, the thirties were a boon to the museum and to Twain commemoration in Missouri. The New Deal addressed preservation concerns at a number of national historic sites across the country and expanded state and local historic sites, like the boyhood home. Additionally, Hannibal put on a great show in recognition of the one hundredth birthday of Samuel Clemens, in 1935. The elaborate tribute that Mahan and the city planned included a temporary museum downtown and a new lighthouse on top of Cardiff Hill (formerly Holiday Hill) that would "shine the light of Twain" across the land. The local Mark Twain Centennial Commission planned concerts, shows, parades, and a pageant called "Mark Twain's First One Hundred Years," which included a cast of more than a thousand participants. The temporary museum inspired by the centennial stoked interest and accepted the donation of hundreds of items associated with Sam Clemens, from first editions of his novels to letters and personal mementos from those who knew him.[41]

A visitor to the house and museum around the time of the centennial would have seen the house much as it was in the twenties, as Donald McKay described it, and quite a bit like it is in the photo taken between 1933 and 1937.[42] Inside the house, visitors could walk through a building that was part museum and curiosity cabinet—complete with all kinds of Mark Twain memorabilia. Rather than recreate the way the Clemenses lived in the house, the front room exhibits and furnishings portrayed Clemens's life after Hannibal and included the often-mentioned "sacred chair" that Albert Bigelow Paine had donated to the museum. In a glass wall-case hung one of Clemens's famous white jackets. On another wall was a large framed photograph of an elderly Clemens smoking on the porch of his final home, Stormfield, outside Redding, Connecticut.

A few years later in 1937, the boyhood home saw support, protection, expansion, and documentation through two New Deal organizations. The City of Hannibal was able to acquire the building directly to its west. With the assistance of the Works Progress Administration (WPA), it was entirely renovated and made into the home for the new collections that the city acquired for its temporary museum during the Mark Twain Centennial celebration.[43] WPA workers constructed a permanent building for the museum with new quarters for caretakers and stone firewall to protect the boyhood home from the fire threat of the nearby Cruikshank Lumber Company. Before the WPA work was completed at the new museum, another New Deal branch, the Historic American

Building Survey (HABS), documented the boyhood home and other historic structures in Hannibal that were associated with Sam Clemens.[44]

After the WPA completed its work on the house next door and the new museum opened in it, the caretaker's former quarters and much of the boyhood home remained empty. Members of the surrounding community donated furnishings that they thought would be appropriate for the upstairs. The Home Board decided to "secure exhibit items in two general categories, one category being things actually owned or used by the author, including manuscripts, first editions, etc., and the other category to consist of items which were in use in Missouri in the Mark Twain era, that is 1835 to approximately 1860." The last "category was to portray the atmosphere [and] social conditions in which Clemens lived in the formative period of his life."[45] Despite this resolution, the house was furnished haphazardly and mostly with cast-offs from the centennial celebration. However, the board and caretakers did their best to outfit the boyhood home in what they understood to be the fashion of good historic house museums, by taking the house back to the "Mark Twain Era."[46] After 1938, the museum building, not the house, presented the life of the adult Mark Twain by displaying his iconic white jacket, a steamboat wheel, the famous chair that Sam Clemens preferred as an adult, and many, many other items. This arrangement of the boyhood home and museum remained unchanged for decades to come.

During World War II, as fuel rationing limited leisure activities, many historic sites in the United States saw plummeting visitation numbers. Even national parks saw their visitation cut more than in half, as was the case at George Washington's birthplace.[47] But the boyhood home was different. Morris Anderson, then President of the Home Board, requested higher wages for caretakers from the city because the museum was busy despite the war. In 1943, 6,334 people visited the house, while in 1944, 10,440 visitors made their way through the museum and the boyhood home.[48] By February 1945, visitation was up 21 percent, and with the end of World War II tourist numbers rose even higher. The little house would see many more visitors each year until its peak in 1978. In 1952 there would be almost twelve times as many tourists making their way through the boyhood home as there had been in 1944. Though visitation during the war years was strong; after World War II, tourism to Hannibal was a verifiable boom.[49]

The Mark Twain sites in Hannibal continued to grow in size and visitation. By 1941, the museum acquired two lots directly east of the boyhood home.[50] This expansion allowed the museum an open area for the contemplation of Sam Clemens and his time in Hannibal. However, the city also destroyed the historic wooden buildings that might have helped a tourist recall that time.[51] As tourism grew, so did the museum. The City of Hannibal acquired several other properties that had some connection to Samuel Clemens, his family, and even characters in the novels. In 1943, the city acquired the "John M. Clemens Justice of the Peace Office" from Warner Brothers Studios. The studio gave the historic building to the City of Hannibal in appreciation for local assistance and expertise in its production of the film, *The Adventures of Mark Twain* (1944).[52] The city moved the building to its current location in 1956; it now sits across the street from the Clemens house.

George and Ida Mahan's only son, Dulany, died in 1937 not long after his father, but his wife, Sarah Marshall Mahan, carried on the family tradition. In addition to the lots east of the boyhood home, Sarah Mahan gave the city "Grant's Drug Store," a massive building across the street and to the east of the boyhood home to the City of Hannibal in 1956. The city outfitted it as a nineteenth-century drugstore and opened it to the public that same year. This building was once home to the Clemens family during a financially difficult time when they were no longer able to afford to live in their house across the street.[53] Sarah Marshall Mahan's gifts may have been largely responsible for the museum's health throughout World War II and during the spike in national tourism that followed. Although some of her gifts led to the demolition of historic buildings downtown, her purchase of the properties protected the boyhood home from the postwar development boom. The same development boom that threatened a number of historic sites across the country also contributed to an explosion in highway construction that made these sites more accessible to middle-class tourists. By 1966, six thousand of the twelve thousand historic sites that had been documented by the Historic American Building Survey—like the boyhood home—had been demolished, but the sites that remained, like the boyhood home, saw the benefit of that same developmental boom.[54] Sarah Mahan's legacy continued, as her father-in-law's had, through her child's spouse. Her daughter, Ida, married John Winkler, who would become a longtime member and chairman of the Mark Twain Home Municipal Board from 1945 until his death in 1977.[55]

By 1953 with John Winkler's help, the boyhood home had long been "one of Missouri's major tourist attractions" with more than 125,000 visitors in 1952 alone. According to a review from that year by George McCue published in the *St. Louis Dispatch*, at the boyhood home, tourists "with obvious delight . . . examined the array of memorabilia intimately associated with Mark Twain's life and placed themselves at scenes fondly remembered from 'The Adventures of Tom Sawyer.'" "Much of this book," it continues, "is biographical and the *authentic* scenes are there—the drain pipe by which Tom stole out at night, the white washed fence, the room where he gave painkiller to the cat, the river island where he and Huck Finn played pirate, the cave where he and Becky Thatcher were lost, Cardiff Hill."[56] The museum still mixed biography and fiction at the site while tapping into visitors' nostalgia. Hannibal aligned itself in many ways as an extension of the museum. McCue pointed potential travelers to Hannibal, where in Sam Clemens's "mellow old home town, the many landmarks and relics connected with Mark Twain and his period have been conscientiously preserved." Unlike earlier visitors, McCue did not focus on Hannibal's "authentic" black culture as a way to understand Tom Sawyer's St. Petersburg.[57] By 1953, in St. Louis at least, African Americans were not quaint tourists' reminders of a bygone era but contemporary citizens asserting their rights. After WWII, with President Truman's executive order 9981 and with the cases that made up the *Brown v. Board of Education of Topeka, Kansas* decision making their way into popular press, depicting black residents as romantic literary characters from the past did not work for St. Louis readers. But in Hannibal, the practice lived on—and was even perpetuated by the Home Board.

While John Winkler chaired the Home Board for most of the more than thirty years he was on it, from 1945 through 1977, he also owned the Becky Thatcher house and a shop on the building's first floor. Winkler's interest in the boyhood home owed to his wife's family, but he also made some of his living off Hannibal's investment in Mark Twain. One of the items he sold in the bookshop over the years was his popular tourist guide, *Mark Twain's Hannibal*. Winkler's 1946 guide to the boyhood home and museum points out relics that would be of interest to visitors. There was the "cherry desk" from Clemens's house in Hartford, Connecticut, on which *The Adventures of Tom Sawyer* was said to have been written.[58] Because the object was connected so intimately with the novel and Clemens's craft, tourists liked to touch it if they could.[59] He also highlighted the infant death-mask of the Clemenses' son Langdon and many other personal artifacts. Winkler pointed out the museum collection's highlights, including locks of Clemens's hair—"tight curls . . . yellow as a child's," handwritten letters, "a bronze cast of the restless hand itself, a multitude of first editions, photographs, paintings, hand bills, newspapers," and "a giant steamboat wheel."[60] Winkler also explained "Jim" and his relationship to Sam Clemens. Hannibal "was a slave-holding town; many of Mark Twain's best anecdotes came from the stories slaves told him, and one of his greatest and tenderest characterizations is that of Nigger Jim in 'Huckleberry Finn.'" He assured his readers, that in addition to the relics above, "[t]here are plenty of negroes around now to give Hannibal a distinctly southern flavor." Winkler equated the authentic relics from Sam Clemens, like his curls and his script, with real live people who, because of their race, supposedly, lent an air of literary authenticity to the town.[61]

Winkler's belief that tourists would be attracted to "negroes" and mannequins must have been strong. His recommendations, published in his popular tourist guidebook, were sold for decades as *the* guide to the boyhood home and all the newly acquired buildings. This guidebook, revised slightly over the years, speaks volumes about Winkler and white Hannibal's commitment to defining the black population through the historic lens of slavery. Winkler also points to the fact that, of the twenty-one thousand people in Hannibal, "about three thousand of those are colored."[62] Through his population analysis, he all but promised the statistical likelihood that the average tourist would be able to experience something like the historic South during slavery.[63]

In the decades of expansion under John Winkler that followed, the museum grew more complex and more difficult for caretakers to handle.[64] New exhibits were carefully planned to minimize caretaker supervision. Despite occasional staff-led tours, most visitors made their own way through the buildings. Members of the Home Board, and sometimes members of the volunteer association, the Jane Clemens Neighbors, led special tours for schoolchildren and interested parties. Sometime after World War II, the boyhood home added Plexiglas partitions and tape-recorded narratives in each room. Visitors had only to touch a button to hear Winkler's voice interpret a scene from Sam Clemens's work. Plexiglas windows and walls kept tourists partitioned away from the artifacts in the boyhood home, John Clemens's law office, and Grant's drugstore. The rooms featured costumed mannequins that represented both Tom Sawyer characters *and* scenes from Clemens's autobiographical writing. The mannequins were designed specifically for the museum. John Winkler ordered the very same costumed mannequins upstairs at his Becky Thatcher House and Book Shop. The main room of John Clemens's law office portrayed the bloody dead body that Sam Clemens stumbled upon as a child and that he described in *The Innocents Abroad*.[65] In the next room, visitors witnessed the courtroom scene from *Tom Sawyer* where Muff Potter stands trial and Injun Joe escapes. The museum juxtaposed Sam Clemens's biographical experience and the experiences of his character Tom Sawyer. Even in the dining room of the boyhood home, Winkler's voice recounted the scene where Tom Sawyer gave medicine to the cat. In the kitchen, it was the story of Sid and the sugar bowl. Nearby, Grant's drugstore and the John Clemens's law office have not changed since these exhibits were installed.[66] The mannequins are now more than forty years old and most of the tape recordings no longer play. The drugstore's second-floor displays have been closed to tourists now for many

Exterior, circa 1937, courtesy Library of Congress, Prints & Photographs Division, HABS

years, and as of 2011, the drugstore's downstairs offerings are also off limits to tourists, because the building itself has become unstable.[67] The mannequins remain, locked in Plexiglas rooms.[68]

By the end of the 1960s, Hannibal business people, like John Winkler, had come to embrace Mark Twain as much as the tourists did. Restaurants and businesses named after Sam Clemens's characters included the Mark Twain Hotel, the Becky Thatcher Restaurant, Mark Twain Dinette, Tom Sawyer Smokehouse, and many more. The Mark Twain marketing that was embraced in the 1910s and 1920s expanded as tourism grew in the 1960s; the town became even more about Mark Twain. During Winkler's time on the board, the museum saw an expansion to many more buildings, and the numbers of tourists that visited the boyhood home grew every year. By 1960, the museum was seeing 200,000 visitors annually.[69]

## "People Like History":
### The 1970s and 1980s at the Boyhood Home

As it expanded, the museum continued to interpret the house as belonging to both Sam Clemens and Tom Sawyer. Meanwhile, at historical sites and museums across the country, historic preservation was developing into a more standardized field. By this time preservation itself was history. The historian Charles Hosmer attempted his first of two massive retrospectives of historic preservation in the United States in 1965. The boyhood home was not the first literary historic site in the United States, but it was one of the earliest. While the Hannibal museum had been expanding, other sites, according to Hosmer, were motivated by the kind of historical archeology work done at places like Colonial Williamsburg and had started "scientifically" restoring historic structures.[70] Using information gained through archeological digs as well as information gained from the buildings themselves, historical architects returned historic buildings to their original condition using period techniques and materials. Clemens's adult home in Hartford, Connecticut, went through a massive historical restoration between the years 1955–1974.[71] In the decade that led up to the national bicentennial celebration, states, counties, and small towns across the United States began to solicit formal histories, some for the first time, and they turned to their historic sites with thoughts of restoration.[72]

By 1977, growth and visitation during the national bicentennial celebration had created real maintenance problems at the boyhood home and museum. The museum's operating funds from the city had never been enough to do more than keep the buildings standing, and some suffered serious structural neglect. When the longtime caretaker Frances Anderson retired and the Home Board president John Winkler died, the remaining members of the board decided to hire a museum professional to look after the site. This person would be the first employee trained in history to work with the museum.[73] The board considered a national search, but opted for a Hannibal native who just happened to be enrolled at the University of Delaware in a history master's degree program that specialized in the decorative arts and historic preservation. In 1978, the board hired Henry Sweets before he was even finished with school. Sweets promised to finish his degree and then come straight back to Hannibal. He has worked at the museum ever since.[74]

Henry Sweets and the Home Board sought to bring the museum and house up to the standards of increasingly sophisticated leisure tourists and museum and preservation professionals. In places like Hartford, tourists went through house museums that had already been painstakingly researched and restored. Historic houses had come to be seen by some as documents that revealed history best when in "original" condition. Some tourists even sought out places where they could watch a restoration in progress.[75] The University of Delaware's program focused on decorative arts, and while Sweets would not find the same kind of high-style objects in his collection at the boyhood home, he brought with him a reverence for the material culture relics of history.

During this time of transition, the Mark Twain Home Foundation was formed at the urging of Herbert Parham, a local businessman and attorney who was interested in helping the museum benefit from nonprofit status. Because the museum was run by the City of Hannibal, many nonprofit funding opportunities had been out of reach. The old Mark Twain Home Municipal Board soon became a city committee that negotiated with the newly formed Mark Twain Home Foundation's board on matters that related specifically to the upkeep of the structures that the city owned. The Home Board negotiated the conditions of a long-term lease of these buildings to the new nonprofit organization. Eventually, the new foundation would govern the museum and its staff, acquire property, and take on the assessment of the museum. While the museum was restructured and became a nonprofit organization, Sweets modernized the collections by cataloguing them according to modern archival standards. Sweets and Parham worked together to connect with local members of the community to preserve the museum's most treasured artifact, the boyhood home itself.

In 1980, Sweets published a short piece in the *Journal of the West* that outlined and celebrated the history of the museum and its buildings. Sweets had discovered that Grant's Drugstore, sometimes called the Pilaster House, was built in pieces and shipped down the Mississippi River to Hannibal where it was assembled. He described the scenes that the museum had interpreted in each building. He recommended a stroll through Hannibal to those wanting to connect the literature of Sam Clemens with the place from which it came. However, unlike his predecessor John Winkler, Sweets did not recommend treating the local black population as though it was part of the setting of one of Clemens's novels. In fact, though he mentioned a number of other characters from Clemens's works, he made no mention of Jim at all. It was a palpable silence.[76]

Sweets began a newsletter called *The Fence Painter* for the Mark Twain Home Foundation in 1981. It kept interested parties and donors abreast of the work that he and others were doing at the house. The newsletter asserted in its first issues that the new foundation sought to work with the Home Board to "restore the Mark Twain Boyhood Home, to improve and enlarge the Mark Twain Museum, and to restore and preserve the 19th Century river town of Hannibal, Missouri, in the area surrounding the Boyhood Home." It went on to define a mission for the new boards "as the stewards of this rich literary heritage, the Mark Twain Home Board and the Mark Twain Home Foundation wish to return this memory into reality and to dedicate to the people of the world this quintessential, river town immortalized by the works of Mark Twain."[77] Part of the foundation's new mission involved preserving the historic structures that the city and others had acquired over the years. However, beyond these buildings, the board's mission was to make memory real—exactly whose memory is never clear. It seems that the museum board still hoped to evoke Tom Sawyer's imaginary memories of his fictional hometown.

One of the most important and immediate goals for the boards was the restoration of the boyhood home. Over the next several years, Sweets evaluated the museum's collection and readied the boyhood home for the 1985 sesquicentennial of Sam Clemens's birth. In 1983, the museum added a new building where visitors might be introduced to the history of Clemens's life and oriented to the boyhood home and other sites. The old museum building was turned into a gift shop. The new building, then called the Museum Annex (and now called the Interpretive Center), offered a short film about Clemens's life and displayed a number of artifacts that were more related to Hannibal's history than the history of Sam Clemens. As a recent director of the museum, Regina Faden, put it, the museum "was full of glass cases with books in them or period items, things not necessarily related to Mark Twain." The collection, though deep and varied, "looked like an accumulation of things over time." Hannibal had never had a local, county, or city history museum, thus the Mark Twain Boyhood Home became the "museum of Hannibal." Faden remembered thinking, "it was one of those old museums where you think, 'Oh, that's old.'" Items in cases were identified with typed index cards. She recalled, "there were guns in there, spoons, women's hand bags, stuff from the Mark Twain Hotel."[78]

## The Mark Twain Sesquicentennial

The museum, by the mid-1980s, had become *the* repository for local history, the place where the "old stuff," that Faden describes found a home. The original Mark Twain Hotel, which had been built to accommodate tourists and the festivities associated with the Mark Twain Centennial in 1935, had long been shut down. Hannibal's economic fortunes had changed significantly by the time Henry Sweets came on board at the museum. Hannibal had few remaining industries and none as profitable as the lumber business. By the 1960s and 1970s, Hannibal's rail lines began to close.[79] Hannibal lost much of its rail service, as more and more goods came to be moved overland by trucks, and Hannibal was not located on a major interstate. The commerce that was still moving up and down the Mississippi River no longer saw Hannibal as a logical access point for shipping goods across country. By the 1980s, during the farm crisis, the smaller communities and individual farmers who lived in the area suffered and were not able to bring their money into Hannibal as they had in the past. Ron Powers, a Hannibal native, Pulitzer Prize–winning journalist, and Mark Twain biographer, revisited his hometown in 1985 and noticed that the historic black business district known as "the Wedge" had been razed.[80] Hannibal saw Sam Clemens as a potential solution to their economic woes. City leaders saw a Mark Twain Sesquicentennial as a potential boon for the area and began developing elaborate celebration activities.

Henry Sweets watched as the city's plans became increasingly outrageous. Planners considered a steamboat race (costly and dangerous), the restoration of the Mark Twain Hotel (to house the anticipated crowds), the world premiere of a musical based on Sam Clemens's life, and a performance of "Mark Twain Tonight" by Hal Holbrook. None of these ideas came to fruition. There was, however, a successful frog race, an art fair, and several concerts staged in a small amphitheater built especially to accommodate them. Hal Holbrook canceled his performance, but a musical about Mark Twain's life would do well a few years later in Elmira, New York.[81] Unscrupulous promoters even planned a new Mark Twain Heritage Theme Park outside of Hannibal, close to Mark Twain Lake and Florida, Missouri, that was to entirely recreate the imaginary landscape of Tom Sawyer.[82] The promoters, like the King and the Duke from Clemens's *Huckleberry Finn*, took the money of local investors, worked up elaborate plans for the theme park, then left town.

Missouri tourism director, Marjorie Benders, saw the sesquicentennial as full of potential. "Why not take advantage of Hannibal's history?" she asked. "People like history. So build on it. Look at Disneyland. Look at EPCOT. Hannibal could be another Colonial Williamsburg!"[83] The City of Hannibal spent more than $26,000 for a promotional video that was supposed to draw in tourists from all over the United States.[84] However, nowhere near as many people came to the celebration as expert consultants predicted, and the City of Hannibal lost enough money on the

scheme that betting on Mark Twain tourism came to be seen as reckless.
As Ron Powers described it, "[a]t times, during the years of slippage and
transition, only one attitude, one common mood, seemed to unite nearly
everyone in Hannibal: a weariness bordering on contempt for the name
and likeness of Mark Twain."[85]

In 1984, amid the sesquicentennial excitement, Henry Sweets commissioned an architectural study of the boyhood home, to see if it could
withstand the expected onslaught of tourists. The report was frightening.
Not only was the house not ready, it turned out to be in imminent structural danger. Sweets made the controversial decision to erect an exterior
viewing platform next to the house where visitors could see into every
room through open windows and doorways but no longer step inside the
house. No longer would the visitor be allowed to come in the front door
to the parlor and imagine him or herself a guest of the Clemens family.
Instead, the visitors would be put in the position of peering into the
home, like a peeping Tom. Though board members and museum staff did
not like this unpopular solution, it was the only way that the house could
stay open through the important sesquicentennial year and allow visitors
to see some part of the boyhood home.[86]

### Restoring the Boyhood Home

The viewing platform was only a partial solution to the house's structural problems. After the architect's report, Sweets and the museum board
had in mind a full-scale historical restoration. No important historical or
archeological research had ever been done at the house. Sweets sought
out both a historical architect and state archeologists to do research at
the site.[87] The plan involved removing the house from its foundations for
repair. The museum replaced the interior and exterior walls and restored
the house to its original condition. Ron Powers described it as an "ingenious project," which filled him "with awe." Although a visitor to many
historic attractions, he "could never shake a feeling of clammy fascination
as I set foot inside this leaning old dollhouse with its tangible, almost suf-
focating aura of occupancy by suprahistorical force . . . the home was the
only shrine that ever felt like a shrine to me." Powers "was appalled and
yet envious of Henry Sweets's audacity at cutting into it," but as "long as
the motives were provably noble, [I] would have liked to take a preservationist divot or two from the old homestead myself."[88] Apparently, many
visitors felt the same.

Noble motives aside, the restoration meant that the house would
be closed for twelve months for research and construction. Historical

archeologists from the University of Missouri, St. Louis, under the direction of Dr. Neal Lopinot, uncovered a more elaborate footprint for the house than was extant in 1985.[89] A two-story addition in the back of the house had been removed sometime between the periods that the Clemenses lived in the home and when the house was given to the city. After Sam Clemens last visited in 1902, Albert Bigelow Paine recorded him saying: "It all seems so small to me . . . a boy's home is a big place to him. I suppose if I should come back again ten years from now it would be the size of a birdhouse."[90] Henry Sweets interpreted both the archeological foundations and Clemens's comment to indicate that the house was once actually larger. Sweets found a photograph of the house that showed the rear addition. Whether this was on the house when the Clemens family lived there or whether it was added on afterward was unclear. If the addition was historically accurate, then the room that the museum had interpreted as the Tom Sawyer/Sam Clemens boyhood bedroom had been wrong since the museum opened. The iconic illustrations of Tom Sawyer climbing out of Sam Clemens's bedroom window had been more fictional than the artists had intended.

Sweets and the board decided to rebuild the addition. In 1988, after years of research, the Mark Twain Home Board engaged Philip Cotton, a "leading preservation and restoration architect in the state of Missouri," to complete their restoration plan.[91] The restoration was not popular with everyone.[92] Hannibal's main tourist attraction, after all, was to be shutdown and carved up. They would have to build a new foundation and dig underneath the old one. These investigations threatened the sacred house. Would it still feel like a holy shrine with new windows, exterior siding, and re-plastered walls? Research into the bones of the house revealed that the WPA had replaced all but one of the floors when they helped build the firewall and the museum building in 1937. Likewise, all of the plaster had been replaced over the years. A small amount of period plaster was found under the new floorboards, and it was from these scraps that Sweets and the researchers determined that the house's interior walls had been painted a terra-cotta color.[93] Would the essence that made Sam Clemens into Mark Twain still be there? The restoration project lasted for most of 1990 and 1991.

*Remembering Tom Sawyer at Mark Twain's Boyhood Home*

When tourists returned to the boyhood home, they found it changed. Most commented on the removal of the exterior shutters and on the new terra-cotta walls inside, but few noticed that the house had increased in size.[94] By 1992 with the opening of the restored boy-hood home, tourists brought in thirteen million dollars to the Han-nibal economy and fifteen hundred jobs.[95] With the media attention surrounding the restoration, to Hannibal there also came a new wave of critical thinking about museums, the stories that they tell, and their impact on community. In the mid-1990s, the museum board began planning to open a separate museum space in downtown Hannibal. The new museum, the Mark Twain Museum, was to draw visitors through the center of the city as a way to improve Hannibal's downtown cor-ridor and as a way provide space for interpretation that could not fit in the boyhood home and the tiny interpretive center. The new building, a historic department store, would also provide space for the museum's archives, staff offices, and community meeting space.[96] Sweets and the board brought in a scholarly advisory board that not only brought them up to date on Twain scholarship, but helped provide the creative ideas to engage visitors with many more of Clemens's texts that could not be covered in the house's interpretive scheme. The museum would eventually install exhibits that allowed visitors to experience Clemens's writing first hand—through experiential displays. Visitors could jump on the raft with Huck and Jim, ride the stagecoach that took Clemens West in *Roughing It*, and peek through into shadow box displays of knights from King Arthur's court.

However, by the middle of the 1990s, the Boyhood Home and Museum, and the city of Hannibal, could no longer deal with Hanni-bal's own history by ignoring it or assuming that Tom Sawyer's history gloss over it. The restoration work at the boyhood home did not help tell the history of Hannibal during the Sam Clemens era as much as some visitors in the 1990s hoped it would, and the new museum looked as though it would largely only interpret Clemens's writings other than *The Adventures of Tom Sawyer* as opposed to telling a larger historical narrative about the city. Both local and national attention pressured the board members and the staff at the boyhood home to tell a history that would include the details of life in a small slave town as a slaveholding family would have experienced it. In other words, people wanted to know where Jim was.

So did Shelley Fisher Fishkin. Fishkin, a Mark Twain scholar and pro-fessor of American studies at the University of Texas, visited the house in 1995 to begin to trace Sam Clemens through the places that were meaningful to him. Her 1996 book, *Lighting out for the Territory,* recounts her trip and took the town to task for its erasure of African American history. Fishkin was especially critical of Hannibal's whitewashing of the ways that Clemens grappled meaningfully with racism and the legacy of slavery in his work. Fishkin visited Hannibal for several days beginning in June 1995. In her resulting chapter on Hannibal, she railed against the town's annual Tom and Becky contests and the daily dramatic renditions of Clemens's works, which erased the character of Jim altogether and gave his "important" lines to white characters.[97] With little mention of Jim in the museum and no mention of him elsewhere, he was the only character that was not grounded in the one-to-one Hannibal historic lore.

When Fishkin asked shop employees, riverboat captains, and people on the street if they had heard of Clemens's antiracism, they had not.[98] As we have seen, the museum, the Home Board, and even the new museum board had chosen to remember only one of Clemens's novels, *The Adventures of Tom Sawyer* at the boyhood home, and even in interpreting that story they chose to remember Jim only occasionally and then with their particular take on Hannibal's slave-town history. Surely, a town just across the river from a free state had a more complicated history, and that history would have had a great effect on a boy, such as Sam Clemens, coming of age as Civil War tensions rippled throughout Missouri.

However, when Fishkin toured the boyhood home, she found it charming. When peeking into Sam's bedroom she found it "beautifully restored" with "nineteenth century hardware, painted with the kind of paint that was used in Hannibal when Clemens lived there, and furnished with authentic period pieces resembling those that the Clemens family was known to have owned." She found the old tape-recorded messages had been re-placed in the boyhood home and that they "provided basic information about how that room was used," but that also still "connected [the house] to specific scenes in Tom Sawyer." Even Fishkin was interested in the objects that might have belonged to the author. She was particularly excited by "a glass case containing marbles that had been found during excavations at the site—marbles Sam Clemens himself may have played with."[99]

With the house restored, the Museum Annex now told a new story based on archeological evidence alongside the old story of the one-to-one relationship between characters in Clemens's novels, emphasizing *Tom Sawyer*. Fishkin seemed untroubled that the house did not depict any material evidence of the Clemens family and the enslaved residents of the household, perhaps because the newly restored house so charmingly matched her vision of Tom Sawyer's house. She was most concerned that the history of Clemens's antiracism was not told in the rest of Hannibal. She came from an era of literary scholarship that considered Sam Clemens's *Adventures of Huckleberry Finn* his most important popular work. For years, the people of Hannibal believed that tourists came to their city to learn about Tom Sawyer and Mark Twain (and perhaps in that order). They might have read *Huck Finn* in grade school alongside the required reading of *The Adventures of Tom Sawyer*, but they may have never thought of their town in relation to Clemens's later works at all.[100]

Outside of Hannibal, college students were reading *Huck Finn* with the legacy of American slavery in mind. Fishkin's groundbreaking book, *Was Huck Black?* (1993), was part of a major interpretive turn in American literary studies. In the 1980s and 1990s, literary criticism had turned from the New Critical and post-structuralist modes of analyzing literature to the current focus on literary history.[101] Many, if not most, college courses that included Clemens, read *Adventures of Huckleberry Finn* and saw it as his response to the racist politics that followed reconstruction in the South. Hannibal, during Fishkin's visit, seemed unaware of this sea change in understanding Sam Clemens's literary legacy.

The interpretation that Shelley Fisher Fishkin had come to understand as commonplace, at least in college literature classes—that *Adventures of Huckleberry Finn* was an antiracist book that responded to the racial injustice that Clemens saw dividing the country in the 1880s—was overlooked in Hannibal. Fishkin pointed out that the gift stores near the boyhood home sold racist figurines, Confederate army caps (as well as Union caps), and bull whips.[102] She revealed in her book exactly where Hannibal had held slave auctions, that John Marshall Clemens had sold one slave "down-south" away from his family, and that Sam Clemens had seen a white man strike and kill an enslaved man on the street in Hannibal, all details about Hannibal history that the chamber of commerce did not advertise.[103] Fishkin did describe slavery in Hannibal as not the "brutal plantation" variety, even though "slavery nonetheless."[104] Although Fishkin admitted that there were many ways to interpret Clemens's works and that there were almost as many interpretations of his biography, she asked "might they [Hannibal citizens] somehow have managed to forget the one that mattered most?"[105] But as we have seen, the city of Hannibal and the boyhood home never chose to remember any version of Sam Clemens or Sam Clemens's past that represented the realities of slavery in Hannibal. In a way, George Mahan whitewashed Clemens's history when the city opened the museum in 1912, by choosing to tell Tom Sawyer's story, not Sam Clemens's.[106] Because the museum's founder was interested in presenting a "positive" portrayal of the New South, the troubling history of slavery was not included at the family-friendly site, but slavery was not included at most historic sites across the country where it might have been. These decisions certainly speak to the kinds of visitors that the museum managers expected and their preferences.

In a 1995 interview with Faye Bleigh, Hannibal native, 1964 Becky Thatcher contest winner, and director of the Hannibal Visitor and Convention Bureau, Fishkin asked which local historic sites made any mention of African American history. Bleigh faltered and could not think of any, but offered to contact a local NAACP member. She tried to explain that they only "did" Tom Sawyer, not Huck Finn. "See, and that's the only part that we promote. His boyhood years. We don't [promote] the part where Huck and Jim are down the Mississippi. We promote only the little boy, when he played marbles, when he whitewashed the fence."[107] The promotion of the boyhood of Tom Sawyer seemed to have erased not only much of the history of Sam Clemens, but also any traces of African American history in Hannibal.

In the wake of Fishkin's visit, some residents of Hannibal did begin to look more closely at its history. A few local historians and residents began asking questions about the history of Hannibal's African American population. Many local people knew that the character Jim "belonged" to Aunt Polly in Clemens's novels, but few knew that the Clemenses had owned slaves themselves. No one locally seemed aware that they had regularly leased an enslaved child, Sandy, for domestic tasks while they lived in Hannibal.[108] But neither the fictional slave, Jim, nor the real Sandy was acknowledged in the house itself. Sometime in the 1990s, very briefly, this changed. Henry Sweets or someone else on staff added a small pallet in the kitchen that might have gone unnoticed, but nonetheless indicated to observant visitors that the household included at least one slave during Sam Clemens's life there. One resident noticed that as quickly as the palette appeared, it disappeared without explanation.[109]

Perhaps the most impressive result of Fishkin's work was that, after reading her book, a local attorney, Terrell Dempsey, who had noticed the city's whitewashing of local history, set out to recover the history of slavery in Hannibal. Dempsey focused on the period when Clemens lived there. His 2003 history, *Searching for Jim: Slavery in Sam Clemens's World,* quickly came to be one of the best-selling volumes in the University of Missouri's Mark Twain and His Circle Series.[110] Dempsey's research allowed the museum and Hannibal's residents to understand, for the first time in recent memory, the real ugliness of slavery in the Hannibal of Sam Clemens's youth. Although his book did not come out until 2003, Dempsey let staff and museum board members know about his research and spoke up about the necessity for local recognition of the history of slavery in Hannibal. He has said that the historical evidence he uncovered, largely newspaper accounts and local and state slave ordinances, was in plain sight, hardly hidden from even the most amateur historian, but local historians had consistently chosen to overlook it.[111]

## Changes at the Museum

In response to these criticisms and with a project already in the works for a brand-new Mark Twain Museum building on Main Street, the board decided to rethink the interpretive plan for the museum.[112] In 2002, the Boyhood Home Foundation hired museum consultant Jay Rounds to study the museum and integrate all its disparate buildings and collections into a narrative that the average visitor would understand and enjoy.[113] The museum had never had a master plan that outlined the goals and the particular historical themes and interpretation that the museum would highlight through the development of exhibits. Until then, Sweet's main interest was in preserving its collection of objects, the primary one being the house itself. Jay Rounds, a professor at the University of Missouri, St. Louis, and founder of the Museum Studies Program there, was the first museum professional to do audience research at the house. He set graduate student researchers to the task of entrance and exit interviews with visitors. He wanted to determine how the average person understood both the museum and Mark Twain.[114] Rounds submitted a master plan in 2003, which board members accepted after much discussion.

Two distinct groups formed within the discussion of changes at the museum: the self-described "fiction camp" and the "biography camp." Because the interpretation at the boyhood home had always been about translating *Tom Sawyer* into the spaces of the house, some members of the board were reluctant to move away from the way things had always been done. The other camp was primarily interested in presenting verifiable biographical and historical facts about Clemens's life. According to Rounds, they worried the museum was "much more . . . about Tom Sawyer and Becky Thatcher than it was a museum about Mark Twain." The fiction camp countered that "people don't come for Mark Twain, they come for his stories."[115] The division between fiction and history had been a tension at the site since Mahan had installed the fictional historic markers. Now the foundation board, presided over by Herb Parham, had to decide how it would unify a site that had been both the historic site where Sam Clemens was a child and the site where the characters from his fiction had been celebrated for more than ninety years.

Jay Rounds was fresh from working as a consultant on a museum exhibition on the nature of human creativity. As a result, he did not see the need for the museum to interpret either only fact or fiction. He saw the museum board's split as an imperative to help visitors understand the creative genius of a man that perpetually intermixed the two. He saw no better way to impart this message to visitors than through simultaneously presenting both biography and fiction. He focused on the 1902 photo-graph of Clemens in front of the boyhood home and imagined what it must have been like for Clemens to visit the small house that he had grown up in.

> Twain had walked into this house after many, many years . . . And he walks up to a place that really is very small, but for decades, in his mind's eye he has been filling this place up with stories and char-acters. So, my idea was that to him, this house is way too small to contain his imagination. It wasn't a physical thing, but that it was absolutely bursting at the seams with all the stories that he's overlaid, all the biographical memories of the different times in the house, the room that contains the piano at one time—the printing press at another times . . . His [Twain's] brain is [so] filled with all this stuff . . . that the space can't contain it.[116]

The 2003 master plan argued that the house should be filled with all these stories at once. In the dining room, visitors would hear a young Clemens being spoon-fed the medicine he received as a sickly child. They would also hear the story of Tom Sawyer dosing the cat with the medicine he takes for his faked sickness. Museum scrims (partially transparent screens that function like curtains), lighting, and audio and visual effects would lead the visitor through a house filled to the rafters with stories col-lected from Clemens's autobiography, letters, and novels. Rounds came to believe that because Clemens was such an unreliable source of infor-mation about his own life, that what Clemens presented in his autobi-ography was largely as much "storytelling" as the Tom Sawyer tales were. "The point is that everything is a story here and the stories are *all* filtered through the creative mind of Mark Twain."[117]

Board members were excited that both fact and fiction would have authority at the site. However, Rounds's idea to use scrims, projections, a full-scale whirly-gig in the kitchen, and other special effects used to "make ghosts walk" upset some of the board members. Many had never seen a scrim used in a museum. Several had not been to a museum that used modern exhibition techniques. "One [board member] made the statement that they were the steward[s] of this national historic landmark and that they wouldn't allow any gimmicks."[118] However, the board was enthusiastic about Rounds's use of the 1902 photograph as a framing device to tell the stories of Clemens's time in Hannibal. They devised a compromise: the house would be *haunted* by the presence of Sam Clemens as he revisited Hannibal for the last time.[119] The museum would deploy Sam Clemens's words to reflect upon his time in Hannibal. They would use white plaster Mark Twain figures in each room to show Twain reflecting on his time in Hannibal. Now when tourists came to the boyhood home, in a sense, Mark Twain would be their guide. Today a large panel, easy to miss as visitors crowd into the main entrance to the boyhood home, explains the white Twains, thus: "In 1902, Mark Twain visited his childhood home for the last time. Enter here to view the home, and meet Twain as he thinks back on his remarkable life." Otherwise, the interpretive frame of Mark Twain looking back on his hometown during his 1902 visit was lost.

Phase one of the master plan went into place in 2005, just one year after the museum board had a hired a new director, Regina Faden, to manage development and community outreach.[120] Rounds, Faden, and other advisors designed a new series of exhibits for the Interpretive Center that presented Sam Clemens's history in Hannibal. The very first exhibit that visitors see when they enter the Interpretive Center—the first stop on any museum tour that orients visitors to the museum—explains that Jane and John Marshall Clemens brought slaves with them when they moved to Missouri. A nearby wall tells the story of slaves in the Clemens household, like Sandy, and has a short paragraph on slavery in Hannibal. In 2005, the museum officially recognized that the Clemens family held slaves, and Hannibal had its first public discussion of the history of slavery.

As a result of these efforts, the Interpretive Center presents Sam Clemens's history clearly and evocatively through timelines, photographs, and interactive exhibits. It still poses the one-to-one relationship between the characters in *The Adventures of Tom Sawyer* and historical persons in Hannibal. It confirms that Tom Blankenship is the basis for Huck Finn, that Laura Hawkins is the model for Becky Thatcher, that Aunt Polly is based on Jane Clemens, Sid on Henry Clemens, and that Injun Joe is a man who lived far into old age named Joe Douglas whom locals called "Injun Joe." But the museum also challenges visitors to answer the question, "Was Mark Twain Tom Sawyer?" The exhibit posits, "not everything in the novels was based on memories of childhood."

The 1934 signs labeling Becky Thatcher's House and Tom Sawyer's fence are still outside. People still look for Tom Sawyer's bedroom. Upstairs, in the boyhood home, they can still find it, but Sam Clemens is there, too. Visitors find the oddest display there. A giant white Mark Twain sits in a rocking chair, hands clasped, reflecting in language from *Life on the Mississippi*, "the things about me and before me made me feel like a boy again—convinced me that I was a boy again, and that I had simply been dreaming an unusually long dream." Meanwhile, just over Mark Twain's white plaster shoulder, a life-sized color cutout of a boy, whom we can interpret only as Tom Sawyer, is readying himself to climb out of the bedroom window.

The white Twains are not in the other buildings yet, but they may be before long.[121] The museum has just begun a capital campaign to restore and reinterpret other buildings that make up the museum's historic block.[122] The Becky Thatcher house is first on the list to receive a new treatment. Here visitors will soon be able learn about childhood in nineteenth-century Missouri.[123] The museum plans to incorporate the stories of Tom Sawyer, Becky Thatcher, Huck Finn, and Jim as a way to talk about how the experience of childhood very much depended upon gender, social class, and race.[124]

The museum under Regina Faden's directorship began to institute programs that were not just about Sam Clemens and his world, but also about the larger community and its needs. Realizing that there was no museum to serve Hannibal and that the African American community had suffered through "Tom" and "Becky" contests that only featured white winners for decades—among many other offensive activities in the name of Mark Twain that had gone on in Hannibal—Faden tried to change things. She instigated changes throughout the museum that include events that celebrated the history of Hannibal's African American residents, such as reunions and oral histories from Douglas High School, which closed its doors in 1959 when the Hannibal public school system desegregated.[125] These changes indicate that museum, and perhaps greater Hannibal, have begun to recover Hannibal's history.

## The Persistence of Fiction

Tourists have been making their way to Hannibal since at least 1906, when Clifton Johnson's guidebook offered tips on visiting the place where the enormously popular Sam Clemens had grown up. When Clemens's boyhood home was opened as a museum in 1912, visitors entered a house that was a largely ahistorical shrine to Mark Twain. More than two decades later, the museum's founder, George Mahan, positioned historical markers around Hannibal that celebrated the supposed sites of episodes in Clemens's fiction, particularly scenes from *The Adventures of Tom Sawyer*. Mahan's decision to commemorate the fictional events of Clemens's writing in front of Hannibal's historic houses and riverfront, beyond blurring the line between fact and fiction, made concrete the local tradition of remembering slavery in Hannibal as kinder and gentler than plantation slavery. Other historic sites, such as Grant's drugstore and the Becky Thatcher House joined the boyhood home in mapping

"A long procession of people filed
through my mind—people whom...I
knew so many years ago—so many
centuries ago, it seems...[T]he
dreaming shades seemed in right accord
with each other, and fitting. Nobody else
knew that a procession of the dead was
passing through...but there it
to me there was nothing un
it; no, they were welcome

Twain figure at dining room table with paper dolls/cutouts and book "stage,"
November 2006, courtesy Seth C. Bruggeman

Tom Sawyer's childhood over sites that were influential to Clemens. In
many ways, because Hannibal did not have a local history museum, Tom
Sawyer's story became Hannibal's history.

Today interpretation at the boyhood home simultaneously embraces
both fiction and biography. In fact, part of its essential claim to Clemens's
origin story has been accentuated in the new interpretation. The museum
now asserts that "The Stories Started Here." The displays in the boyhood
home reflect a postmodern interpretation that subverts the chronology

Huck Finn house, August 2007, compare with Image 6

of Clemens's experiences at the house and creates a discontinuous display. For instance, we see an adult Clemens crafting characters like paper dolls at his childhood dining room table. Each "story" told in the house loses its historical context and becomes one of many overlapping stories, each with equally unstable historical and contextual meaning. The interpretative message does not bury Hannibal's past in Clemens's fiction, but suggests that all stories that are told about the past are subject to interpretation by visitors. The exhibit embraces tourism studies' postmodern understanding of tourists' desires for interaction with "authentic," though not necessarily period, objects. The white plaster Twains and other displays may not date to the Clemens period, but they encourage visitors to wonder how the house served as inspiration over the years for Clemens. Still, how visitors understand the history presented at the site is unclear. Because studies have shown that visitors to museums trust historic sites more than any other source of historical information, the museum must be careful with its display, cognizant of the power the site has to influence visitors' understanding of history.[126] If tourists believe the events depicted in the house—like the adult Clemens playing with paper dolls at the table—actually happened, they may have a very different understanding of Clemens and Hannibal history than the museum planners hoped.

Critics, like Dempsey, still believe that the museum should do a better job depicting the realities of slavery in Hannibal during Clemens's childhood. There is now, however, a place where the museum *might* be able to answer Dempsey's criticism and depict the history of slavery in Hannibal, possibly even through the lens of fiction. In 2006, the museum built a new two-room stone-and-clapboard building. The replica "Huckleberry Finn house" was dedicated and opened to the public in 2007.[127] According to the new marker outside on the lawn, "[t]he house that once stood here was believed to be the home of Tom Blankenship, named by Mark Twain as a model for Huckleberry Finn." Local lore held that on this site was the building that housed the whole Blankenship brood and was the same structure where Nellie Smith once lived. Recall the picture of the house with Smith out front, and you will see that the house looks quite different. There is no second floor as described by Clifton Johnson in his 1906 account. The house looks so tidy and new, that it is hard to imagine the hardscrabble Huck Finn living in this nice little cabin, let alone his historical counterparts, Tom Blankenship and his seven siblings.

Despite its newness, the Huck Finn house could be a perfect place to interpret the history of antiracism that Shelley Fisher Fishkin sought and found missing during her visit to Hannibal in 1994. It is currently partially furnished and houses displays that tell the story of the Blankenship family and outline some of the controversies surrounding the novel, *Adventures of Huckleberry Finn.*[128] Here visitors could *almost* get the story of Jim told in one of the "historic" sites. Although visitors do not get much information about Uncle Dan'l's daily life in the Quarles household near Florida, Missouri, they do learn the basic story of the novel. They discover that "Huck wishes to escape his father's drunken abuse" and that "Jim seeks his freedom" as they travel along the Mississippi River. They also learn that "[a]s they travel together, Huck begins to shed his learned prejudices and acceptance of slavery," and "[i]n the end, he is willing to risk society's and, he believes, God's condemnation to protect Jim." Little is said about why Jim might be trying to escape or what slavery meant in Hannibal or even in the fictitious town of St. Petersburg. Nevertheless, the museum staff has presented information on the history of slavery and engaged critical debate over the censorship of *Huck Finn* and arguments about whether the novel is racist or antiracist. Visitors are invited to "Decide for yourself. Read it [the novel]."

With its interpretive plan and help from the outside advisors and members of the community, the museum has managed the transition from a historic site that very recently either ignored Hannibal's history of slavery or exploited its black population as part of the scenery, to a museum that attempts to argue that the history of slavery in Hannibal is an essential element in the creation of Mark Twain. That the board and staff decided to discuss race and the legacy of slavery is a triumph for history and literary fans alike, and it seems possible that future exhibits will do more to depict the historical realities of slavery in Hannibal. Jim and Huck have made their way into the museum at last.

Ultimately, the story of Sam Clemens's boyhood home and its transformation into a museum and tourist destination is significant for those interested in literary tourism because the museum and even the city of Hannibal—through its acceptance of the historical markers—allowed Hannibal to be interpreted as Tom Sawyer's hometown of St. Petersburg for so long. The struggle that literary sites face in the decision between depicting fiction or "fact," between balancing biography and biographical interpretation, bring up many important questions for literary sites and literary scholars. Can we understand literary inspiration through understanding a writer's childhood? Can we understand an important literary work by understanding the cultural and historical condition of its production? Ultimately, the questions that these sites pose are the same questions that literary scholars have wrangled with over the years. Understanding a literary work is not a finite or discrete process—it requires research, imagination, and interpretation, and such work is never finished. Translating literature onto a historic site requires the same kind of critical intervention and revision.

Other places that have chosen to preserve fiction in homes of literary figures face similar challenges. The childhood home of Lucy Montgomery on Prince Edward Island teeters on becoming a re-creation of *Anne of Green Gables*. Beatrix Potter's home is frozen in time as though she lived there among her cast of literary creatures. The House of the Seven Gables for many years put forward an interpretation that the events of the novel actually took place in the house, with very little mention that Hawthorne was even the author of the story. Recently, Willa Cather's childhood town, Red Cloud, Nebraska, has similarly chosen to embrace her novel *My Ántonia* as a lens through which to understand local history. Red Cloud has even started preserving houses that "belonged" to the characters in Cather's fiction—in much the same way that Hannibal's residents preserved the Becky Thatcher House. In each case, these places thrill some visitors and are off-putting to others.

The story of the museum at Sam Clemens's boyhood home can provide a picture of both the hazards and the benefits of interpreting fiction at literary sites and the risks that literary interpretation poses for local history. However, Hannibal's interpretive success is now its history. The town has been promoting the idea that Mark Twain's "stories started here" for a hundred years. Of the many historic sites devoted to remembering Sam Clemens, Hannibal is the only place where his literature trumped historical evidence, and it is the only place where the literature itself is of primary interest. It seems that literary tourists want to visit Tom Sawyer's town. Visitors can get on a raft and imagine that they are on the Mississippi River with Tom and Huck, and they can jump in a stagecoach and try to see the West as Clemens did. Visitors encounter a mixture of the authentic object of their quest—in the boyhood home itself—and they have the experiential process of making sense of the white plaster Mark Twains that they find there. This museum is a place that now obliges the participation of its visitors. The interpretation that is presented today in the boyhood home, the mixture of fact and fiction with the postmodern interpretive frame of an adult Clemens looking back at both his childhood and his literary creations, seems to work. It walks the line between fact and fiction, but it does so by requiring that visitors do the work to sort out what is going on for themselves.

## Chapter Three

# The Right Stuff

### *Mark Twain, Material Culture, and the Gilded Age Museum*

See it in furnishing: A stone or block of wood to sit on, a hide to lie on, a shelf to put food on. See that block of wood change under your eyes and crawl up history on its forthcoming legs—a stool, a chair, a sofa, a settee, and now the endless ranks of sittable furniture wherewith we fill the home to keep ourselves from the floor withal. And these be-stuffed, be-springed, and upholstered till it would seem as if all humanity were newly whipped.

—CHARLOTTE PERKINS GILMAN (1910)

f all the Twain sites, Samuel Clemens's only surviving adult home—the place where he lived his most productive years—is the site that has most successfully pulled off the central trick of the historic house museum. It approximates with near scientific accuracy what the house would have been like in the 1880s and 1890s, and it does not interpret his literary creations. It does not quite create the feeling that the family has just stepped out for the afternoon, but it gives the impression that the housekeepers have just straightened up and have readied the house for company. Because the house has such a gloriously gilded interior—with Louis Comfort Tiffany and Associated Artists stenciled wall treatments and other splendid interior decoration—it must be a surprise for the average Mark Twain reader who expects that Clemens lived his adult life in a "grown-up" version of the little white house in Hannibal. I described the Hartford house to a friend—an "average" reader—who

Mark Twain house in Hartford, 1950, courtesy of The Mark Twain House and Museum, Hartford, Connecticut

responded, "how disappointing."[1] Today, to non-scholars, Mark Twain seems separate from the Gilded Age he lived through and wrote about. He has become timeless and ubiquitous—his visage and words associated with every possible product and cause—that it is hard to think of him as a man who lived in an elaborate Victorian house.

This chapter sets out to understand this gilded house and how it came to be a public space: first a library, then a museum, then a shining example of historical restoration. The history of this site is neither as complicated as the story of Mark Twain's many birthplaces nor as interpretatively complex as the stories at Mark Twain's boyhood home in Hannibal. Rather, Mark Twain's house in Hartford is a museum historian's dream. The museum staff largely presents the "facts." There are no ghostly white plaster figures in the rooms, and there are no skeletons hidden in institutional reports about the structure's questionable authenticity. This is a house museum devoted to Sam Clemens's biography and his life as a family man in Hartford. Of all his houses, it is the one that is most directly tied to the efforts and choices of Sam and Olivia Clemens.[2]

The house has always been a showplace and an extreme example of architectural taste and literary display. The house itself was reviewed in the press even before its construction was complete—almost as if it were one of Clemens's publications. Two primary periods in the house's life are important in the discussion of this house as a site of literary tourism. The first is that of the house's preservation under Katherine Seymour Day. The second spans the house's "renaissance" and restoration from 1955 to 1974. In each case, the house served as a showplace for the ideas of the board of trustees much in the same way that it served as a showplace for the Clemens family while they lived there. The decisions that the board made over the years point out how influential a board can be for a historic property and how important its reactions are to the shifting needs of literary tourists. The Hartford house did not suffer from the same interpretive stagnation as the birthplace—a state site that was victim to the budget problems of a large regulated system, with no individual founder to see to its care. And it is unlike the boyhood home which though city-owned was under the interpretive supervision of a single family for more than sixty-five years. The Hartford house only faltered when its staff and board became so devoted to the authentic recreation of the house as it was during the Clemens family's residence that they forgot the literary and community connections the house could provide.

## The Mark Twain House and Museum

Most readers know very little about Sam Clemens's adult biography other than two facts, that he once captained a steamboat and he was a writer. When they, like my friend who had never seen the Hartford house, imagine Mark Twain's home, they imagine a house much like the one in Hannibal. It fits the mold because Clemens, Norman Rockwell, and others made the mold so well.[3] Perhaps that is why the boyhood home is still the most visited of all the sites devoted to Sam Clemens. The Hartford house, on the contrary, is a grand formal museum and sees the second largest tourist numbers to a historic site in all of Connecticut.[4] In Hannibal, visitors lead themselves through the buildings; at the birthplace, they peek through the windows of the tiny cabin. In Hartford, visitors park their cars in a newly surfaced lot, take the grand staircase up to a giant visitors' center, and look around at the impressive travertine walls, which are inscribed with Mark Twain quotes while they wait in line to buy tickets to a guided tour of the house.[5]

When it is time for the tour, visitors stand in line with up to eighteen people to look inside the house.[6] The tour guide enlightens visitors about

Sam Clemens's life in Hartford, his daughters, and his wife, Olivia, who all the tour guides call by her more familiar name, Livy. The Clemenses lived a joyous life at the house. Guides inform visitors about George Griffin, the Clemenses' butler and his antics, and the tour goes through the house room by room. Most of the rooms are open to walk through, but a few are partitioned off. The house is quiet, beautiful, dark, and smells like wood polish.

As in most house museums, guides point out specific attributes of the house as the focal points for stories about the residents. In this case, the marble-floored, formal entryway becomes a place to talk about the Clemenses' and Edward T. Potter's complicated architectural design style. The chimney for the grand fireplace in the entry hall is used as an example. Potter placed an interior window that connects the parlor with the impressive entry hall—splitting the chimney into two flues on either side of the window. The formal dining room with its three-paneled wooden screen, set up to provide house staff with a place to hover attentively but invisibly during meals, becomes the site for stories about George Griffin's badly timed laughter at Sam Clemens's jokes, as his laughter often came before his punch lines. The fantastic Scottish mantel and the bric-a-brac placed upon it in the library is a site for tales about Clemens as a storyteller and family man. Here, he would, at his daughters' request, construct tales that involved all the objects placed on or near the mantel. The conservatory that adjoins the library is where guides discuss the challenges of restoring the house to exactly how the Clemenses had it. The upstairs master bedroom with its ornate and richly carved Italian bed becomes a place to recount stories of Sam Clemens as a consumer. The story often told here is that Clemens spent so much on the bed that he decided to sleep in it backward so he could admire the elaborate carvings on the headboard.

Throughout the house, the furniture is ornate and includes many decoratively carved pieces, and all of the seating is covered in rich upholstery with generous stuffing.[7] The wood paneling and the doors in the public rooms are covered in intricate and varied silver and gold Orientalist stenciling designed by Louis Comfort Tiffany and Associated Artists. The study and children's playroom on the second floor is awash in oriental rugs, deep red pillows, children's toys, and schoolbooks. It is this place, the tour guides explain, where Clemens tried to work, but where his three daughters' continual presence led him to loaf and play instead.

By the time visitors begin to take it all in, the tour moves up to the third floor. Sam Clemens did his writing in the billiard room on that top-most floor, and it is here that the tour makes its final stop. Among his cigars and pool cues, the author wrote much of *The Adventures of Tom Sawyer, The Prince and the Pauper,* and *A Connecticut Yankee in King Arthur's*

*Court.* It was from the small balcony that Clemens sometimes conversed with fans down in the yard, or hid from them when they rang to see if he was home. He stepped out on the balcony so servants could accurately say he had "just stepped out." Yet even here, among the masculine display of Clemens's objects, there are stenciled designs on the ceiling and etched decorative windows, each adorned with pool cues and pipes.[8] Visitors cannot venture far into the room—for this is one of the rooms with a velvet rope—but off in the far corner is a small, modest, and messy desk. This is where the genius happened.

I wanted a closer look when I went through on my first visit, but with the seventeen other visitors, I barely filed into the roped-off section of the room before the tour moved on and out of the house. We passed the next tour group as we made our way out of the house and down the back servants' stairway. If visitors want to see the servants' wing of the house, they have to pay for another, separate tour, and most visitors do not opt for the added expense and time.[9] The house is striking and large, and by the time visitors get their bearings, the tour has ended.

The Clemens house has always been grand and was surrounded by houses that were only slightly less elaborate in the past. Samuel Clemens's house in Hartford became a tourist site even before his family moved into the twenty-five-room mansion on Farmington Avenue in 1874. Their closest neighbors and friends in Nook Farm—their tight neighborhood in Hartford—considered the house daring and innovative. Nevertheless, many others in Hartford saw it as a garish architectural oddity. In this way, Hartford's reaction to the house was much like its reaction to Clemens himself. He and the house were accepted and embraced as innovators among some and seen as merely entertaining and a troubling sign of modern times by others.

People who admire the house today describe it as "high Victorian Gothic," and love the exterior near arts-and-crafts "stick-style." The literary critic Bill Brown has recently called the house "German gothic style."[10] Others still repeat the rumor that the architect designed the house to resemble the steamboats that Clemens once piloted up the Mississippi River. It is a hard house to describe. It is a massive home, warmly Victorian and truly gilded in its restored splendor. Its brickwork is elaborately patterned, as are its decorative roof tiles, and its many gables and chimneys contribute to the vertical pull of the three-story house. It is the house of wealthy people, not a nouveau riche Vanderbilt or Rockefeller mansion, but a house outside the daily experience of most of its visitors then and now.

The house in Hartford served as the Clemens family's primary residence from 1874 until 1891. In biographical sketches of the Clemenses' lives, their move away from their beloved home in Hartford is always depicted as a great family tragedy. Olivia and Sam Clemens, by all accounts, loved their house and found it difficult to be away from the home that they had so carefully designed and decorated, and in which they had raised their family. Hartford could be a difficult place to live in the last decades of the nineteenth century. At the time, it ranked as "the richest city" in the United States, and as a result, it was exceedingly expensive for anyone to live and to entertain the way that the Clemenses did.[11]

## A House "Reviewed" like a Book

While the builders finished the house and the Clemens family traveled abroad to buy furnishings, reviews circulated widely. Response to the unique Clemens home was not universally favorable. One critic called the house "preposterous . . . the oddest piece of architecture in the city," and went on to say, "the style is indescribable, being a sort of between a Mexican adobe hut and a Swiss cottage."[12] The house does not resemble an adobe structure in any manner, but its patterning is exotic and its brickwork might recall a red and black Navajo rug made for tourists. Another local review offered, "it is one of the oddest buildings in the State ever designed for a dwelling, if not the whole country."[13]

Even in Elmira, New York, Olivia Langdon Clemens's hometown, the paper printed a rebuke of the house before the family had a chance to move in. The author detested the Medieval gothic style and the Victorian exterior and called it "a small brick-kiln gone crazy, the outside ginger breaded with woodwork, as a baker sugar-ornaments the top and side[s] of a fruit loaf." The writer went on to argue, "there is positively no style, unless it is 'conglomeration'" in the house's design. The experimental "conglomerated" style so offended the reviewer that he or she accused the architects of "trying to invent . . . purely American architecture."[14] Apparently, the author thought their attempt, and perhaps any such attempt, absurd.

The Clemenses' interest in building a truly American-styled home reflected their belief that American homes had a distinct quality and Clemens discussed it in a section of his autobiography from 1892:

> There is a trick about an American house that is like the deep-lying untranslatable idioms of a foreign language—a trick uncatchable by the stranger, a trick incommunicable and indescribable; and that elusive trick, that intangible something, whatever it is, is the something that gives the home look and the home feeling to an American

house and makes it the most satisfying refuge yet invented by men—
and women, mainly by women.[15]

Though he is unable to translate the essential quality of an American
home that makes it a satisfying refuge, he was clearly an admirer of the
American home and all of its conveniences. The Clemenses and their
closest friends likewise cherished the Hartford house, even if it did not
necessarily meet with the aesthetic approval of all.

Sam Clemens oversaw some of the details of the building of the house
and as it neared completion, seven months after the review above, wrote
to his wife. "It is a quiet, murmurous, enchanting poem done in the solid
elements of nature." To him the house and barn seemed "as if they grew
up out of the ground & were part & parcel of Nature's handiwork." The
harmonious result enchanted him and he declared that, "it is a home—&
the word never had so much meaning before."[16] Clearly, Clemens did not
think his house was an artless conglomeration of styles. He saw the house
as organically part of the nature of the Nook Farm landscape. Clemens's
admiration for the house, its design, and location are clear. He never wrote
about any of his other homes as lovingly or as descriptively. By the time
the builders finished it, the house began showing up on tours of Hartford,
as a celebrity oddity—as an object for general sightseers as well as Mark
Twain enthusiasts.[17] While the Clemenses lived there and long after, the
house made its way into all varieties of New England guidebooks.

The authors of these guidebooks and reviews speculated about and
critiqued the interior of the house as well. In 1876, accounts of the
house's interior began showing up in print. In one such review, a bust
of John Calvin in the library caught the eye of a Presbyterian minister visiting the house. The bust had been defaced by "some sacrilegious
hand," which had "penciled a swirled moustache and goatee" on Calvin's
face. "After gasing [*sic*] around the oddly arranged room" the minister's
"indignation became unbounded," and "with one blow of his cane he
shattered mustache, goatee and bust, scattering its dust over the apartment in the greatest profusion." According to the account, "Mr. Clemens,
who came in shortly after, upon viewing the remains, slowly remarked
that it was a pretty rough handling of Calvin, but was possibly, all things
considered, the appropriate thing to do."[18] It probably mattered little that
the article pointed out Clemens's ambivalence toward organized religion
and the Presbyterian upbringing of his youth, but the report's remark
about the "oddly arranged room" cannot have sat well with either Sam or
Olivia Clemens. Twain scholar Kerry Driscoll has pointed out that Sam
Clemens was surprisingly sensitive about the arrangement and furnishing of the Hartford house. Isabella Beecher Hooker, a sister to Harriet

Beecher Stowe, in her diary from 1876, mentioned a heated discussion with Clemens over a lampshade. Hooker reported that she joked about not liking a lampshade and, in response, Clemens became not only defensive, claiming that he trusted reputable shops to help him make such choices, but that "his eyes flashed & he looked really angry."[19] Driscoll points out that Clemens seemed to be anxious about making choices about other household items as well.

Another critique a year later called the house "architecturally midway between a mediaeval church and modern game of baseball." The writer went on to describe the library, "the appointments of which are characteristic of the owner's originality. The tints are all neutral and the furniture of the homeliest and plainest description."[20] Homely and plain cannot be language that either Sam or Olivia Clemens thought best described their decorating style. It is possible that such coverage sent them on a quest to outfit their residence with stylish, eclectic European furniture and bric-a-brac that many well-appointed neighboring Hartford homes already had and to engage Louis Comfort Tiffany and Associated Artists to redecorate their house.[21]

Kerry Driscoll argues that the Clemens family's trip abroad between April 1878 and August 1879 was intended, in part, to purchase the *right* items for the house.[22] The house was finished and decorated by that time, but as Driscoll points out, the Clemenses had not yet distinguished themselves as stylishly worldly and educated people through the acquisition and display of eclectic objects in their home. As they were in the process of setting up the house in Hartford, Sam Clemens was in transition, too. He had published two successful books based on his travel writing. He had tried his hand at editing a Buffalo newspaper and failed and had not yet established himself as the author of *The Adventures of Tom Sawyer*. His profession and even reputation as a writer was in flux when they first settled on living in Hartford.

It is likely that Sam and Olivia Clemens saw the Hartford house as a place to raise their family in comfort and set up their ideal author's residence. The Clemenses had visited Shakespeare's birthplace in Stratford on a trip to Europe between 1873 and 1874.[23] The Clemenses were aware that the "authorial home" was not an uncommon subject of reflection. Nicola Watson, a scholar of English literary tourism, has argued that the end of the nineteenth century coincided with a rise in literary tourism in England, a phenomenon of which Americans were particularly fond.[24] It seems the Clemenses were not immune. Some of Clemens's least favorite writers had elaborate writerly residences that were open to the public.

Sir Walter Scott's extravagant home, Abbotsford, had been a historical showplace for the author. American literary tourists, including

Washington Irving, came to know Scott as an excellent host to his own domestic exhibits of Scottish history and biography.[25] Scott's house was famously more a museum to his grand subject—a romanticized Scottish history—than a comfortable writer's retreat. The writer who was most often the victim of Clemens's wrath and perhaps the only writer that Clemens disliked more than Scott, James Fenimore Cooper, visited Abbotsford and returned to revive and restore his own familial home, Otesego Hall, in Cooperstown, New York.[26] Additionally, scholar Erin Hazard has argued that Washington Irving's visit with Scott at Abbotsford contributed to his design for his home, Sunnyside.[27] It is not clear that the Clemenses were similarly inspired.

Sam and Olivia Clemens visited Abbotsford while they were in Scotland in 1873, before they completed the house in Hartford. Despite Clemens's distaste for his prose, they came back with two complete Abbotsford editions of all of Scott's works.[28] While in Scotland, they not only visited Scott's "ancestral home" but also purchased, from another old estate, the pivotal piece of decoration for their impressive library, a massive palatial carved wooden mantel that had to be divided into two separate pieces to fit into the Hartford house. Despite Clemens's vehement hatred of all things Scott, he and Olivia must have spent some time thinking about Abbotsford given their visit, its popularity, proximity, and its abundant mementos and postcards. However, it is doubtful that the Clemenses thought much of Abbotsford's decorating scheme when they hired Associated Artists to redecorate the interior of their house. The Clemenses did not seek to create an ancestral hall, like Cooper and Irving, and refused to name their home. Clemens offered that the house "has a number, but I have never been able to remember what it is."[29] Instead, they used Olivia Langdon Clemens's money and money from the sales of *The Innocents Abroad*, and eventually his other novels, to furnish and decorate their home extravagantly.[30] By 1883, they had a very different house on the inside.

In an 1885 issue of *Harper's New Monthly Magazine*, George Parsons Lathrop prominently featured the Clemenses' house, among dozens of Hartford sites and landmarks, in his article, "A Model State Capitol."[31] After covering Hartford's various cultural, educational, and industrial institutions, Lathrop settled in quickly on Hartford's literary neighborhood, Nook Farm. Most of Hartford's famous residents appear in inked portraits, but Mark Twain's visage was inked from a bust. It was likeness of a likeness—for a man already immortalized through hundreds of print images. Clemens's house was featured prominently, as if it were already a museum. In an illustration of its exterior in *Harper's Magazine*, a man seems to wait for a carriage in front of the house, and a small group is

Illustration from George Parson Lathrop's "A Model State Capital,"
*Harper's New Monthly Magazine.* October, 1885

touring the grounds. The house, it seems, was a lively attraction for people
interested in visiting Hartford and a necessary point of interest to anyone
who wanted to know more about the city.

Mark Twain and Hartford, by this time, were already well linked in the
press. Clemens himself led Lathrop through the house, providing commentary about the use of each room. Much had changed at the house
since its "homely" state. The house was now a "charming haunt." It was
"full of easy-chairs, rugs, cushions, and carved furniture that instantly
invite the guest to lounge in front of the big fireplace." The Clemenses'
"house [was] made for hospitality." Lathrop described the drawing room
as "luminous," "elaborate," "genial," and "seductive," with the new Tiffany
and Associated Artists' interiors and he lingered over the elaborate mantel
that the Clemenses had shipped from Scotland.[32]

With Sam Clemens as his guide, Lathrop's tour through the house culminated in Clemens's third-floor work space. Then Clemens explained
why he could not work in the formal study that he and Olivia designed

on the second floor and explained why the second study he outfitted over the carriage house could not work for him, either. The problem was, there were too many social and familial distractions. Finally, Lathrop described Clemens's home office. In the "billiard room . . . there [he] writes at a table placed in such wise that he can see nothing but the wall in front of him and a couple of shelves of books."[33] Lathrop's descriptions showed a family with a carelessly luxurious, sophisticated home—a home full of rejected writing spaces—where in one bare, masculine room, Clemens could smoke cigars, cavort with his male companions, and, on occasion, turn toward the wall to write. The house itself had transformed from plain and occasionally offensive to a place that was so lovely and charming that the author had to turn away from its luxuries to get any writing done.

By 1902, literary tours throughout New England that had once focused on only the houses of "elder" eastern poets now included the Clemens house on their itinerary.[34] Edwin Bacon's *Literary Pilgrimages in New England* included the Mark Twain house as a site with which most of his readers would have been familiar. Published after the Clemens family no longer lived in the house but before they had sold it, Bacon described a house that had become famous. It had appeared and was elaborately illustrated in *Harper's* and other widely circulated magazines.[35] Bacon went on to write that "visitors are wont first to seek because of its fame through repeated descriptions."[36] Thus by 1902, the house had become so represented in print, included in tour guides, illustrated and reviewed that it needed little description. Bacon argued the house was "constructed . . . as to be unique among its neighbors, as is the author among his fellows." The "preposterous" house was in perfect balance with its well-known writer-owner. Who else could own such a house? Though Bacon was careful not to insinuate that the average visitor could get a peek inside the house, clearly he had a sense of the house's lay-out, its design, its plush interiors, and its life as the author's workplace.[37] He went on to describe Clemens's second-floor formal study, which had been converted into a playroom for Clemens's daughters, and his "real" work space in the billiard room. Bacon even insinuated that those not in the know, "the uninitiated," might assume that this house was the happy home of Clemens's best writing efforts. Bacon hinted that Clemens often had to seek out quieter, less social spaces to get his writing done. Clemens occasionally "locked himself into a little room in an office building downtown." Bacon described the unoccupied house as seeming "to invite literary labor under the most delightful conditions."[38] Today, the tour guides at the house tell a similar narrative.

These accounts reveal the house as a kind of literary text, often cited and revised over the years. Harald Hendrix, a scholar of French literature, has argued, "writers' houses have meaning beyond their obvious documentary value as elements in the author's biography. They are medium of expression and of remembrance." Hendrix points to the ways that authors have sought to create, consciously or not, literary texts in the spaces that they inhabit. He sees these places as pure forms that give us access to the "architectural fantasies and fictions" of writers and a rare chance to see a writer "experiment with a mode of expression fundamentally different from his own."[39] In many ways, Hendrix would be right about the Hartford house. However, it was as much a showplace of Samuel Clemens's architectural, decorative, and authorial fantasies as it was Olivia Clemens's. There is no doubt that both Clemenses saw the house as a means of expressing who they were and whom they most wanted to present to others.[40] The house was a domestic sphere, a workplace, and a stage where Clemens would effectively perform Mark Twain for his guests. Additionally, the house served literally as a stage for family dramas and performances among friends.[41] Although Clemens had not yet affected the white suit and all the iconic trappings that we know him for today, his reputation was growing, and by the end of his time in Hartford he was perhaps the city's best known citizen and a full-blown celebrity. His house was part of the show.

## The House after Clemens

The Clemenses could not keep up the show at Hartford's incredible cost of living, and in 1892, they sought more affordable living abroad.[42] Eventually after the death of their daughter Susy in 1896, they decided to sell the house. It was a very difficult house to sell. Elaborate residences like theirs quickly went out of style in Hartford, where the colonial revival came into fashion early and stayed a favorite for decades. The house cost the family between $1,000 and $2,000 a month to maintain. Sam Clemens wrote angrily to his Hartford agent, F. G. Whitmore, in 1903, "for the Lord Jesus H. Christ's sake *sell or rent that God damned house.* I would rather go to hell than own it 50 days longer."[43] Eventually, Whitmore was able to arrange the sale of the house, though at a great loss.

In 1903, the house sold to the vice president of the Hartford Fire Insurance Company, Richard M. Bissell. The Bissell family inhabited the house until 1917 and simplified the interior while there, covering over the elaborate Tiffany and Associated Artists' interiors with grass paper and removed the wall-to-wall carpeting, adding wood flooring throughout the house.[44] After the family resettled in suburban West Hartford, Richard Bissell leased the house to the Kingswood School for boys. The school turned the library and formal parlors into neutral classroom space and set up dormitories for the boys in the upstairs bedrooms. It is tempting to imagine a house full of Tom Sawyers and Huck Finns, but photographs do not reveal such hijinks. Most of the house's gilded splendor had been toned down by the mid-twenties, and after the Kingswood School relocated for larger accommodations, Bissell sold the house to real estate developers.

In 1920, New York developers J. J. Wall and the brothers John and Francis Ahearn planned to raze the house and construct apartment buildings in its place. When Emile Gauvreau, then editor of the *Hartford Courant,* learned of the developers' plan, he took up the cause in his paper. Later, reflecting upon the house in his memoirs, Gauvreau claimed to have discussed the house's historic value with the Ahearns, who "tried to appease [him] with the assurance that Mark Twain's profile would appear in a plaster plaque over the new entrances" to the apartment buildings. Gauvreau was convinced that the people of "Hartford would rise up in arms to prevent the outrage" when he publicized the development plans in his paper.[45] He was wrong. In 1920, few were interested in saving the house. The resistance to saving the house had as much to do with Sam Clemens and his tenuous connection to the Hartford elite outside of the Nook Farm neighborhood as it did with the fact that by the 1920s the house was largely seen as a particularly gaudy Victorian blemish in an otherwise architecturally tasteful Hartford. Many Hartford residents were even irate with Gauvreau for taking up the cause of the hideous house, and others were merely uninterested in Sam Clemens. After all, Clemens was not, in the estimation of the Hartford elite, a "real" Hartford resident.[46]

Some of Emile Gauvreau's own employees at the *Hartford Courant* tried to explain the historical context to him. "Hartford never liked Mark Twain," they explained; "it is ashamed of him." Gavreau alluded to the fact that many Hartforders were still upset with Twain for his political stances, particularly annoyed that he had supported Democrat Grover Cleveland for president. Gauvreau later came to blame his campaign to save the Clemens house for his short stay as editor in chief at the *Hartford Courant.* He believed that he had made "influential enemies" with his "little battle" to preserve the house. One Hartford resident put it this way: "Mark Twain spent his time laughing at people and finally he had to move out of here. What in the world possessed you to stir up all this mess about his house?"[47] Clemens's status as an "outsider" made locals suspicious. Some of those who had known him and disliked his public political stances were still active in the 1920s; they did their best to keep the house from being saved.

Gauvreau was, however, successful in stirring the state government to pass an injunction, which kept the new owners from tearing the house down. Instead, the new apartments went in right next door on land that had been sold as part of the same parcel. The apartments were completed in 1926 and a bas relief of Sam Clemens was placed above the entryway just as the developers had promised. Wall and the Ahearns still expected to be able to demolish the Twain house for the valuable real estate beneath it. Eventually, they found a way to make money on their stalled investment. They offered to sell the house to preservationists for more than twice what they had paid for it just three years earlier. In the meantime, to make money from their frozen property they converted the house into apartments. Although the house was transformed into single rental units, the footprint of the house remained essentially the same. Somewhere under the grass paper and years of school and rental wear and tear, the Clemenses' beloved Associated Artists' gilding was still there.

### The Clemens House and Katharine Seymour Day

The Mark Twain house in Hartford is the Twain site that most follows the conventional historical trajectory for historic house museums in the United States. The house was "saved" from development in 1929 by Katharine Seymour Day; it was lovingly restored from 1955 until 1974; and it is now a biographical house museum of the highest order with a state-of-the-art visitors' center and a massive institutional debt to match.[48] By the time Day saved the house in 1929, she had already decided to dedicate the later years of her life to preserving Harriet Beecher Stowe's house and legacy in Hartford. Day was the grandniece of Harriet Beecher Stowe. She was moved to purchase Stowe's last Hartford house in 1924 and set about collecting papers and items that belonged to her great-aunt, her family, and Stowe's important literary circle in Hartford. Day moved into the Stowe house in 1927, and from there she saw to it that Stowe's and, as a result, Mark Twain's literary legacy in Hartford would not be forgotten.[49]

Katharine Seymour Day was born in 1870 and knew the Clemenses from her childhood in Hartford. She often played with the Clemens daughters, Susy, Clara, and Jean, and as an adult she often asked about them in her letters home to her mother.[50] Day, like the Clemens girls, spent a good deal of time abroad. She was presented to Queen Victoria's court in 1893, as well as to the courts of the King of Württemberg and the "Khedive" of Egypt. She traveled extensively. She marched for women's suffrage in New York City and London, and she studied painting in Paris and in New York with William Merritt Chase. She participated in progressive efforts to fight corruption in New York City's notorious Tammany Hall, and, when she was in her mid-forties, she enrolled at Radcliffe and finished an undergraduate and a master's degree in five years.[51] Day was not the average "ladies association" woman. She was not interested in costumed tea parties in colonial houses, although she was not above dressing up in support of her preservation efforts.[52] After a rich life as a highly educated artist and social activist, Day settled down to preserve the legacy of her radical ancestors.

Day presented her plans for Nook Farm in a letter to her mother, Alice Day, in 1925. She wanted to "develop this idea of special libraries, & get as much Beecherania (is that the way to spell it) as possible, in the future people can come from all over for reference to things they couldn't find elsewhere."[53] Day advertised her plans to friends and family, and one acquaintance, Mrs. Slade, offered to contact a friend, one of Olivia Langdon Clemens's nieces, to look into "the state of the Clemens [house]" on her behalf.[54] Just a few years later after relocating to Hartford, Katharine Day formally took up the cause of the Clemens house. She, with other concerned citizens, founded the Friends of Hartford, an organization designed to raise money to buy and "save" the house and to use it as a branch of the local public library.

Her preservation efforts came just a few years after Gauvreau's attempt and were met with similar resistance. In a letter to the editor of the *Hartford Courant*, one local resident, Clara Langdon, still believed it was a ludicrous idea to save the Twain house. She offered, "if the talk of raising a "shrine" to the writer of books who made the world laugh could be cut out and the idea of a fine library be put in its place I am sure more people would be interested." She argued that "when it comes to erecting 'shrines,' let them be to the men who, by their writings[,] have made men think." After all, in her estimation, "Artemus Ward made the world laugh but I have not as yet heard of his neighbors and friends insisting upon raising a shrine to him." The belief that Twain was not a thinking man's writer, but merely a popular humorist not worthy of attention, haunted Day's efforts as it did Gauvreau's. Langdon did not only reject the idea of a shrine to Mark Twain, but went on to write, "surely everyone would like to see the front of the Twain house demolished and a fine library put in its place." She believed that "to restore it to its original condition would be a crime"[55] So though the idea of a new branch for the public library became very popular, the house was still seen as an eyesore with no historic, literary, or aesthetic value. The architectural value was a constant worry to those who wanted to save the Twain house because of its literary associations, and they often found themselves in aesthetic, rather than literary, debates. These debates were not just about the Clemens house. Victorian architecture of all kinds was so reviled by the Hartford population that even twenty years later preservationists could not get the

Connecticut Historical Society to join their cause to save the neighboring George and Lily Warner house.[56]

### The Mark Twain Memorial and Library Commission

In 1930, after a two-year local capital campaign, Day's Friends of Hartford succeeded in raising just enough money to secure a $100,000 mortgage from a local bank.[57] The Connecticut Assembly approved the incorporation of the Mark Twain Memorial and Library Commission, a nonprofit organization designed to run the memorial and facilitate a branch of the Hartford public library through an elected board. The commission's charter specified that the Mark Twain Memorial and Library Commission was organized "for the purpose of acquiring, conducting and maintaining a library, museum and memorial in the city of Hartford as testimonial to the literary achievements of Samuel L. Clemens."[58] The commission's board became responsible for the mortgage payments on the loan that the Friends of Hartford had secured to save the house.

Making these payments was a struggle for the new organization, but the rental income that still came in from the subdivided apartments helped financially.[59] The renters were largely elderly, female residents, a number of whom had a keen interest in Mark Twain. Their rents, along with the rent that the Hartford Public Library paid for its two rooms downstairs, *almost* paid the interest-only monthly mortgage payments and the necessary upkeep for a house that had been sorely neglected in the years since the Clemenses lived there. The Mark Twain Memorial and Library Commission struggled to keep the house in a habitable condition and the duty often fell to individual members of the board.

With no hired staff to show visitors through the house, most early visitors saw just the entry hall and the whitewashed library, where reading tables filled the rooms that had once been the Clemenses' library, conservatory, dining room, and parlor. When people curious about Mark Twain and his house visited, they could see the rooms that were part of the library downstairs. Occasionally, Katharine Day would venture from her house next door to run a tour and talk about the Clemens family. Although Day did not want to be seen publicly as the head of the commission and declined its presidency, she served as "First Vice-President" and "Acting President" for more than twenty-five years, and she organized nearly everything that went on at the house in the early years.[60] She approved repairs, donated almost all of the early furnishings from her personal collection, paid for maintenance of the grounds, and often financed large repairs to the roof and plumbing. Although she invested much of her own money into the house, she and the board did not pay off any of the principle of the mortgage.[61]

The organization's financial difficulties and the larger financial crisis of the Great Depression led to an interesting bout of creative fund raising throughout the 1930s.[62] Day and the other women on the board organized theatrical performances based on Clemens's works and the broader, historical literary life in Hartford. In at least two performances of the *Pageant of Letters in Hartford*, Day played her own mother, Alice Beecher Hooker (Day), while her cousin, Charlotte Perkins Gilman, played the role of Harriet Beecher Stowe.[63] Another member of the board dressed as Mark Twain and another played Jim from the *Adventures of Huckleberry Finn* and *Tom Sawyer* in blackface.[64]

Board members also performed the roles of the Clemens family and neighbors at another event. This time they performed as characters from books by Mark Twain and other writers, and held a series of "Living Book Reviews." The Living Book Reviews fell somewhere on a spectrum between book club meetings and living history performances. Participants read, performed, and discussed Daphne DuMaurier's *Jamaica Inn*, Stowe's *Uncle Tom's Cabin*, and *The Prince and the Pauper* at one such event. Once again, the board took on the roles of literary and historical characters. Day played her mother, Alice Beecher Hooker, and Gilman played Stowe, but this time, board member Seth Holcome performed in blackface "as colored butler, George" Griffin, the Clemens family's famous servant. The newspaper accounts of the "living book reviews" show that they ran from 1937 through 1939. Unlike the pageant, these events were held at the Mark Twain house and sometimes, weather permitting, performed on the lawn. Sarah Wheeler of New York organized the Living Books Reviews, and as the characters read their lines, or recited passages from the novels, they carried with them a gold frame—to enclose and highlight their performance.[65] Board member Charles E. Burpee dressed as Mark Twain and served "lemonade and cakes" to his guests.

That the commission board would stage blackface performances in Hartford, once an abolitionist capital, seems odd today. Blackface performances were still extraordinarily popular in 1930s America. Hartford, despite being home to famous abolitionists, was no exception. Day, pageant writer Inez Temple, and Sarah Wheeler deployed blackface at the Clemens house events because their Hartford audience would have been comfortable with it.[66] The pageants and performances echoed other celebrations of Sam Clemens, like the 1935 Mark Twain Centennial celebration in Hannibal, Missouri. These performances did not last long in Hartford, perhaps because they blurred the lines between fact and fiction, or perhaps because they were too old fashioned for most residents.[67]

## The House Museum Movement and the Colonial Revival

The 1920s and 1930s saw a boom in the preservation of historic houses. Between 1895 and 1932, "more than four hundred" house museums opened their doors. Lawrence Vail Coleman, director of the American Association of Museums (1927–1958), then housed in the Smithsonian Institution in Washington, D.C., led a national effort to save historic structures.[68] He believed American houses were instructional tools, tools that educated Americans about their own history and architecture. Coleman visited Mark Twain's Hartford house in 1932, not long after it opened to the public. As a result, he listed it among house museums that led the way for significant preservation efforts in the United States. He noted "where fame makes its home . . . [these] for the most part are the places chosen to survive." Most historic house museums were preserved because of their biographical connection to a great man. As Coleman pointed out, "James Whitcomb Riley, Brigham Young, Mark Twain, Walt Whitman, Grant, Lee, John Brown, Lew Wallace, Woodrow Wilson, Roosevelt and a score of others less illustrious have already given recent houses immortality."[69]

Coleman saw the survival of houses as imperative for citizens who sought out knowledge about the United States "not only to *use* but to *know*—to *understand* American houses of the past. This is not a revival but an awakening; its result is education."[70] To know and understand houses of the past through their preservation was a relatively new impulse in the United States. By the beginning of the twentieth century, in the wake of the Civil War and the national Centennial Exposition in Philadelphia, historic buildings began to gain national attention for preservationists. To "understand" a historic house, as opposed to a public building, in the 1930s meant understanding domestic technologies that had just been outdated. By the 1930s houses regularly had telephones, electrical service, attached garages for automobiles, and other modern conveniences. Understanding domestic life before these inventions was a way to understand life in preindustrial America. In 1932, the former Clemens home was merely fifty-eight years old, but it had been outfitted with all the modern conveniences of the 1870s and 1880s. The Clemenses had a telephone, a kitchen in the front of the house, and spacious modern bathrooms. What visitors to the house might "understand" about American history had more to do with Sam Clemens as a turn-of-the-century family man than the house as a site of important historic events or nostalgia.

Coleman and Katharine Day believed American houses were key to understanding the American past and its important historical figures, historical moments, and literary achievements. Coleman's list elevated houses belonging to poets and presidents side by side. In his support and advice

to preservationists, he was part of the first formal wave of American commemoration that included Day, Henry Ford, and John D. Rockefeller
Jr. While Day restored her aunt's neighborhood, Ford and Rockefeller
preserved, or fabricated, entire villages at Greenfield Village and Colonial
Williamsburg in the 1930s. Although Day's primary interest in preservation was limited to Stowe's and Twain's houses—and neither house
had colonial roots—the movement she was swept up in had the same
positivist take on American history as the Colonial Revival.[71] Lawrence
Vail Coleman pointed out that those interested in the movement to create historic house museums were not necessarily "revivalists."[72] Coleman
showed sensitivity about the term "revivalists" because he did not want
preservationists to be seen as women who merely participated in costumed teas or men who "reenacted" history as noncritical admirers of
the romantic American past. He hoped to elevate the preservation of
architecturally significant buildings and buildings associated with historic
figures, while Day cared about the same issues as "revivalists," just not
necessarily with the same architecture.[73]

In a way, Katharine Seymour Day simply carried on a family tradition. Revivalists believed that right and proper ways of living might be
learned from the historic houses of the past. As she preserved Harriet
Beecher Stowe's papers, she must have felt some continuity in preserving
her great-aunt's house. It was the material evidence of years of Stowe's
advice literature. Harriet Beecher Stowe and Catherine Beecher advised
their readers about the "formation and maintenance of economic, health-
ful, beautiful and Christian homes" (Beecher and Stowe).[74] They offered
advice about "right" ways of living through their book, *The American
Woman's Home* (1869). Their nieces, Charlotte Perkins Gilman and Katharine Day, saw houses as learning tools as well. Whereas Gilman designed
kitchen-less homes as a way to free women from the constraints of the
household, Day wanted to preserve Stowe's place within the domestic
sphere and within the world of letters for posterity.[75] Day's commitment
to saving a historic structure associated with a woman, even her famous
family member, was as radical as much as it was conservative.[76] Day's preservation ethic was complicated, and because it spanned from the mid-
1920s until her death in 1964, it no doubt evolved as she did.

Katharine Day was never a preservationist merely for the sake of preservation. Although Day had participated in progressive politics and had
worked devotedly toward women's suffrage, she worried about immigra-
tion and assimilation to "American" values. Later in her life, Day believed
"that what is best about the present is derived chiefly from the example
and experience of the past."[77] In her way, Day denied the present through
her celebration of the past. Walter K. Schwinn, a journalism professor at

Trinity College and longtime board member and two-time president of the board of trustees, began writing a history of the Clemenses' Hartford house sometime in the mid-1980s. In his history, Schwinn speculated that Day's goal was not to make "a great point of restoring the house to the state in which it was when the Clemenses occupied it. The house was to be used, but not restored."[78] When it came to the Mark Twain house, Day believed that the house should be "saved" from destruction by real estate speculators, but she did not believe it old enough or historically important enough to be restored. She thought it should be *used*. In 1964, she left the Mark Twain Museum and Library Commission $3,000 while it was in the midst of full-scale restoration and revival.[79] She chose to leave the great bulk of her estate to endow a research institute in honor of Harriet Beecher Stowe and located in the Day house, where all of the original letters and objects she had amassed over the years might serve a higher historical purpose. She also left instructions that the Stowe house be restored as best it could be to the era of Harriet Beecher Stowe's occupation.[80]

## Opening the Twain House to Tourists

Hartford, like other northern cities in the 1920s and 1930s, changed a great deal with the Great Migration from the south. Before the Civil War, Hartford's black population was almost entirely Connecticut born, by 1870 the percentage of the black population born in the south rose to 25 percent, and by 1900 "blacks who were descended from New England pre-Revolutionary families composed a very small proportion" of the black population.[81] The little neighborhood of Nook Farm residents and their descendants thought of themselves as antiracist and activist leaning, but the city struggled to provide an infrastructure to support the changes brought about by the migration. In 1904, just one year after the Clemenses sold their house, Hartford was caught up in a race riot and near lynching believed to have been instigated by a recent southern émigré, Joseph Watson.[82] In the wake of World War One and during the Great Depression, Hartford went from being one of the richest and whitest cities in the country to having a significant African American population and dealing with a devastating loss of industry. And in 1934, according to Weaver, there was "what amounted to a three-day race riot" brought about by tensions between the Irish and black populations in Hartford.[83] White flight from the city was almost immediate and destructive, and West Hartford boomed as an all-white destination.

Some of the white residents who did not leave the heart of the city during the 1930s white flight devoted themselves to preserving it. By

Interior of the Mark Twain House, 1955, courtesy of The Mark Twain House and Museum, Hartford, Connecticut

the late 1930s, a significant number of visitors had started coming to the house who were not just checking out books at the branch library. They came to see Mark Twain's house. The Mark Twain house received other attentions as well. Franklin Delano Roosevelt's New Deal sought to aid various institutions that were of national interest, and the Mark Twain house briefly hosted WPA workers one day a week. One worker assembled elaborate scrapbooks of all of the Sam Clemens and Mark Twain house-related items that Katharine Day had snipped and collected from local and national coverage of her efforts in Hartford.[84] But after an initial increase in visitors, in the 1940s, the Mark Twain Memorial and Library suffered as most historic sites in the United States did during WW II.

The trustees tried to make the most of what they had. To draw visitors and library patrons alike, the commission began opening up more rooms to sightseers. Clara Clemens inspired the opening up of Sam and Olivia Clemens's upstairs bedroom when in 1940 she gave the commission the elaborately carved bed that had belonged to her parents.[85] At some point over the next few years, the commission opened the upstairs bedroom and started charging ten cents to see the room and its furnishings. Day and the other board members decorated the bedroom, arranging it as best they could to look like what they thought the Clemenses' bedroom *should* have looked like.

The commitment to the full restoration of the house to "the Clemens period" only came about after Day's power on the board began to wane in the 1950s. Although she would live well into the 1960s and see a new board vote to fully restore the house to the "Twain-era," Day was in her late eighties and nineties when restoration on the house began. Change came to the Mark Twain house with a new group of trustees. Day found that "raising money for the Mark Twain Memorial [was] so much more difficult." Day assumed that it was more difficult to raise money for the house in the 1950s because there were fewer people still alive who knew the Clemens family personally. Her successors would see things differently. Day believed that "the present generation doesn't have the same feeling for him."[86] She was right. They did not dismiss Mark Twain as an outcast of the Hartford elite, but saw him as a subject of fascination and as a potential tourism draw for the whole city.

In 1953, after the death of Day's brother and longtime trustee Arthur P. Day, Day announced her desire to retire from the board. She and the board began an extended series of discussions about the future of the Mark Twain Memorial and Library. They brainstormed about ideas for the Mark Twain house's future and generated a long list of options. Some believed the house should become "an education center" that focused on "the study of American History and American Literature," or that it might become an "Institute for [the] American Idea." Some trustees hoped the house might be converted into a "graduate school for work in American Literature [because it] already [had] the nucleus of a library." Some held out hope that the little branch of the public library could stay open. Many argued that it should become formally connected with nearby leading educational institutions, specifically Yale University or Trinity College.[87]

A number of trustees also wondered if the "building [should] be restored to the 1870–1890 period." They debated about whether the house could be both a museum and an education center. Because many served on the boards of both houses, some consideration was given to a potential consortium between the Stowe house and the Twain house. Several trustees thought the house needed to bring in visitors and that in order to do that it needed to be "more interesting." What board members meant by "interesting" is not indicated in their minutes, but there seemed to be a consensus that the more Twain-related the house could become, the more interesting the memorial would be. It was clear that something new needed to happen to inspire visitors and new trustees. All agreed more people needed to be involved with the house to bring in more money. Ultimately, the board decided to bring in more, and younger, trustees, and it would be these trustees who would officially change the scope of the mission for the house.[88]

The board of trustees, under the stewardship of its youngest member, Mary Shipman, began to carefully select new members. Mary Shipman became a board member by reason of proximity in 1951. She and her family lived in the George and Lily Warner house, and because she was young and willing, Shipman took on many of the most important tasks of the commission. She helped bring on new members and transitioned the older trustees (the "Old Guard," as she called them) to new roles as "honorary trustees." During the transition and long into the 1960s, Mary Shipman and Edith Salsbury ran things behind a false front of male presidents.[89] In 1954, they added an architect to the board to assess the condition of the house. They added businessmen and bankers to help order the Mark Twain Memorial and Library Commission's finances. The total number of board members doubled to allow for a shared burden and financial responsibility.[90] Day could not help but notice that "a group of younger people have become members of the Board and we have great hopes and plans to make the house one of the most important literary shrines in America."[91] Her excitement at the shift appears genuine. Although Day was the most difficult member of the "Old Guard" because of her proximity and founder status, Mary Shipman was able to smooth over most of the new board's changes with Day's grudging consent.[92] In an attempt to convert the library and memorial into a true "literary shrine," the new board members decided that they would need more room for the Mark Twain collection that Day and other trustees had been amassing over the years.

To make room for the expansion, the commission claimed more rooms for museum space over the following years as building tenants died or moved into assisted living.[93] Later in 1954, the board decided that it was necessary to cancel the lease with the Hartford Public Library and, for the first time, to charge an admission to the house.[94] In addition to managing and reclaiming the interior of the house, the new trustees made one of their first priorities to pay off the remaining amount of the original mortgage on the house. In 1955, in an effort to publicize the board's financial need, the *Hartford Courant* ran an article that pointed out that since 1930, "the mortgage has been reduced by only $5,000."[95] This time the *Courant*'s pleas for funds were heard, and heard especially by the friends and neighbors of the new trustees.

## Norman Holmes Pearson and the Restoration

The Mark Twain house presented an ambitious restoration project. The once-lavish house had changed a great deal in the fifty-two years since the Clemenses sold it. Any restoration project requires thousands of choices about how exact a restoration is possible and practical. Research into a house can be exacting or mere historical estimation. The trustees at the Mark Twain Memorial and Library Commission chose to do the most exacting research and an exhaustive restoration. They reviewed and uncovered what remained of the Mark Twain–era decoration in the house and discovered that peeling back the layers could never return the house to how it was when the Clemenses lived there. Removing the carpeting and grass paper and stripping the woodwork would only take the house so far. They consulted board member Norman Holmes Pearson, a professor of literature and American studies at Yale. Pearson recommended an extreme course of action.

That Norman Holmes Pearson became involved in the restoration of the Mark Twain house spoke to his interest in literary detritus. Pearson, an Office of Strategic Services (OSS) agent in London during World War II, became an extremely influential editor of modernist poets and novelists. His longstanding relationship and correspondence with H. D. (Hilda Doolittle)—whom he befriended during his time in London with the OSS, William Carlos Williams, Ezra Pound, and others provides some of the most valuable insights into the everyday lives of these writers, their processes, and the work of their editors. Pearson is also credited with having preserved much of this correspondence for future scholars through his influence at the Beinecke Rare Book and Manuscript Library at Yale University. As a scholar, he found the correspondence of canonical "American" authors like Hawthorne fascinating, all the while making sure the modernist poets made their way into the canon through his work as the editor of the *Oxford Anthology of American Literature* (2nd edition, 1938). In the case of Clemens, he was also interested in preserving the legacy of American authors through the "texts" that they had inhabited.[96]

Pearson was the board member who inspired the organization's devotion to the minute details of the Clemenses' original belongings, and insisted that the house as a text itself was worthy of scholarly editing, explication, and illumination.[97] He was determined that the restoration recreate the perfect authentic text in the house. His idea that a historic structure should be treated as a primary historical document, that it should be preserved as historical text that brings to life the material reality of an author's life, rather than a space that merely memorializes or celebrates the author, was unheard of in the 1950s. His ideas inspired the staff as they devoted themselves to the meticulous restoration of the house. His guiding principle—that the board should "only restor[e] to the original text"—led them to invest in the idea that "the house [was] a document . . . not our house, it's [Clemens's] and we should only reflect what he did."[98]

The board carefully laid out restoration principles that kept the house from becoming the pet project of any particular person's interpretive agenda. As Bill Faude, the curator of the house during a portion of its restoration put it, "it is a purist philosophy, formulated by a scholar, and it imposes severe restrictions," which "also prevents important donors, however well meaning, from inflicting on the restoration furniture, paintings, or decors which do not belong." Devotees like Faude believed these restrictions protected "the credibility of the work." In their minds, if it was "not a restoration, why spend all that money and effort on a figment of imagination."[99] In addition to guiding the staff in research and in its preservation philosophy, Pearson eventually instructed the board as to Clemens's proper literary reputation as well. He advised them "that Mark Twain be referred to as a *writer* not a humorist."[100] He set the interpretive tone at the house through his own understanding of Clemens. Pearson's devotion to the perfect restoration of the house also seems to reveal an absolute belief that the house could become the authentic object of a literary tourist or scholar's quest and reveal something about the origin of Clemens's genius.[101] Faude and the rest believed Pearson and that they could accurately represent the historic reality of the Twain era through near scientific research and reasoning. This kind of devotion to a method provides its own interpretive schema. In the 1950s, the trustees believed, at least in their collected notes, reports, and newsletters, that they were part of "a true restoration," and that this restoration was what visitors wanted to see when they came to the Clemens house.

Bill Faude, who was brought into the restoration as a high schooler during his summer vacations, saw the trustees under Katharine Day as "playing house" in the museum.[102] It is likely that many of the new trustees saw the earlier efforts at the memorial similarly. Because Day had spent time in the Clemens household as a child, her arrangements were considered accurate enough. At that time, most house museums' staff did not have the expertise, time, or money to do in-depth research about specific wall treatments, flooring, woodwork, and linens. They did their best to arrange period objects in ways that evoked historic interiors and inspired visitors to think about the house's occupants. In the same way, the boyhood home in Hannibal arranges its objects today to evoke small-town Missouri life in the 1840s, and Mark Twain's birthplace in Florida arranges its objects to estimate modern versions of what museum professionals believe a pioneer Missouri house would have looked like in the 1830s. However, no historical house museum then, and few now, offered the "perfect" arrangement of interiors through the kind of systematic research that the trustees and staff performed at the Twain house between 1955 and 1974.

Unlike Sam Clemens's childhood homes, his adult home in Hartford had been carefully planned and documented in the Clemenses' correspondence.[103] At the time, people were still alive in the 1950s who had visited the house while it was owned by the Clemenses and the Bissells. The house itself was profiled in a number of publications, as we saw earlier. Importantly, the Clemenses' acquaintances were a literary bunch, and the trustees' careful review of their letters and diaries revealed details of the house. Moreover, the authentic object itself—the house—was able to tell the restorers much about what it had looked like. The grass-paper wall coverings had inadvertently preserved the design of much of the original wallpaper and stenciling done by Tiffany and Associated Artists. Inspired by the rise of historical archeology at places like Colonial Williamsburg, board members carefully extracted, recorded, and preserved the layers of the house.[104]

With this in mind, in 1955, the new board voted to "make the Mark Twain House in Hartford not only a memorial to him but also a literary center in keeping with Mark Twain's standing as a world figure in literature" and "to maintain the house and grounds in *perfect* order in keeping with the Mark Twain period." They decided to "restore the house and outbuildings as they were in Mark Twain's day and to maintain and develop them as a museum and library and to provide a Curator and librarian and other suitable staff." They also resolved to "foster literary, cultural or other research of the Mark Twain period and conduct seminars, lectures, courses of study and other activities along these lines." The board came up with a new set of guiding principles based around the accurate and careful study of the house as a primary text. These principles were radical in their day. At the time, almost no house in the United States had put such academic restrictions on itself. Moreover, no house devoted to an American or perhaps any author had ever been so painstakingly researched and restored. What started with the vote in 1955 was not completed until almost twenty years later in 1974.[105]

In addition, the new committee voted to pay off the remaining $100,000 mortgage on the house as quickly as possible, to focus on the restoration.[106] The new trustees were not fazed by the fact that so much of the original loan remained unpaid. They paid it down themselves through donations from friends and family. Much to their advantage, in the decades following WW II, Hartford's insurance industry boomed and fund raising was much easier for these trustees than it had been for Day and her partners during the worst years of the Depression and World War II.

In the postwar years, there was renewed interest in visiting historic sites across the United States. Most importantly for those at work on the house, Mark Twain was newly admired. He was no longer the subject of disdain by members of the Hartford elite. Hal Holbrook began his popular performance of Mark Twain in 1954 and was featured on the *Ed Sullivan Show* in 1956. Holbrook performed as Mark Twain all over the country and even behind the Iron Curtain, and he stirred up interest in Clemens as he went. When Holbrook came to the Mark Twain Memorial and Library, the trustees found that the popularity of his performance could be used as a fund-raising tool for the board. Holbrook had also spent time trying to speak with every living person who had known Clemens, to get a sense of his voice and mannerisms. Along the way, he uncovered information and connections that were useful to the researchers at the Twain house. His performances, by 1960, were already seen as directly responsible for Mark Twain's renewed popularity and the "yearning for yesterday" that his image evoked.[107]

### Performing the Restoration

The restoration process itself drew tourists to the house. Many visitors wanted to peek around as workers completed projects. The process was carefully staged so that visitors could watch the performance of the skilled craftsmen as they restored the house. The restoration crew focused on two rooms at a time, so that most of the house could be open to curious visitors and so that funding could be found project by project. Throughout the twenty-year project, the house became a showplace for restoration techniques, and the board made public its search for artisans who could do the historical work to restore the house. They also publicized the house's restoration by sending parts of it out into exhibitions, as they did with a door from the house, which was sent to a 1958 Louis Comfort Tiffany exhibition in New York.[108] At the Clemens house, a visitor could see craftsmen restoring the grand Victorian past and see the setting for Clemens's domestic world come to life room by room.

The board of trustees decided that it was better to fund the restoration one grant and one donation at a time than to incur debt—they learned this lesson from their predecessors. This smart decision kept people interested in the project as it unfolded, and it inspired contributions as visitors and community investors could see that the work being done was done well. It became possible, for instance, for one individual donor to pay for the restoration and partial reconstruction of the bookshelves in the library, while another could pay for the molding that encased it. In addition, most of the donations brought into the project were set up to serve as matching funds to large-scale grants from the Hartford Foundation, the Gannett Foundation, the Coe Foundation, and eventually, the National Trust for Historic Preservation. The National Trust for Historic Preservation, though founded in 1949, had not been in a position to actively assist historic properties until almost a decade later.[109] The expansion of the role of the National Trust throughout the United States during this period kept national interest in preservation high. Although the grants from these organizations did not pay for all of the restoration and research, they inspired local people to contribute their money and to take the project seriously.

By limiting their restoration to the "Mark Twain period," or roughly the seventeen years when the family made the house their primary residence, the board focused its efforts within a manageable range of years. Because the Clemenses had redecorated the house so extensively a few years after they moved in, it was unclear at first which version of the Mark Twain period the board of trustees would attempt to restore. They could restore the house to exactly as it had been in 1874 when the Clemens family moved in, or they could restore the house to the period after the Clemenses' hired Associated Artists to redecorate.[110] The board decided to focus on the period after the Associated Artists had decorated the house and as a result, became one of the first institutional collectors of Victoriana and Louis Comfort Tiffany work in the country. The rest of the country was still suffering from its extreme distaste for the decorative arts of the Gilded Age and Victorian era.[111] However, the choice to restore the house to the Associated Artists era meant the board chose to take on a much larger and more expensive project, and choosing one era over another (instead of providing a layered view of the house over time) was an interpretive choice—a choice that continues to affect the way that we understand Mark Twain and his domestic life today.

The trustees' interest in the relationship between objects, decorations, and Mark Twain made sure that careful research led to not just the authentic object, but also the right object in its right place. The trustees became archivists for the Clemens home, believing that the proper research and arrangement of archival materials could uncover all they needed to know about the Clemens house—what furniture went where, what wallpapers were used, and what activities dominated each space of the house. The right object, the right place, and the right interior conditions would bring about the proper interpretation and take visitors back to the days when Sam Clemens lived in the house. They believed that arranging the right internal elements of the house would bring about the truest understanding of the house itself, and the perfect house would create a more perfect picture of Sam Clemens the man.

The board hired a graduate student from Yale, Albert Stone, who under Pearson's direction interviewed people who had known the Clemens family.[112] Stone's research was some of the first oral history used in the restoration of a historic building, let alone some of the first oral history used to create a deeper picture of an American writer's domestic life. Amateur historians on the board of the memorial did most of the research that went into the house, but they took their research seriously and wanted to get every possible detail right. They bemoaned, for example, that "the Hartford Gas Company and the insurance agent would not allow the restoration to illuminate the house by gaslight."[113] Members of the board, especially Edith Colgate Salsbury, made themselves experts on Sam Clemens's time in Hartford.

Edith Salsbury visited nearly every known repository of Sam and Olivia Clemens's letters and mined them for information about their lives in the house. She got to know Olivia Langdon Clemens's surviving niece and nephew and developed a strong relationship with the Langdon family that would bring many Clemens and Langdon family treasures to their collection. Salsbury spent time with prominent Twain scholars and sorted through the correspondence of not just the Clemens family but also of all its known associates. Salsbury's efforts, aided by Pearson's direction and influence, made the restoration of the house a "science" rather than a merely enthusiastic estimation and celebration of Victorian interiors. Salsbury created her own archival principles for the information that she acquired. She organized folders for every room of the house to include every historical mention of the room, its furnishings, and what went on there. These folders revealed that life at the house was never static. As a result, the museum board over the years has been able to recreate the house at different moments and has been able to imagine, for instance, what the house was like at Christmas, when the Clemenses had company, and when a child was sick.[114] Salsbury, Stone, and Pearson's research fueled the project for nearly twenty years.

Though she was not as vocal a leader as Day, Salsbury made her mark among Twain scholars and historic preservationists. Her book, *Susy and Mark Twain*, which wove together Susy Clemens's biographical writings about her father with excerpts from both Susy's and Sam Clemens's letters, was accepted by Twain scholars as a "substantial" work of research as well as "entertaining and unusual." Harper and Row considered it a popular enough subject to publish in 1965, and it was such an impressive work of scholarship that Frederick Anderson, then editor of the Mark Twain Papers at Berkeley, endorsed it with an introduction.[115] Salsbury was one of the first to publish on Mark Twain and his domestic sphere and influenced a generation of literary scholars who would come after her.[116] The Mark Twain house staff has since taken Susy's short life as a special topic for interpretation and focus.

For many years, Susy's death was the tragic explanation for why Sam and Olivia Clemens never returned to the Hartford house even after Clemens had earned enough money to pay back his creditors. Susy did not accompany her parents to Europe in 1895, but planned to visit Hartford and stay with friends. She contracted spinal meningitis and became fatally ill while her parents were away. In a feverish state and delusional from her illness, Susy wanted to be in the family's Hartford house. She died in the house before her parents made it home from England. In the retelling of this tragic story, the staff often quotes Clemens's letter to his close friend the Reverend Joseph Twichell:

> Ah, well, Susy died at home. She had that privilege. Her dying eyes rested upon nothing that was strange to them, but only upon things which they had known and loved always and which had made her young years glad . . . If she had died in another house—well, I think I could not have borne that. *To us, our house was not unsentient matter—it had a heart, and a soul, and eyes to see us with; and approvals, and solicitudes, and deep sympathies; it was of us, and we were in its confidence, and lived in its grace and in the peace of its benediction. We never came home from an absence that its face did not light up and speak out its eloquent welcome—and we could not enter it unmoved.*[117]

The italicized portion of the letter above has quite often been used in promotional material for the Hartford house and even for the boyhood home in Hannibal. After Susy's death, the Clemenses largely abandoned the Hartford house and nearly abandoned the hope of ever selling it. They left most of their furnishings and a number of household goods behind with the house, which were eventually sold at auction in 1903.[118] In part, the research that Salsbury completed in her book became the basis for scholars' late-twentieth-century interpretations of Clemens's work as having two distinct periods, the period before Susy's death and the period afterward, when his work was less light-hearted.[119]

For the trustees and curators the 1903 auction was the "Holy Grail" of the Twain house. Unfortunately, no one has been able to locate an auction inventory or sales list. Despite the missing concordance to the house, the board of trustees in the 1950s wanted to understand every piece of the household. As they came across a mention of a toy or an item that any of the Clemens family owned, they sought out items matching the description throughout their networks in Hartford. According to a 1956 newsletter, the trustees were "becoming expert sleuths with the result that original furniture is being tracked down from California to Maine." They actively sought out "authentic pieces which are unavailable at the moment."[120] All of their research was strategically planned. If they were not able to secure the authentic pieces right away from their current owners, their enthusiasm quite often led to the gift of the items eventually. They sought to "acquire every single original item that we can find and afford, and, by degrees we want to replace with *the perfect specimen* objects which have been loaned as stop-gaps."[121] By raising the profile of the house in local newspapers, producing a coordinated newsletter, and eventually through regional travel reporting, news got out that the memorial was interested in the pieces that had belonged to the house. Accordingly, those pieces started showing up.

In 1957, a man near Redding, Connecticut, telephoned the museum to tell the staff that in his barn he had the Scottish mantel the Clemenses had installed in the Hartford library. House staff initially believed the man deranged. By all accounts, it was believed that the Scottish mantel had been lost when Sam Clemens's last house, Stormfield, burned to the ground in 1923.[122] The elaborate fireplace surround had been one of the personal items that Sam and Olivia Clemens shipped from Hartford to their new residence. Clemens moved the mantel into Stormfield, the house near Redding, Connecticut, he had built after Olivia Clemens's death. The board members quickly found out that it *was* the same mantel that had been in the Hartford house. It had been salvaged as the house was in flames by local residents and been stored in a nearby barn for nearly thirty years. The "owner" of the mantel asked for $2,500 cash or a car in trade for it.[123] It was too good a deal for the board to pass up. These kinds of surprising finds made reading through the newsletters of the Mark Twain Memorial and Library Commission in the 1950s like following a treasure hunt, and the newsletter accounts stirred up even more interest in the house.

## The Social House Again

The new trustees believed that the social life of the house could not be neglected. They believed that their "perfect" restoration should be used. To get to know one another better and to raise interest and money for the restoration, the board held grand social events.[124] The board replaced annual educational membership meetings held on Mark Twain's birthday

Mantel, circa 1980, courtesy Library of Congress, Prints and Photographs Division, HABS

with elaborate balls and waltzes in the house. Sometimes costumed affairs, pictures of these events flooded the *Hartford Courant*'s society page. Attendees drank cocktails and smoked cigars in the house. The board members' interest in restoring the house did not preclude their enjoyment of it. For the public, they added an annual frog jumping contest and other programs.[125] By 1959, their fund-raising appeals and events had earned enough money to pay off the last remaining portion of the 1929 mortgage. That year the annual board and members meeting culminated in a mortgage burning ceremony inside the house.

By the early 1960s, things had changed drastically. The board in its outreach and research efforts had collected hundreds of photographs and letters about the house and hundreds of items relating to Mark Twain. Visitation had increased so much that the board let their local site manager go in order to hire someone with professional museum and library experience.[126] It hired a professional architectural historian to complete the historic research into the stenciling on the third floor, and they made sure that the house got on the National Register of Historic Landmarks. By 1963, the Mark Twain house was a functioning historic house museum in the throes of scholarly research on its primary object—the house itself. All three floors of the house and much of its basement were open for the public to tour. Researchers had tracked down every piece of furniture relating to the "Twain-period" that they could, and the house was full of "the right stuff." At one point, the house was so perfectly appointed that you could open a drawer—not that the average visitor was permitted to—and find period linens, clothing, and toiletries right where they would have belonged.[127]

The board planned to complete the restoration by 1974 in time for the house's centennial. What the board had begun with its decision to restore the house to the "Twain-era" in 1955, other historic house museums across the country began to contemplate in the decade that led up to the national bicentennial. In 1956, 1,328 visitors toured the house, and within a year of the appointment of the new board, the numbers rose to 5,000.[128] By 1963, more than 18,000 visitors were making their way through the Clemens house annually, and the board voted to change the name of the organization to the Mark Twain Memorial.[129] As one board member put it, "people come from far and wide, all types, all classes, Brownies, Girl Scouts, tourists, students, scholars, lady bowlers, printers, accelerated school groups, slow groups, delinquents—all enjoy the three floors of the museum."[130] By the early 1960s, the house received regular coverage in New England newspapers and the national press, and the house really did see visitors from "far and wide."[131] By 1967, the house had 40,000 visitors a year.[132]

By the mid–sixties the Twain house was no longer unique. The 1966 Historic Preservation Act made a national priority of the kind of work that had been going on for a decade at the house and began to "curb the rampage" of construction that tore down historic neighborhoods and buildings in the name of postwar "development."[133] The National Park Service began to revamp the national parks in an attempt to get sites in order in time for an anticipated boom in historical tourism that would come with local and national celebrations of the bicentennial.[134] These national bicentennial efforts, in turn, inspired smaller house museums and historic sites, like the Mark Twain Boyhood Home in Hannibal to update their interpretive programs and to begin the careful scientific process of architectural research that Hartford finished in the mid-seventies.

However, the boom in visitation can only partially be accounted for by postwar travel, or even by the rise in Mark Twain popularity brought about by Hal Holbrook's portrayal. The reputation of the house itself and the work going on inside became a primary draw during its restoration. As the house became more and more the Gilded Age gem it had been, as workers spent months carefully measuring and then reapplying the gold and silver stenciling inside the house, people flocked to the museum to see the process. Each step of the restoration was met with a "grand reveal" event that both honored the donors involved and served as a teaser for work that was yet to come. Local interest in the museum skyrocketed as people demanded to see what was going on inside. The museum became so popular that the staff instituted a "free" day for people who could not afford admission.[135] New Year's Day was chosen, and for several years, the staff served hot cider inside the house as droves of local people made their way through the museum. The free admission day was so popular that people often stood outside in the snow for hours waiting. The Memorial's board and staff kept up this practice until the numbers grew too high for all the visitors to make it through the house in the hours it was open.

## After the Restoration

The Mark Twain House and Museum was a calmer place after the restoration. Staff developed educational programs, the board stopped holding parties in the house, and it quit holding annual frog jumping contests to quiet reports of animal abuse. The memorial became once again like a museum rather than a social club. But, as the foundation for the Mark Twain house became more solid, the city of Hartford saw decline. As the Mark Twain House and Museum Web site explained in its short institutional history:

Visitors waiting outside for the New Year's Day Open House, courtesy of The Mark Twain House and Museum, Hartford, Connecticut

The neighborhood began to change as signaled by the insertion of the Mark Twain Apartments on Farmington Avenue in the 1920s and again more considerably in the early 1960s with the arrival of Hartford Public High School on Forest Street. The latter triggered the destruction of several Nook Farm period houses, and the texture of the immediate surroundings of the Twain House was sharply compromised. While a good neighbor and partner, the high school's physical presence dwarfed the historic landmarks nearby and effectively terminated the sense of a 19th-century setting to the south.[136]

Katharine Day had petitioned to stop the high school from moving in next door. During the community zoning debates, she argued in the press, that "it would be absurd . . . this has always been a great cultural street—not at all a school street. We want to keep it as it was."[137] Day seemed to have conveniently forgotten that the Mark Twain house was itself the Kingswood School not long before she purchased it. It is quite possible that she meant that Farmington Avenue had never been a "public school" street. But in 1960, the high school was built and even Mary Shipman lost her house—the former George and Lily Warner house, also built by Edward Tuckerman Potter.

The high school changed the neighborhood. After all, what could be less conducive to the Victorian era that the board was trying to evoke than modern-day teenagers? The Hartford High School interrupted the park-like calm on the grounds. Eventually, the school building expanded to the very edges of the city's property. Today the new visitors' center abuts so snuggly against the school that there is little room to maneuver between them. Parents pull into the Twain house's east lot in the morning to let out their children just as staff come in also looking for parking. What the museum's brief institutional history does not tell you, is how *exactly* Hartford changed since Day's time.

The museum's growth coincided with some of the most turbulent years in Hartford's long history. This turbulence was born of racial discord. Local white supremacists raged against the 100 percent postwar growth of the black population. At the same time, Hartford's total population did not increase at all and actually shrank due to white flight.[138] The National Association for the Advancement of Colored People (NAACP), Congress Of Racial Equality (CORE), and Southern Christian Leadership Conference (SCLC) members came to Hartford throughout the 1960s to try to calm racial tensions. CORE worked on building relationships between white employers and potential black employees. The increase in the black population was blamed for the need for a new Hartford high school, the very high school that went in next door to the Mark Twain House and Museum, despite a total population *decrease* in the city over this decade.[139] The pressures that led to the new high school came about because of school overcrowding. Moreover, the school overcrowding was the direct result of the demolition of an old high school, which was razed to make way for an overpass that connected the white suburbs with downtown Hartford.

In the years immediately following Katharine Day's death, the city was engulfed in several race riots, the worst being the "Labor Day" riots of 1969 that originated in the Hartford Puerto Rican community's call for safe and affordable housing.[140] Hartford faced the same problems that urban areas across the United States experienced in the wake of massive deindustrialization and white flight from the urban core.[141] Hartford, once the richest city in the country, became one of ten poorest cities per capita in the 1980s and 1990s.[142] As one Hartford resident put it, "Stowe's cozy, fat Hartford can be lean and cruel today."[143] During these years, the house museum and its mission became less meaningful to Hartford residents. It was not alone. A number of urban historic house museums faced similar challenges to connect with their cities' changing population.[144]

Front hall after restoration, while still used as a lobby and gift store, courtesy of The Mark Twain House and Museum, Hartford, Connecticut

## Public History and Perfection

Elsewhere by the 1970s, a new cohort of public history profession-als rose to leadership positions at historic sites. Academically trained as historians, they were interested in spreading their scholarly and activist investment in New Social History into the public sphere. These historians challenged the indoctrinating influence of the historic house museum by focusing on histories of working-class men and women of all races. Places like the Lowell National Historic Site began to take on the chal-lenge of making tourist sites "attractive" without "trivializing or erasing difficult and complex histories." But some sites clung harder than others to the top-down model of history. Even sites like Colonial Williamsburg that set a radical New Social History interpretive agenda, according to ethnographers Richard Handler and Eric Gable, fell short in their front-line interpretation in everyday interactions with tourists.[145] Likewise, the New Social History had a difficult time making its way into interpreta-tion at Mark Twain's Hartford house. Because the board had been so intensely focused on the house as a primary source text, it missed opportunities to connect with the changing Hartford community. It is difficult for any literary site that celebrates a single great author to make connections with complex social history. But Clemens's creative texts provided ample opportunities for literary scholars to engage in the literary-critical work equivalent of the New Social History—Marxist criticism, the new literary history, feminist critique, reader-response criticism, and cultural studies. However, the house stayed a shining example of what wealth and genius could build.

Perfection had become the reigning interpretation. Hal Holbrook wrote in 1974 to a board member: "I have the profoundest respect for all who have placed your hearts and your labor and your taste for perfection into Mark Twain's beautiful dream house."[146] The board's "taste for perfection"—inspired by Norman Holmes Pearson's insistence on scholarly research standards—had become its highest goal and this pursuit ended up being as binding an interpretive method as any other. By 1976, board members believed the house was "the greatest 19th century house-museum in the United States," because of the restoration and their careful attention to Victorian details, almost despite Sam Clemens's residency there.[147] Even though the stories of Sam Clemens at the house were full of details that would lend themselves to literary scholars who were interested in women's history, cultural studies, and African American studies, the house itself was so vibrantly transformed by the restoration that it came to tell the story of the decoration of the house itself.

Edith Salsbury, shortly before she died in 1971, encouraged the board to hire a young man with a degree in history who had long been involved as a volunteer and part-time employee at the house, Wilson Faude.[148] In the 1970s while Bill Faude was the lead curatorial influence, his research into Tiffany and Associated Artists became a driving force at the memorial. He published his research results in the leading scholarly decorative art journals, including *Winterthur Portfolio*. However, his research was not really about the Clemens family. His research concerned the people who designed the Clemenses' wallpaper and stenciling—the individual designers who made up Associated Artists.[149] Because the board had sought out Victorian pieces to fill the house and along the way had started collecting work by Tiffany, they came to own one of the most impressive collections of Tiffany works in the United States. Their acquisitions policy evolved from just pieces associated with Sam and Olivia Clemens and their circle to including the objects and documents associated with the artists who worked on the house. In 1977, for instance, they acquired the kitchen table and chairs that Louis Comfort Tiffany had designed for his own home, which Faude enthusiastically described as "medieval vogue" in the

Hartford press.[150] Although a fascinating set of furniture, there is no evidence to argue it connects directly to Sam Clemens, his family, or friends in Hartford. The board and curator's "taste for [aesthetic] perfection" may have undercut the site's local connections.

Collections have a way of determining the fate of a museum. Today most museums have highly structured and vetted collection protocols to manage not only their limited budgets, but also their unconscious and conscious desires to collect—to seek out the next authentic object in a series, to "complete" a collection. The Mark Twain Memorial started out collecting only materials that related to the "Mark Twain Era" at the house, but somewhere along the way, the staff could not refuse Tiffany-related gifts, and a collection of Tiffany, like a collection of anything, clamored to be completed or expanded.[151] Then there was the secondary trap, if they collected Tiffany, they ought to collect the work of other designers related to Associated Artists. Faude's research set the institution on a path toward becoming a broader museum of Victoriana and decorative arts.

## The Mark Twain House and Its Futures

The Hartford Twain house is an interesting place to study because, among other reasons, it was the place where Norman Holmes Pearson's American studies and literary scholarship methods entered the realm of public culture. At first the techniques and research focus on the house were blessings for those involved in its preservation. Pearson's methods inspired Edith Salsbury to look at the relationship between Sam Clemens and his daughter Susy, and her research and the careful preservation of the house, in turn, led to new thinking about Clemens as a family man fully participating in the Gilded Age. But the quest for the restoration of the Twain era at the house eventually made interpretation a scholarly exercise. Despite its initial popularity, the approach separated Hartford's population from activities at the house. It was a scholarly trap. With the restoration completed, the museum board and the growing professional staff were left to ask, what's next? In an effort to reconnect, and show off some of the museum's Tiffany collection more permanently, the museum under the direction of John Boyer and with the board's full support, built a "35,000-square-foot $14.6 million [visitors'] center" that is "three times the size of the Twain house."[152]

This building has been blamed by the press and by board members for the museum's current and very public financial troubles. The board's decision to build such a large building on the historic landscape that Day, Shipman, and others had tried so hard to preserve as part of a historic district indicates a break from the authentic-object scholarly approach. In the mid-1990s during the "dot.com boom" and after years of quiet and responsible educational program expansion, the board of trustees and Boyer believed it was a good idea to build a new visitors' center. There the museum could facilitate outreach programs, and larger museum exhibits, like a Tiffany exhibit, could be displayed. The visitors' center would include a thoroughly up-to-date archive, temperature-controlled rooms for the collections, and research space for academics who wanted to study Mark Twain and his times. Researchers found the house and its collections an amazing window into the life of Sam Clemens and took him seriously as an important American writer, just as Pearson had believed that they would. By the time that the board and staff had decided to expand, it only seemed fitting that such an important, perhaps *the* most important, American writer's house would have the whole museum package: a fully restored house museum, a series of educational programs that fit the institution's mission that had been laid out in 1955, and a new space to house everything that could not fit or did not belong in Sam Clemens's great house.

Today, the Hartford house may be taking a lesson from Hannibal's boyhood home, which since 2005 has incorporated interactive exhibits for young people into its museum building. In Hannibal, children can jump on the raft and pretend that they are on the nearby Mississippi River and they can walk through the larger-than-life pages of an open copy of *The Adventures of Huckleberry Finn.* Today in Hartford, the massive new building facilitates beer tastings and authors' readings, seminars, and research. There is ample room for school group workshops, lunches, and tours of the house. There are spaces where classes can discuss Huck Finn and Clemens's literary legacy. There is a gift shop, a theater that shows portions of Ken Burn's documentary on Mark Twain, and a kid-friendly exhibition on Clemens's worst investment, the Paige Compositor. In recent exhibits, in an earnest attempt to connect with the general public, the museum staff has created two new exhibits in the visitors' center. There is the "Stories by the Fireside: A Readers' Room" that invites readers to "relax on sofas, or on the floor and read Twain's books." Or "they can simply play: There are blocks, word searches, connect the dots and coloring games." Visitors are invited to watch "the Mark Twain channel" on the television in the exhibit, which plays only documentaries about Sam Clemens and rare silent footage of Clemens at Stormfield. The staff has provided "copies of Mark Twain's books" and appears to want young tourists to feel at home. They have even arranged to have student art depicting scenes from Clemens's books to be put "on the wall shortly before the students themselves visit—so they can see their handiwork hung in a museum, with elegant curatorial labels on the wall nearby." According to chief curator

Patti Philippon, "we wanted a space in the Museum Center where visitors could sit down, relax, and experience Mark Twain."[153]

By allowing the student work to hang in the same museum space as Tiffany glass and large-scale portraits of Sam Clemens, the museum overtly included young people in its process and, in effect, revealed that what goes up in a museum is a curatorial choice. They are encouraging people, children and adults, to *read* Twain and attempting to assure that there are people who know and love Sam Clemens's work in the future. Though the house is still the main attraction, it is no longer necessarily the only place where visitors are challenged to think hard about the historical and contemporary meaning of Clemens's work. Such community outreach is a good thing for the museum and has helped to raise funds to keep the doors open.[154]

In a way, the Hartford house is still the perfect house museum. It tells the story of Sam Clemens at the house, it does not seem to mix fact with fiction, and it never implies that Tom Sawyer or Huck Finn were real people that lived in any house. In its fidelity to the biographical and material "truth" and object authenticity, it nearly lost its footing.[155] It may not be out of the woods yet. When I started the archival research for this chapter in 2008, I sat in the archive requesting scrapbooks and meeting notes while trustees met in a flurry in the background, and staff confessed to me that they worried about the security of their jobs.[156] However, in its new approach, the museum board and staff may have found a way to make the perfect arrangement of the objects in the house matter to a new generation of readers. As a result, Hartford remains an example of "best practices" in the field of literary and historic site development and management. Its recent troubles speak to the larger hard times that historic sites face today, and the museum board was smart to reveal its financial shortfall before the current economic crisis.

With museums suffering in the current economy, and with house museums already tormented from "malaise" in the tourism markets, the Hartford house's story raises important questions for museums and public historians.[157] How does the role of a literary site's board of trustees affect the direction of literary interpretation at the site *and* how does it affect literary scholarship? What is the proper role for a literary site today? What are the connections between an author who lived a hundred years ago and the current residents of any city, state, or nation? How can literary sites update and expand their missions to serve their diverse stakeholders? And how is a literary house museum almost always a form of advocacy of an author and his or her works?

Perfect preservation at any historic site cannot exist. Even if the board and curators at the Mark Twain house had not become interested in collecting outside the "Mark Twain Era" at the house, a successful site cannot be all Twain all the time. A site—even in its attempt to provide an absolutely accurate and objective arrangement of historical interiors and exteriors—is not without interpretation. Just as any historical or scholarly narrative is constructed with biases, theoretical constraints, and through the careful arrangement and selection of unstable "facts," so is the preserved or restored house museum. The house in the end was its most effective when it was in transition during its restoration, when visitors could see the work being done on it. In this way the visitors had both the object of authenticity—the house and its content, and a meaningful authentic experience with the house—the site of the performance of the restoration. The interpretive message that the house tells today, and that it has told since the board decided to make the house more "interesting" in 1955, is that the most "authentic" site is the best site, the most interesting attraction, and that it imparts a message to its visitors about how the past really was. But in the past three years they have added to their message. It also matters that visitors enjoy the experience of reading the works of the literary figures that we enshrine.

*Chapter Four*

# Quarry Farm

*Scholars as Tourists*

Owners of historic houses that are not even open to the public find no way of keeping their doors closed to interested strangers who deserve to be admitted and have come with no other purpose. These visitors are not revivalists. They are eager people intent on finding out all they can.

—LAWRENCE VAIL COLEMAN (*HISTORIC HOUSE MUSEUMS,* 1933)

When I went to Elmira, New York, in January 2008, I knew only two things about the city. First, I knew that Sam Clemens had spent many summers with his family and in-laws at nearby Quarry Farm. Second, I knew that the city's economy had been among the worst in the United States.[1] Even so, literary tourists visit this remote town in southern New York to better understand Sam Clemens, and I wanted to know why. Clemens's study is the only site in Elmira that is open to the public, though only regularly during the summer and by appointment at other times. There are no "real" museums dedicated to Twain here, nor are there visitors' centers, LEGO exhibits, restored houses, or rafts to jump on with Huck and Jim. Nonetheless, while I was in Elmira during January and February 2008 visiting the sites associated with Sam Clemens, I took more pictures of Clemens sites than I took at the birthplace, the boyhood home, and the Hartford house combined.

The only thing I did not take a picture of while I was in Elmira was Clemens's study. I took pictures of the view from his sister-in-law's front porch, of her barn, of the milk bottles from her short-lived dairy, of carved details in the bookshelves in her house, and of the ancient "Regulator" clock in her kitchen. I took pictures of the city of Elmira, of the decaying old homes, of the downtown churches, of the signs that pointed to "Mark Twain Country," of Clemens's grave, and of tourists taking pictures of his grave in the middle of a very cold Sunday in February. However, I did not take a single picture of the famous study.

There were several reasons why I did not take a photograph of the study. It was icy out and getting close to the study required parking and walking in the extreme cold. Yet, I took a ridiculous number of photos at Clemens's grave, a good number of which included my own mitten in the frame. I could say that the study was not really on the way anywhere, but I drove by it at least six or seven times. Although the study is closed in the winter to "drop-in" tourists, Director Barbara Snedecor of the Center for Mark Twain Studies at Elmira College will make arrangements to show literary tourists like myself the study. I saw it on my first day in town. Still, on that tour, I did not snap a single photo.

I did not know what to think about this pretty little building. I asked questions. I learned about the history of the study. Clemens's sister-in-law, Susan Crane, had the study built in 1874 as a workplace for him during summer visits. She conceived of the octagonal study with Edward T. Potter, who built the Clemenses' home in Hartford, Connecticut. Built on a hill above her house at Quarry Farm, the study overlooked the farm and the city of Elmira and provided Clemens with a place where he could write.[2] A former caretaker, Gayle Early, told me that, while Susan Crane was still alive, boys would ride their bikes up the steep East Hill to play at the study. One boy recalled decades later sneaking up to Clemens's study with a friend, and being caught by Susan Crane. She ordered the boys to come with her, marched them down the hill to the house, and punished them with milk and cookies.[3] After Crane's death in 1924, the house passed to her nephew, Jervis Langdon Sr.

It is sometimes confusing to keep track of the Jervis Langdons in the story of Quarry Farm. Jervis Langdon (1809–1870), abolitionist, Elmira College founding trustee, and father to Olivia Langdon Clemens purchased Quarry Farm originally in May 1869 as a summer retreat for his family from their city home in Elmira. The farmhouse at Quarry Farm was significantly different when he purchased the property, but the grounds and the site were optimally situated to catch the cool breezes on East Hill. Jervis Langdon barely had time to remodel the house before his death in 1870, when the house was willed to Susan Crane, his daughter. After her death in 1924, the house went to her nephew, Jervis Langdon Sr. (1875–1952), and after his and eventually his wife Eleanor Sayles Langdon's death in 1960, the house went to his son Jervis Langdon Jr. (1904–

2004). Jervis Langdon Sr. lived in the house off and on, sometimes using the house as a full-time residence and sometimes as a summer home. The nearby study was always a literary and architectural curiosity. In 1952, despite years of Crane and Langdon hospitality, a vandal destroyed an antique chair in the study and burned it in the historic fireplace.

The Langdons had tolerated visitors carving their names on a desk in the study and in the study's woodwork, but the fire was too much. Jervis Langdon Sr. realized that his family could no longer protect their home from fire or vandals, and he decided to move the study to where it could be watched more carefully. In 1952, Langdon donated the study to Elmira College so it could be in a public place. His sister, Dr. Ida Langdon, was a professor at the college. His grandfather, the first Jervis Langdon, had been a trustee and one of the founders of the college. And his aunt, Olivia Langdon Clemens, had gone to the day school at the college before she married Samuel Clemens in 1870. It seemed like the right place for the study.

When the Henry Ford Museum learned that the study was going to be moved, curators there believed it would be better suited for their collection. More people could see Clemens's study at the Henry Ford Museum, and they could place it alongside Thomas Edison's studio and Menlo Park laboratory. It could be included among their exhibits on American genius. But Langdon refused their generous offer. He wanted to keep the study close to the place where Clemens had done so much of his famous writing. If it could not be kept at Quarry farm, the Langdon family believed it should be kept in Elmira.[4]

The study is the only Clemens historic site in Elmira open to tourists today. I tried to imagine what crowds of summer tourists visiting the site fifty years ago would think and feel as they peeked inside. Even though I did not take a photograph of the structure, I came home with many images of it, including post cards, printed drawings, and digital images of the building from Elmira College's archives. Like the boyhood home in Hannibal, the study has a pictorial life of its own. Bryan Reddick, the college's retiring vice president and dean of faculty, told me that the study was not only popular with tourists interested in Mark Twain, but also popular with newlyweds who posed in front of the study for a picture after taking their vows. The study has become one of the college's most important symbols. It lives right next to Cowles Hall and a small pond, affectionately referred to as "the puddle," that is a popular student hang-out in good weather.[5]

Tourists flock to the study throughout the summer months and listen to student ambassadors tell the story of its removal from Quarry Farm and explain Sam Clemens's relationship with Elmira. The study still bears

Quarry Farm, January 2008

The Mark Twain study as it was transported away from Quarry Farm, 1952, courtesy Mark Twain Archive, Elmira College

the marks of its early visitors, but today, a tourist could not deface the structure without being tackled by campus police. But, despite its popularity, the study is only one of the sites that Twain scholars come to see. By the time I reached Elmira, I was so interested in seeing the other— Quarry Farm—that the study was merely an interesting stop on the way to the main show.

## Quarry Farm—Destination

At Quarry Farm, the history of the commemoration of Sam Clemens is quite different from the other sites in this study, or at least it seemed so at first. The house and the grounds have not been returned or preserved to the time when Clemens and his family summered there. Instead, they are frozen in 1983, when the college received the gift. The Langdon family kept most of the house intact and was conscious of its significance to literary scholars and Twain enthusiasts. Primarily a family home, it grew and changed with the Langdons as they adapted the house to meet their needs and aesthetics.[6] However, with a little imagination, visitors can see many elements of the house as they existed during Clemens's time there.

Today, the house and its furnishings are adapted to serve its current residents, Twain scholars. At Quarry Farm, scholars are truly guests. The Center for Mark Twain Studies at Elmira College invites scholars to stay at the house as research fellows.[7] In other Clemens houses, a literary pilgrim can only dream of spending time alone walking the halls, sitting on the furniture, and peaking into all the corners unobserved. At Quarry Farm, Twain scholars live, eat, sleep, and write where Mark Twain did. Limited access to the site means the house is preserved as a residential living archive and library rather than as a museum.[8]

I went to Quarry Farm as a Twain scholar on a research fellowship, though I was not there to study Sam Clemens. Because I was interested in how Quarry Farm had served as a site for scholarly tourists, and because the founding of the center was such a recent phenomenon, I may have made the staff there a little nervous. They were used to helping scholars answer research questions about Clemens and even the Langdons and Cranes, but they were less certain how to answer questions about their own roles in preserving Clemens's legacy. Barbara Snedecor introduced me to Irene Langdon, Gretchen Sharlow, Mark Woodhouse, and former caretakers and staff who had been essential in maintaining Quarry Farm for its visitors. My main research goal while there was not to discover a new understanding of Clemens's work, but to determine why it was that scholars have been so stimulated by this place. They seem to experience a deeper connection to Clemens at Quarry Farm than at the other sites that celebrate his life. More than fifty-two scholarly books have come from research and writing stints at the Center for Mark Twain Studies, including several books on Clemens and religion, women, volumes of Mark Twain's letters, Terrell Dempsey's *Searching for Jim* and Shelley Fisher Fishkins's *Lighting out for the Territory*, and other books that I have used in crafting this study all came out of time scholars spent at Quarry Farm.[9] As Barbara Snedecor put it succinctly in a recent newsletter from the center, the house has "served as a catalyst to promote and encourage scholarship in Mark Twain studies."[10]

Quarry Farm was not quite what I expected. I thought that I would want to see a house of such historic value and literary significance opened to the public. A historic site that was set aside for preservation, but only open to an elite population of scholars, rubbed me the wrong way. My attitude changed once I arrived. The house was not a museum. There were no tour guides, no carpet runners, and no velvet ropes. It was just a wonderful house and I felt lucky to be there. The setting, seclusion, and the list of scholars who had stayed in the house impressed me more than the fact that Clemens had summered here. It is such a lovely place, that I felt and feel that almost anyone could be a great writer given a few months residence at Quarry Farm. I was torn during my visit as to whether the house should ever open to the public. The stories that scholars have been able to tell through the site and its archive and library are important and largely reliant upon the house remaining closed to the public.

The Sam Clemens who was "resident" at Quarry Farm was a very different Clemens than the one interpreted in Hannibal and Hartford. He was neither the homespun storyteller nor the Gilded Age materialist that those places present. He was a man with time to think and space to reflect. Seeing the house, the site of the study, and the grounds might shed light on Clemens's writing process and the *genius loci* that inspired many of his works. The easement agreement for the gift of Quarry Farm to the college required that no commercial activity take place at the site, that it be "a center for the study of Mark Twain, his works, and influence upon his and later generations," and a "temporary home for such students of Mark Twain as may be designated from time to time by the President of Elmira College."[11] Jervis Langdon Jr. expressly did not want the house to be open to the public lest it become a popular tourist destination like Hannibal, Missouri.[12] Local people interested in Clemens and Quarry Farm visit events held by the center in the renovated barn, but they cannot ordinarily tour the house. The center organizes special lecture engagements to create opportunities for public access to the site, but the house itself is still largely off limits.

## Quarry Farm and the First Pilgrim

Unlike other literary sites devoted to Sam Clemens, Quarry Farm and its caretakers have not produced decades of travel guides, promotional materials, and interpretative plans. The house has remained below the radar of *most* tourists. The Clemens family spent more than twenty summers at Quarry Farm and, as a result, spent perhaps more time there than they did at any other single residence. During that time, the press occasionally followed Sam Clemens to his "summer home," and eventually even some of his devout fans made their way there as well.[13] Rudyard Kipling was one of the very earliest literary pilgrims to Quarry Farm. He enjoyed telling people that he had traveled all the way from India to visit Clemens. Kipling's account of his trip to Quarry Farm is notably modern, self-effacing, and is written with asides throughout that remind him, and his readers, that he really is there with his idol, Mark Twain.[14] In many ways, his account foreshadows how other literary pilgrims would encounter Quarry Farm.

When Kipling arrived in the summer of 1889, he had no idea if Clemens was in Elmira, and, if he was, where he would be. The morning after he arrived, someone pointed him toward Quarry Farm on East Hill. East Hill, as its name implies, lies due east of downtown Elmira and overlooks the small city that lies in the scenic valley of the Chemung River. Kipling hired a driver to take him up the "awful hill, where sunflowers blossomed by the roadside and crops waved." He pointed out that even the local livestock stood "knee deep in clover, all ready to be transferred to photogravure" for *Harper's Magazine.*[15] For Kipling, every detail of Quarry Farm was suitable for publication. He sensed that he was not the first to pursue Sam Clemens up East Hill and assumed that "the great man must have been persecuted by outsiders aforetime and fled up the hill for refuge."[16] There is no doubt that Clemens and his family did enjoy their time in Elmira, in part, because it was remote from their more public life in Hartford and elsewhere.[17]

Kipling's account, aside from being an entertaining piece about a young man's quest to find his literary hero, provides an early description of Quarry Farm:

> It was a very pretty house . . . clothed with ivy, standing in a very big compound and fronted by a veranda full of all sorts of chairs and hammocks for lying in all sorts of positions. The roof of the veranda was a trellis work of creepers and the sun peeped through and moved on the shining boards below. Decidedly this remote place was an ideal one for working in if a man could work among these soft airs and the murmur of the longeared crops just across the stone wall.[18]

Kipling portrayed Quarry Farm as though it would have looked at home on the pages of a design book by Andrew Jackson Downing. By most accounts the Quarry Farm house was an attractive "farm house," thanks to Susan Crane's landscape decisions. The architectural historian Lorraine Lanmon has pointed out that it was likely that Crane was aware of Downing's extraordinarily popular design books—her sister, Olivia Clemens, surely was—and Crane may have modeled Quarry Farm on the cottage styles found in his books. The proliferation of elaborate and romantic outbuildings at Quarry Farm is a sure sign of Downing's influence.[19] Despite not being able to see Sam Clemens's study, Kipling pronounced Quarry Farm a perfect workplace. By including the essential description of the porch, Kipling also showed the house as part of the ideal middle landscape. Quarry Farm was perfectly situated between the city and the wilder reaches of New York's wooded hills. The view from the house was set up so that all who lived there could enjoy the picturesque slice of the hillside, valley, and river below.

Despite the inviting scene, Kipling did not linger at Quarry Farm because Clemens was not at home. He eventually tracked Clemens to the Langdon mansion on Church Street in downtown Elmira and spent the afternoon with him in conversation. Though Kipling was overjoyed and felt "blessed" to be in conversation with Clemens, he could not keep himself from coveting some object of Clemens's as a memento. "I would have given much for nerve enough to demand the gift of that pipe, valued five cents when new," and "I understood why certain savage tribes ardently desire the liver of brave men slain in combat." Kipling half convinced himself that the "pipe would have given me, perhaps, a hint of his keen insight into the souls of men," but Twain "never laid it aside within stealing reach of my arms." Kipling restrained himself, but he seemed to want more than personal contact with the writer he adored. He wanted a memento, a talisman of the man. Like a true religious pilgrim, he imagined mystical powers in the "relic" that would be transferred to him upon his possession.[20]

*The Center for Mark Twain Studies and*
*Quarry Farm at Elmira College*

Since Kipling's visit in 1889, others have made their way to Elmira over the years to trace Clemens's time there, but few were granted access to Quarry Farm. Many years later, scholars occasionally discovered the location of Quarry Farm, made their way to the house, and either drove by or stopped and ventured tentatively onto the grounds. Some were even occasionally welcomed by the Langdons. Quarry Farm, like Clemens's study, now belongs to Elmira College and is part of its Center for Mark Twain Studies. Following his father's example, Jervis Langdon Jr. donated Quarry Farm to the college and the center itself was founded in response to the gift in 1982. The center does not and cannot provide public access to Quarry Farm, despite the fact that it has promoted the house and grounds as one of the most important historical landscapes in Sam Clemens's life.[21]

The original gift agreement for Quarry Farm included strict regulations about who can and cannot visit the house and under what circumstances. The house may be used *only* as a private residence for researchers interested in Mark Twain and his times. Over the years, directors have pushed the restrictions to include creative writers, but the Langdon family response was swift. Jervis Langdon Jr. lived until 2004, more than twenty years after the gift of the farm to the college, and he made sure that the college met the gift agreement's specific requirements. Since his death, his widow, Irene Langdon, has played a larger role at the center. The farmhouse, barn, outbuildings, and more than six acres have been preserved as a place where scholars can live while working on research projects related to the author and his times. A flip through the guestbook at the house reveals that almost every Mark Twain scholar of note has spent at least a night or two at Quarry Farm over the past twenty-five years. Scholars and researchers can walk the same floors that Sam Clemens and his family did and look out at the same view of the Chemung River valley from the house's wide porch.

Elmira College was the recipient of the property after protracted negotiations between Jervis Langdon Jr., the National Trust for Historic Preservation, and the Chemung County Historical Society. Langdon reportedly offered Quarry Farm to the Chemung County Historical Society and the National Trust for Historic Preservation and neither wanted to single-handedly manage the site, but both agreed to serve as watchdogs for the college. The relationship between the college and Quarry Farm has a long history, but the college's struggling financial status in the early 1980s may have made it Langdon's third choice.[22] The college relished its historic relationship with the study. As early as the 1910s and 1920s, women from Elmira College would hike up East Hill to the Mark Twain Study at Quarry Farm on "Mountain Day." Classes were canceled and the students would climb up the steep hill, picnic on the grounds, and spend time in the study.[23]

The founding director of the center, Herb Wisbey, was already a professor of American History at Elmira College in 1982 when the college created the center. He had been instrumental in encouraging local interest in the connections between Sam Clemens and Elmira. He and local resident Robert Jerome had started the Mark Twain Society in Elmira in 1975. Wisbey and Jerome collected accounts of Clemens's time in Elmira and documented Olivia Clemens's branch of the family. Jerome and Wisbey published *Mark Twain in Elmira* in 1977 and found that the little volume made available through the Chemung County Historical Society was devoured by Twain scholars and local residents interested in history. They reissued the volume and began the *Mark Twain Society Bulletin* to continue their research from the book.[24] Herb Wisbey stepped down from the directorship in 1986 to serve as an advisor and curator for the Mark Twain collection at the college library in his retirement.[25] The college appointed an unlikely new director, an individual with no background in the study of Mark Twain, but with unbridled enthusiasm for the topic and the organizational expertise to propel the center to national status. Director Darryl Baskin was a professor of political science at the college with an interest in American culture and religion. The college's president, Thomas Meier, an English professor, saw Baskin as someone who could expand both the center's standing in the community of Twain scholars and saw the gift of the house as a way to bring Elmira College back from the brink of financial collapse.[26] While the college struggled, the city faced the financial downturn that plagued a number of rust-belt industrial cities throughout the 1980s. Both the college and the city saw Mark Twain as a way to bring in dollars and interest.[27]

Darryl Baskin assembled an advisory board of local residents, Jervis Langdon Jr., and a select group of interested Mark Twain scholars. The group he organized helped determine the path of the center. Among them, Twain scholar Alan Gribben served as an influential advisor to Baskin in his quest to establish the center as the leading institution in support of Mark Twain scholars. Gribben's dissertation research, which reconstructed Sam Clemens's library, led him to Quarry Farm and the volumes that Clemens had encountered while visiting Susan and Theodore Crane.[28] He guided Baskin in creating a community through which Twain scholars might share their work. At the University of California, Berkeley's Bancroft Library scholars were able to access the largest trove of Clemens's letters, diaries, and other writings. But the editors of the Twain Papers at Berkeley were not in a position to serve as hosts for scholars beyond regular archival requests and research. Gribben and Baskin understood that scholars desired a place to learn about one another's research, a place where they might meet, study, and write, and a place where they might be at home with the subject of their scholarship.[29] Darryl Baskin promoted the Quarry Farm Fellowships and began the popular visiting lecturer series called "The Trouble Begins at Eight," named from a line on fliers advertising Clemens's own first major lecture tour (1866–1867). He began a highly successful series of National Endowment for the Humanities funded workshops for teachers interested in reading Twain in the classroom and began an international conference on "The State of Mark Twain Studies."[30] The Center for Mark Twain Studies was designed to be the preeminent place for scholars to think about Clemens, his times, and his work.

## The Real Literary Pilgrims and Hauntings

The center's programming was a draw for scholars and locals interested in Sam Clemens, but the real draw to events was Quarry Farm itself. Why, one hundred and twenty years after Rudyard Kipling's visit to Quarry Farm, does the desire to get close to the *things* of Mark Twain still obsess readers, fans, and scholars? Over the last two decades, it seems that scholars have gained a great deal from Quarry Farm, and like Hartford, the collective understanding of Clemens has changed as a result. Investigations into Clemens's relationships in Elmira have led scholars to believe that Elmira, and his circle of companions and in-laws there, changed the way Clemens understood the legacy of slavery in the United States. It was at Quarry Farm that Mark Twain both heard and wrote "A True Story" that documented Mary Ann Cord's life as a slave and the devastation she experienced as her children and husband were sold away from her. It was also here that Clemens took up the tale of Huck Finn again and finished it.

The Center for Mark Twain Studies celebrated its twenty-fifth anniversary in 2008, the same year that I visited. Barbara Snedecor asked individuals who had spent time at Quarry Farm to reflect on their experiences for an anniversary edition of the center's newsletter, *Dear Friends*. One described Quarry Farm as a "Mecca," another said it was a "living memorial," and yet another repeated the popular sentiment that the residence provided a way to "meet" Sam Clemens through a "trip into the past."[31] The centerpiece of many scholars' commentaries was how their individual experiences at Quarry Farm changed how they felt and thought about Clemens and his work. Not all of the scholars had stayed overnight in the house—some had just visited for conferences on "The State of Mark Twain Studies." The ones who had stayed overnight gushed that the experience of living in the space occupied by Clemens and his family made them feel as "at home at Quarry Farm—as Mark Twain did."[32] These scholars were "able to *meet* Sam Clemens on this very real common ground" and more than a few referred to the house as a "shrine."[33]

Quarry Farm accommodates the kind of literary tourists that Nicola Watson has seen as seeking out literary sites "to savour text, place and their interrelations."[34] The Quarry Farm fellows are exactly the kind of literary pilgrims that David Herbert saw as a subset of tourists to sites like Chawton, those "well educated tourists, versed in the classics and with the cultural capital to appreciate and understand this form of heritage."[35] These scholars who visit Quarry Farm have made their work the business of Sam Clemens, his writing, and the historical context of his times, and they are able through fellowships at the center to spend time in a domestic archive unlike any other in the world.

One such literary pilgrim, American studies and literary scholar Shelley Fisher Fishkin, wrote about her experiences at Mark Twain sites across the country in her 1996 book, *Lighting out for the Territory: Reflections on Mark Twain and American Culture*. In a very personal account, she traced developments in Clemens's thinking about slavery, racism, and race through the geographic trajectory of his life and works. While she found the motivation for *Tom Sawyer* and *Huckleberry Finn* in Hannibal, Missouri, she found the roots of Clemens's antiracism and anti-imperialism in Elmira, New York. Olivia Clemens's parents, Jervis and Olivia Langdon, were abolitionists, and Fishkin believed that Clemens's time in Elmira led him to reevaluate his ideas about race.[36] Much of Fishkin's book is a form of critical literary pilgrimage and speaks to what it is that literary scholars do when they visit these sites. They look for traces of the literary figures that they "know" through their work. Scholars find evidence of an author's work, whether it is in primary source materials or in the atmosphere of the place itself. Fishkin visited Elmira to "savour" Clemens's texts, but also to supplement them with the connection she personally forged with Clemens through time at Quarry Farm.[37]

In this way, Fishkin, and many other scholars who visit Quarry Farm to find evidence of Sam Clemens, fits perfectly with Aaron Santesso's discussion of ideal literary tourism. His best model of literary tourists are scholars educated enough to understand an author's texts, times, politics, and the particulars of a literary place. Santesso cites Henry James's reflections upon "meeting" Hawthorne in Salem as the best form of communication between reader and writer as mediated through a historic place.[38] These interactions can only happen when a literary site is relatively undeveloped. Each literary pilgrim has to experience the author's place in relative seclusion. Places like Stratford and Hannibal do not allow interested visitors to experience the site with the feeling that they are encountering a place unmediated by the tourism industry's interpretation, while places like Quarry Farm allow visitors to feel a connection to a seemingly undeveloped place that evokes their literary and scholarly imagination.

## Meeting Clemens's Ghost on Common Ground

Many Quarry Farm fellows have felt that they "met" Clemens at Quarry Farm. Some have even gone so far as to say the place is "haunted" by the "spirit of Twain." While these literary scholars hardly ever mean that Quarry Farm is actually haunted, they suggest the trope often enough that it deserves noting. The guest books over the years provide a window into their responses to the house and their sense of connection to it. Some visitors, like Jules Merron and Lousia Seraydarian, mentioned that Quarry Farm allowed the "turning back [of] the hands of time." However, other scholars have found less distinct and more ghostly influences. As David Smith found after his time at the house, a number of visitors believe the "humane spirit of a great writer seems to inhabit this house." As research on Quarry Farm has been widely published, and scholars have uncovered just how meaningful Elmira was for Clemens, the cast of ghosts at the house has expanded. Visitors like Mary Boewe have seen the house as haunted by a whole cast of historical characters. She wrote in the *Quarry Farm Guestbook* that there was "a mingling of presences, past *and* present: Auntie Cord is here in the kitchen, bending over an iron cookstove." Elsewhere she heard "Sue and Theodore [Olivia Clemens's sister and brother-in-law] speak low in their spacious bedroom lest others waken," and offered that there are "so *many* voices here!—And over all, the presence of Livy and her 'Mr. Clemens,' our Mark Twain . . . They are in the front parlor, where he reads the day's creative output."[39] While most visitors did not elaborate on these ghosts' activities as much as Boewe did in her reflections in the Quarry Farm guest book, many acknowledge that the elite group of tourists at Quarry Farm are "apostles of St. Mark." These disciples sense "the shadows of the muses—when walking with the ghosts of Quarry Farm [and]—when in the presence of greatness."[40] Many visitors, at least according to their accounts in the guestbook, are both scholars and devoted disciples in search of near religious inspiration from the landscape at Quarry Farm.

## House as Literary Evidence

Ghosts are not all that scholars have found at Quarry Farm. Over the years, they have uncovered letters and marginalia, and a long-lost traveling trunk that belonged to Clemens was found in the attic of the house. Every inch of the house and barn at Quarry Farm has been scoured for its Mark Twain treasures and for evidence of Clemens's life and work. Visitor Scott McLean found "there is no amount of reading about Clemens that can quite equal a few nights spent in the guest room and sitting on the porch."[41] For McLean the place itself replaces scholarly interpretations and research—supplanting the critical approaches to Clemens's work. Quarry Farm is its own interpretation. Over the years, the works that have come out of research stints at the Center for Mark Twain Studies seem to indicate that Quarry Farm itself has been an evidentiary influence on Twain scholars. The resulting scholarship is distinctly connected to the place. Scholars who visit other archives, like the Mark Twain Papers in the Bancroft Library at Berkeley, may declare their gratitude to the archivists and archive in their acknowledgments, but they almost never mention that the archive itself and its atmosphere contributed to their work. Here Quarry Farm seems to have evidentiary resonance.

Twain scholar Susan K. Harris and others came to see the Chemung River as the inspiration for the Mississippi River that Huck and Jim travel on in *The Adventures of Huckleberry Finn*.[42] Joe Fulton found the subject of an entire book on the shelves of the Langdon family library at Quarry Farm. Though visiting the center for another research project, Fulton stumbled upon Clemens's notes in the margins of W. E. H. Lecky's *History of the Rise of the Spirit of Rationalism in Europe* and *A History of England in the Eighteenth Century*. These marginal notes, along with others in books that had belonged to Susan and Theodore Crane, led to Fulton's book, *Mark Twain in the Margins: The Quarry Farm Marginalia and A Connecticut Yankee in King Arthur's Court*. Such studies have promoted Clemens as a deliberate and careful writer, countering the long popular conception he was an author who largely drew upon wit-infused autobiography alone to craft his writing.

Beyond the scholarly evidence that Quarry Farm provides, the place itself has come to signify a meaningful step in a scholar's academic trajectory as a "Twain Scholar." As Jan McIntire-Strasburg put it, "his presence is everywhere here, and I've never felt more like a Twain scholar (or more grateful to have chosen my course of study wisely)."[43] Quarry Farm has become essential not just as a gathering place and refuge for scholars but also as an essential piece of their identities as Twain scholars. As the late, preeminent Twain scholar Louis Budd put it succinctly, "those of us even dimly in the know sign off with 'See you in Elmira.'"[44]

*The Work of Scholar as Literary Pilgrim*

The literary scholar Diana Fuss, in her 2006 book, *The Sense of an Interior: Four Writers and the Rooms That Shaped Them*, gets close to describing the scholarly impulse to be a literary pilgrim. She describes her scholarship that drew upon authors' homes as her "attempt to encounter these writers where they live, *to meet them*, to what extent possible, on their own ground and on their own terms."[45] Fuss, like the scholars who visit Quarry Farm, was interested in places where she perceived that she could "meet" the writers she admired, but she overlooked the difficulty of "meeting" an author at a historic site that is mediated by curators and site staff. She reflected:

> It is not every day that one gets to sit in Emily Dickinson's cupola or to lie on Sigmund Freud's couch. Some research projects are pure wish fulfillment, intellectual enterprises that gratify both mind and fancy. This book was such a guilty pleasure, the culmination of a persistent desire to occupy, if only for a moment, the private lives of celebrated authors.[46]

Fuss's persistent desire to occupy the private lives of the authors she studies speaks to the idea that a house, a living space, an office, or a desk can somehow provide the actual "life" of an author. Occupying the spaces of literary figures gives some scholars a kind of access to the origin of the literary mind, real or imagined. Fuss, while in Emily Dickinson's cupola and bedroom, rejoices in the material detail of her life, door jams, and bed stand. She uses Dickinson's material traces to make nuanced architectural readings of her poetry. She is never critical about the objects themselves or their curatorial arrangement in the house. When she visits Emily Dickinson's house, The Homestead, she sees only Dickinson's poetry and the long history of feminist and psychoanalytic interpretations of her poetry. Her account of being at the house takes for granted that Dickinson left her desk just as it is today next to her window, and somehow Fuss is able to ignore the display of Dickinson's white dress within a glass cabinet. Fuss overlooks a long history of museum intervention at the site.[47] Perhaps scholars have to purposely ignore the curatorial elements of literary houses in order to achieve the effect of understanding a literary figure through his or her house. While at Elmira, Shelley Fisher Fishkin did something similar as she wandered around the Quarry Farm family home interested in every chair, every book, and every nook that might hold clues about Clemens. However, she, like Fuss, was never terribly self-reflexive about why she was made happy by being near the Langdon and Crane family belongings.[48]

This kind of origin seeking is part of the work that goes on at literary sites, and it sometimes provides links to the evidence that scholars need to do their work. The evidence that scholars find in the setting is part of their desire to be close to the things and landscapes associated with the writer, to be able to see as the writer saw, and perhaps to be able to *remake* the same connections that a writer makes with his or her surroundings. In these places, scholars overlay the fine details from the writer's life and work, and through this comparison find some essential elements of place and text that exist in both. The author's house (and even his or her summerhouse) and its surrounding environment are a type of primary evidence to be considered and weighed in understanding a literary work and life, but they are a special kind of evidence. Because Americans are obsessed with houses and how they assert, display, and allow for the performance of the personalities of their inhabitants, they provide a wealth of information—about both the daily lives of writers and how authors portray themselves through their domestic spaces. While Harald Hendrix has argued that houses can be the "architectural fantasies and fictions" of writers, this house is not that.[49]

It could be argued that Clemens's Hartford house might be that rare chance to see a writer "experiment with a mode of expression fundamentally different from his own" that Hendrix and other literary critics desire to analyze as a literary text.[50] However, Quarry Farm does not quite fit this mold, because the house never belonged to the Clemenses. Because it belonged to Susan and Theodore Crane, it was not likely they were concerned with the construction of an ideal author's home. As a result, the house provides rare evidence of a landscape and environment that was inspiring to a writer without being an architectural fantasy devised by him. It provides evidence of Susan and Theodore Crane's life there, provides evidence of the Langdon family's time there after Susan Crane's death, and most importantly for this study, it provides evidence of how the Center for Mark Twain Studies and its directors and staff have anticipated their scholar-visitors' needs and expectations.

Today, the house, like the other house museums in this study, provides evidence of site managers' intent to make the house what its visitors desire most. The house, whether it seems so or not, is designed to interest Mark Twain scholars, to be evocative, and to provide an excellent writing experience for visitors, which creates a concrete way for visitors to connect with Clemens *as a writer* at Quarry Farm. Some scholars come alone to work, and others bring their families. If they bring their families, they create a situation that replicates Clemens's where they are surrounded by the people they care about *and* have support for scholarship, research, reading, and writing. The house itself, with its workspace and library, its stocked kitchen, its comfortable reading chairs, computer, printer, and view, provides enough solitude and stimulus to make the act of writing in the space itself a form of literary touristic ritual. Like the literary tourists that stack stones at the site of Thoreau's cabin and create a ritual of repeating Thoreau's retreat into the wilderness, literary scholars at Quarry Farm partake in a ritual of writing in the place where Clemens wrote.

This ritual is made more perfect by the careful maintenance of the house at Quarry Farm. Though it appears as if the site is merely a family home thrown open for scholarly guests, all houses—in their decoration and design—present information about the people who live or lived there. The house at Quarry Farm is such a marker of the Cranes, Langdons, and now the center's and the scholars' time there. This house, like Clemens's other house museums, can reveal something of the intentions of its designers. The center's directors have decorated the interior of the house over the years to maintain the Victorian divide been public and private spaces in the house. Downstairs, three rooms are maintained in near-museum quality.

Upstairs, private spaces are arranged for scholars. The parlor, dining room, and downstairs library are outfitted with historic furnishings. Some date to the Clemens and Crane period, and some pieces have been acquired by the center to flesh out the house with period essentials. The sofa where scholars sometimes pose for photos was donated by a local family and has no connection to the Cranes or Langdons, but it fits the interior design. Staff has placed original chairs throughout the main floor, which are carefully marked with paper signs requesting that visitors refrain from sitting on them—further signifying their relationship with the Clemens period.

In the downstairs parlor, in front of the secretary, is a chair in which Clemens sometimes sat; next to it resides a framed photograph of the parlor, with the chair, as it was when the Cranes lived there. Scholars can compare the photograph to the room that they experience in the present day. Around the residence are other photographs of the house as it was during the Cranes' residence and pictures of Sam Clemens in various locales on the grounds. Though the house is not a museum that attempts to recreate the exact environment that Clemens would have encountered while summering there, the period furnishings and arrangements evoke that period. The photographs provide reinforcing evidence that scholars are in the "real" place and that authentic objects surround them, even though the photographs of Sam Clemens in various Quarry Farm locales likely would not have been situated around the house.

Upstairs in the house the arrangement is less precisely historical. The bedrooms are simple and openly arranged for the comfort of scholars and their guests. The upstairs resembles a pared-down bed and breakfast more than a historic house museum. The furnishings are simple, the wallpapers and paint light and airy. The scholar's study, arranged to maximize space for the library of books about Clemens and workspace, provides a computer, printer, wireless Internet access, and a television with cable. However, even upstairs there are carefully placed objects that are meant to evoke the house's status as a site of pilgrimage. In the scholars' study, for instance, there are several photographs of Clemens in his study and an illustration of the study's interior. Writing is the way that visitors can connect with their subject while visiting Quarry Farm. Although they cannot spend time writing in Clemens's study because it has been removed to Elmira College, they are surrounded by images of it and the works that he created there.

Other ambiguously old objects are artfully arranged throughout the house. There is an early typewriter in one of the bedrooms, an old treadle Singer sewing machine, a dresser that is decorated with silk flowers in a vase and an old iron key, and rotary phones. Most of these items might not relate to the "Clemens era" but they are arranged carefully to evoke a sense of the past. Even the rotary phones, which clearly do not date to Clemens or Susan Crane's time at the house, serve to remind the scholars that they have stepped out of the present day and are occupying a place between Clemens's time and their own.

This careful staging of Quarry Farm as a historic house, as a scholarly refuge, and as a place that is in-between times is effectively an interpretive schema as much as any at the other historic house museums in this study. Although no curator has designed a formal interpretive plan, the staff at the Center for Mark Twain Studies has carefully assessed the needs and desires of their particular visitors and sought to meet them. Early in the center's history, like the Hartford house, the staff at the center put out calls among its friends for items that would set the right tone at the house as well as provide needed equipment like computers and printers that today's writers need to be productive. They acquired rugs and small appliances, and they tastefully reupholstered the furniture that they collected.[51]

In the kitchen at Quarry Farm you can begin to tease out the center's and the house's long relationship with Clemens. An enormous wood-burning and coal-burning stove is set into the west wall and dates to the Clemens period. It is an impressive appliance, a Richardson-Boynton & Co. iron stove that is marked "Our Favorite" across the top ovens and woodbox. It is reported to be the stove over which Mary Ann Cord, the inspiration for Clemens's "A True Story," once cooked and warmed the bath water for the Clemens daughters. It stands next to a more recent model that dates to Jervis Langdon Jr.'s last residency at the house and this is where scholars warm the water for their tea and cook while they are visiting. In the cupboard, someone left a set of Mark Twain-inspired 1980s collector's glasses that feature scenes from Tom Sawyer. There was one drying in the dish rack when I arrived for my visit, and the oddness of the mass-made Twain-keepsake-glassware was striking at first. Katty-corner from the cupboard is a little nook with a tiny photograph of Clemens and his family on the long eastern porch at their house in Hart-ford. The kitchen is the one room in the house, and perhaps of all the sites where Twain is celebrated, where the broadest continuum of Twain commemoration was displayed. The house is no longer a private home and it is not quite a museum. It is an evocative gallery, sprinkled with memorabilia and authentic objects that are meant to inspire visitors to think about Clemens in all his forms. But because the visitor can interact with these objects—from the fast-food retail collectable glasses to the decorative vases that were present at Sam and Olivia Clemens's wedding, the house also provides scholars with that elusive existential authenticity that is hard to find in literary tourism and in literary research.

The house and grounds at Quarry Farm provide the full package of literary tourist experience. It feels like an undeveloped site, despite the photographs and clues otherwise, because the deliberate markers of inter-pretation—signage and informative text—are missing. Each tourist to the site is prescreened through the fellowship application and nomination process and known by site managers to be in possession of the back-ground information necessary to make this site meaningful. The site itself is set up to replicate for the tourist-scholars the rituals of writing that they most associate with Clemens. Though the site feels unmediated by curatorial forces, the house itself is a text articulating an interpretation of Clemens that fits right alongside the rituals that scholars perform. Schol-ars come to see connections between themselves and Clemens because these connections are carefully constructed through the house and center. Some of these rituals are played out at the quadrennial conference as well. There is often a "coming-together . . . on the site of Mark Twain's fabled octagonal study."[52] Here scholars share a drink, and some smoke cigars. At a conference in August 2009, the pilgrims on the hill all sang a rousing rendition of "Will the Circle Be Unbroken" with Hal Holbrook.[53] The rituals at Quarry Farm speak to the ways that scholars imagine them-selves reenacting events in Clemens's spaces.

### House within House

What struck me most about the house in considering it for this study is how well the staff has placed photographs of Clemens around the house. These are "snapshots" of one of the most famously photographed men in American letters. Many Americans might not have read Sam Clemens's novels, short stories, or autobiographical pieces, but most will certainly

Image from before the 1924 edition, similar to how the house would have looked during Clemens time these, courtesy the Mark Twain Archive, Elmira College

recognize a photograph of him. Moreover, Twain scholars are not likely to forget what he looked like either. The house sets up a careful display of images that argue Sam Clemens lived among the people he loved, and he loved Quarry Farm. Images of him in his Quarry Farm study and paused on the stone steps up to his study show him as a man relaxed among peers, not posing for a profile portrait of an author. Though some of the photographs in the house were taken elsewhere, they fill the house with Clemens and allude to not just his writing or fame, but also to the way he lived with his family.

It is odd, then, that the second most pervasive photographic subject in house, the study, is missing from Quarry Farm. The fact that the study was moved to Elmira College in 1952 has left a hole at the site. Alan Gribben, as early as 1987, recommended that the study be moved back to Quarry Farm as part of the development of the new Center for Mark Twain Studies. He specifically recommended, in a letter to then director Darryl Baskin, a "reunion of the study with its environment."[54] All of the pictures of the study throughout the house may be an attempt to fill its absence as much as they are to inspire scholars to write as Clemens did at Quarry Farm. After all, might the center be able to more perfectly recre-

Early postcard of Quarry Farm, from the author's collection

ate the ritual of writing at the site if it was able to provide the exact space where Clemens sought refuge to write? If scholars had his study, the little table that he wrote on, and the view outside his windows, might they not come to understand even more about his writing process?

Gribben had imagined a grand event when the study went "home" with a helicopter ride for the little building as it was placed back on East Hill. He even imagined that the center would be able to provide public access to the site in its "new" old location. A small parking lot could be built, a little bookstore that sold the best of Twain scholarship could be added in the barn, and a tour guide that made his or her hourly wage from ticket sales to the interested public. Gribben wanted public access and the ability for scholars to visit the study at its original site at Quarry Farm.[55] Darryl Baskin kept Gribben's recommendations from his advisory board because he knew that such a plan, a plan that charged a fee to see Clemens's study and that built a parking lot at Quarry Farm, would upset the delicate balance on the center's advisory board. Any action on such a plan would explicitly break the gift agreement. Baskin did pass a copy of the letter along to Elmira College president Thomas Meier and to others who might see a nonprofit but for-fee future for Quarry Farm.

Quarters at Quarry Farm decorated with images of the study, 2008

Part of the reason I neglected to document my own tour of Mark Twain's study was because its environment was so extreme. It was not just the cold and ice, but rather the removal of the extremely private space to an entirely public space along Elmira College's main thoroughfare. It was a bit like seeing a rare bird at the zoo. It was lovely and fascinating, but stilted and flightless in its new environment. It seems impossible to imagine Clemens writing in the building in its current location. No wonder Gribben thought it was destined to come back to Quarry Farm.

### The Future of Quarry Farm

At Quarry Farm, scholars may notice the subtle arrangement of the house that influences their time there. When they remark that they "meet"

Quarters at Quarry Farm decorated with images of the study, 2008

Mark Twain at the site, they do not necessarily mean that they *literally* encounter the ghost of Clemens. But many do feel that Quarry Farm, through the literary pilgrimage it can provide, brings them closer to understanding the man and his writing. In turn, Quarry Farm is affected by the research that these scholars produce. In a sense, scholars meet Twain at Quarry Farm because the center staff understands and incorporates their work into the site. The center can then provide the best possible conditions for conjuring him to meet their particular audience's desires. In turn, scholars provide input into changes at Quarry Farm. Because the center strives to meet their needs, the house changes to suit them. These changes are as small as adding wireless Internet service or putting a new photo on display, but they effect the way scholars understand Clemens at the site.

For instance, the one photograph that may have shaped my experience at Quarry Farm was not one that establishes the house as primary

Relic from the Mark Twain Boyhood Home and Museum's Mark Twain Centennial Celebration, displayed at Quarry Farm, 2008

evidence of where Clemens lived and wrote, but one that provides evidence of how Clemens and his houses have been made into sacred sites and shrines. The small framed photograph that surprised me hangs in the butler's pantry off the kitchen. It is the same 1902 image of Clemens as an old man, standing in front of the house on his last trip to Hannibal that the Boyhood Home and Museum has recently used as its central narrative device.

However, this photo print dates to 1935. On the faded gray mat surrounding it there is a handwritten inscription that explains that the City of Hannibal presented the photograph and frame as a gift to Jervis Langdon Sr. on the occasion of the centennial celebration of Sam Clemens's birth in 1935.[56] Perhaps George Mahan, the museum's founder, sent it along himself. Most important, the frame surrounding the photograph was constructed from the original floorboards from the boyhood home. In a house full of authentic relics of Clemens's adult and family life there is plenty of evidence of his commemoration, but this relic provides the keenest evidence that this house is like the others—sacred because of its association. A visit to Quarry Farm allows access to a treasure trove of relics that scholars learn from and incorporate into their work. The frame made from flooring at the boyhood home indicates just how connected these places have been in maintaining Sam Clemens's reputation over time. The Langdon family contributed objects to the collections at Hannibal and Hartford, and now the best object in their collection—Quarry Farm—is part of an effort to expand Clemens's reputation among literary scholars.

This place, like any other site that celebrates Mark Twain, is the result of decisions made over time and presents a narrative about the origin of Clemens's writing that has resonance with literary scholars. The Langdon family's express desire in opening the site to scholars was that the house be used to "promote and encourage scholarship." The house and the center have done precisely that.

We cannot know what the future holds for Quarry Farm. Perhaps Alan Gribben's dream from twenty years ago, to see the study returned to the farm, will happen, accompanied by a parking lot and gift shop to accommodate tourists. Overt commemoration at Quarry Farm is still quite young. Quarry Farm has not had the crises of representation that the other house museums struggled through over the years, but likely, it someday will. This site's history is just getting started. If we know anything from the histories of Florida, Hannibal, and Hartford, we know that interpretive regimes at historic houses that celebrate American authors are hard to change, but that they do. Careful study of how Quarry Farm adapts over the next decades will reveal what Twain scholars as literary tourists want. The center will have to continue to strike an interpretive balance between meeting the needs of its scholarly literary pilgrims, making local stakeholders happy, and staying within the bounds of the gift agreement. However, as Lawrence Vail Coleman asserted intuitively in 1933, "owners of historic houses that are not even open to the public find no way of keeping their doors closed to interested strangers." Quarry Farm may someday find itself in the same position and may have to agree that these literary pilgrims "deserve to be admitted."[57]

S

# Epilogue

## *Marking the Spot*

Americans are obsessed with houses—their
own and everyone else's.

—Dell Upton (*Architecture in the
United States*, 1998)

A century after Sam Clemens's death, Mark Twain is going strong.
Weeks before the 2010 release of his "new" autobiography Sam
Clemens topped the *New York Times* and American Booksellers
Association's nonfiction bestseller lists. Fans still celebrate the author and
his work in exhibits, library programs, and by visiting any number of
Mark Twain destinations worldwide. In the United States, Mark Twain
literary tourism is especially big business. Tourists believe that they can
learn something about the author or his work by visiting the places where
he lived. At his houses, now museums, Clemens remains as popular as he
ever was during his lifetime.

The appeal of Clemens's house museums should not surprise us. Literary historic sites pin their claims to authority, after all, on the promise
of unique insight into authors and texts through firsthand experience.
In 2010 Edward Rothstein, the *New York Times* cultural-critic-at-large,
suggested that those interested in Clemens should "go first to the Twain
House" in Hartford, Connecticut.[1] According to Rothstein, the house
unravels many of the mysteries surrounding the author and even reveals
the secret to the complexity of *Huckleberry Finn*'s ending. While he
does not advocate that visitors eschew literary biography and history,
he believes that if you visit Clemens's house, you will find the evidence necessary to understand Clemens critically. He is not alone in
this belief.

Since shortly after Clemens's death, local boosters, Twain fanatics, scholars, and others, like Rothstein, have put a great deal of faith in the author's house as critical text, as a place where they could access an almost archival glimpse of the "real" writer and his or her work. It is natural that they should assume so, because we believe that where and how we live reveals something about who we are. Clemens's houses seem to reveal the life of the author at different stages in his life. Some even work to illuminate the lives of his characters as much as his own.

As tempting as it is to accept Rothstein's argument or to accept the authenticity of Clemens's homes, however, we must understand that house museums are not reliable critical texts. All historic sites, literary or otherwise, are fiercely mediated places. This is to say that Clemens's homes, by merit of being house museums, cannot really provide archival insight into the author and his works. Rather, as I have shown throughout the previous chapters, his homes, like all literary house museums, are carefully constructed spaces designed to satisfy visitors. Their portrayal of Clemens changes frequently to accommodate our own expectations of the author and his work.

I am a literary tourist, just like the people who visit Sam Clemens's houses. Sometimes I visit sites where I know a great deal about the authors and want extratextual context for their literary work. But I also go to house museums because I'm nosey and obsessed with houses— just like all Americans, as Dell Upton asserts.[2] I like to see how people live and have lived, or at least as much as I can tell about how they have lived from their houses. And I believe that where and how people have lived matters. I think that house museums matter a great deal, too. Museums such as the Lower Eastside Tenement Museum, the House of the Seven Gables, and even Clemens's birthplace, historical claims notwithstanding, tell us a great deal about what has mattered to the people who preserve them. This alone means we should note them, and it means that they deserve our scrutiny. Museum making is serious business, and the narratives that are enshrined in our federal, state, and local museums are hard to change because they have a physical place that asserts itself in communities.

I am also fascinated with why Clemens's houses persist while other literary houses have not. Why do we have so many house museums devoted to Mark Twain and not a single museum of any kind devoted to Langston Hughes or Ralph Ellison? If it is acceptable to build replica houses, why hasn't someone "reconstructed" a Langston Hughes childhood home in Lawrence, Kansas; a Ralph Ellison house in Oklahoma City, Oklahoma; or a T. S. Eliot childhood home in St. Louis, Missouri? And why are there so few literary house museums devoted to women? These questions cannot be answered by only looking at how the American literary canon is formed and maintained through scholarly production. Nor does my investigation of only four literary destinations answer these questions, but it does suggest that their answers may be discovered in institutional histories. As we've seen, many times, house museums come about because of state and local promotion, community and economic development, nationalism, personal and familial interests, and, occasionally, happenstance.

Literary houses are especially interesting to me because I am fascinated by both houses and literature. Historic house museums tell the stories of the people who have designed, built, and inhabited them. Literary house museums can tell us even more. Because these houses engage the imaginative world beyond a writer's biography, they are fascinating places to study the origins of national and regional identity. Like their historical counterparts, literary house museums also tell the stories of the people devoted to their preservation. Clemens's houses tell us a great deal about Dad Violette, the Mahan family, Katharine Seymour Day, the Langdons, and all the individuals who have restored these houses or influenced interpretation at these sites.

Historic house museums, and history museums in general, have received considerable scrutiny in the last fifteen years. Especially since Roy Rosenzweig and David Thelen's *The Presence of the Past: Popular Uses of History in American Life* (1998) found that Americans trust historic sites more than any other single source of historical information, historians have cared a great deal about the work that museums do. But literary historic sites have not seen the same attention from literary scholars. I do not advocate that we police literary sites for accuracy. I do think, however, that if Americans trust these sites as much as historic sites, then the stories they tell must concern us a great deal. Most Americans are probably much more likely to visit a literary site than to read literary criticism or even the biography of a literary figure. These sites can serve as extra-literary texts that supplement popular and scholarly understandings of literary figures like Clemens. They allow tourists and scholars alike to visit the American literary canon. Discovering the cultural work that they accomplish means keeping in mind how these places mediate the relationship between author, literary text, and literary tourist through museum interpretation.

It is not reasonable, however, to hold public literary historic sites up to the same scrutiny as academic studies of literature and literary history. When Shelley Fisher Fishkin went to Hannibal in 1995, she pointed out that Hannibal got the facts wrong. At times, she even poked fun at the local population for not taking Clemens's important antiracist critique seriously. Other scholars have similarly faulted literary sites for falling

down on the job. Historian James Loewen faults tour guides and historical markers for not incorporating up-to-date scholarship about historical
events and figures. Similar critiques may certainly have helped historic
sites make important interpretive shifts, but most critics and literary historians seem unaware that these sites and markers often have long complicated interpretive histories of their own.[3] Ultimately, it is not fair or
productive to assess these places solely on the accuracy of their historical
analysis, or even on their ability to bring a literary text to life. A large part
of any museum's mission is to provide resources for its community, and
these places often do much more as institutions than just interpret literary
figures to critical readers.

At Hannibal, for instance, the Mark Twain Boyhood Home and
Museum has been the city's central tourist attraction since 1912. Heritage
tourism is a risky business, but it ensures that tourist dollars come into
the town. While other postindustrial factory towns along the Mississippi
River suffer, Hannibal offers the Mark Twain Dinette, the Becky Thatcher
Restaurant, the Holiday Inn, and every other business in town that benefits from Hannibal's tourism industry. Although visitation to the museum
peaked in 1978, through community events like Music Under the Stars,
its first Fridays film festival, and traveling exhibits from the Smithsonian,
Hannibal's Mark Twain museum provides meaningful cultural activities
for much of its community. Although many scoff at Mark Twain's visage
reproduced on everything from vending machines to cement trucks, they
are expressions of a community that is truly proud of its native son.

If judged in terms of civic engagement, Hannibal has begun to succeed,
whereas the Mark Twain House and Museum in Hartford, Connecticut,
is just beginning to reconnect with its community. Because the scholarly
rigor of its restoration excluded the involvement of the Mark Twain Public Library early on, the museum has struggled to find a role for itself in
greater Hartford. The irony, of course, is that the house museum began
as a library intended to serve its immediate neighborhood. In 2009, the
nearby Mark Twain branch of the Hartford Public Library closed due
to citywide budget cuts. It reopened in 2011 in the high school directly
next door to the museum. In the interim, while the museum encouraged
children who visit to read Twain, neighborhood children had no access to
free books.[4]

More drastically, the Mark Twain Birthplace State Historic Site, in
Florida, Missouri, does not seem to connect with any local community
beyond occasional vacationers from Mark Twain Lake. Quarry Farm and
the Center for Mark Twain Studies in Elmira, New York manages somewhat better to strike a balance between its two audiences: scholars and
locals. In the 1980s, as Elmira suffered through a number of factory clos-

ings and its tourism bureau lured tourists to see "Mark Twain Country," pressure mounted for public access to Quarry Farm. Lectures and teacher workshops allow community members to observe the historic house even if not directly. Today, Quarry Farm's scholarly activities benefit the community too. The center's reputation, for instance, has improved the standing of Elmira College, which has become an important local employer and now offers a graduate certificate in Mark Twain Studies.

Despite their contributions, these sites can also obscure community problems like racism and class conflict. For instance, while Quarry Farm attracts scholars from around the world, their work hardly concerns working-class Elmira, which remains economically depressed and with few employment prospects beyond the college and two nearby prisons. In Hartford, the disconnect between the historic house and its hardscrabble surroundings is immediately evident. The house that was once, in Clemens's eyes, in perfect harmony with its environment, is no longer. The museum staff works hard to stage community events like beer tastings and literary readings that focus less on décor and more on the serious and playful matter of Sam Clemens's work and history. However, currently, the museum does not seem to be reaching its immediate neighbors.

In Hannibal, despite increased attention to the history of race and slavery and outreach to black residents, the Mark Twain Boyhood Home and Museum still obscures the persistence of racism and class tensions very much rooted in Clemens's time. One need look no further for its traces than the kitschy tourist stores next to the museum that set out Mammy figurines in their shop windows. In this regard, the museum's assertion that "The Stories Started Here" may be more true than it's willing to accept. Although the powerful history of Mark Twain in Hannibal is a community story that some take pride in and rally around, other histories are hard pressed to find space for their narratives.

All of these contradictions and complexities only demonstrate how such places are important to study because they provide insight, beyond literary discourse, into how literary figures become canonized. Clemens's place in the American canon was uncertain at the founding of three of these four sites. Hannibal originally celebrated Clemens because he was a local boy who had used his wit to make the world laugh, not because he had been declared "the first true American writer." Florida followed suit. Katharine Seymour Day's commitment to the Mark Twain house in Hartford came more from loyalty to Harriet Beecher Stowe's family legacy than from Clemens's literary accomplishments. In the end, these house museums may have done as much for Clemens as he did for them. Only the Center for Mark Twain Studies at Quarry Farm was founded in the full flower of Clemens's literary reputation. One might, in fact, wonder whether Twain's legacy would be so well established had it not been for these house museums and their appeals to tourists and readers alike.

Mark Twain is a moving target. Each of the four places that I studied lays claim to Clemens's legacy, seeks to define what he means, and locates him in a place. But even they cannot achieve the "comprehensive exhibit of American character" that Charles Tilden Sempers imagined in 1901. Because his life, fiction, and popular image are so intertwined, Clemens is impossible to tie down at any one museum. Consequently, these sites adapt to visitors' needs as much as they adapt to our shifting understanding of the author. The result does begin to convey the complexity of his domestic life. Although the birthplace may be a replica, for instance, it does illustrate the poverty of Clemens's early life, a situation that was not uncommon in Missouri during the 1830s. The birthplace might also someday elucidate the legacy of slavery and racism about which Clemens was so concerned. His boyhood home, through its interpretation of *Tom Sawyer*, has come to symbolize more than either Sam Clemens's childhood or Tom Sawyer's childhood. The house's iconic status has made Hannibal a symbol of small-town America. In fact, today its official motto is "America's Home Town." Meanwhile, the Mark Twain Museum in Hartford shows Clemens at the beginning of his fame and fortune. Although the Clemenses would leave the house, largely because they could not afford to live there, the house museum shows Sam and Olivia Clemens grappling with issues of status and authorial representation in Gilded Age America. Meanwhile, Quarry Farm offers a glimpse of the Clemenses' lives when they were among their closest friends and family. For scholars, it provides a rare personal encounter with Clemens's writing space.

Though these literary house museums provide access to the famous homes that we associate with Clemens, they are nonetheless mediated objects. Houses cannot display Clemens's domestic life without managerial interpretation. Staff at house museums that interpret literary lives must grapple with the same interpretative choices that all house museums deal with. Managers must decide what biographical information to present and what not to present. They decipher, with a corps of interpretative specialists and research associates, how to communicate why the house was important in the life of the author. But literary houses have the extra burden of explaining how the house was central to the author's literary creativity. Staffs have to articulate a connection to a literary text, to a specific writerly space, or to an atmosphere that was particularly important to the writer's literary production. And, at places like the Boyhood Home and Museum in Hannibal, managers can *choose* to interpret literature. The tensions among these many choices and the individual motivations of visitors are what makes literary houses different from many historic house

museums, and they are what make the narratives that they create so fruit-
ful to study.

These houses are vital texts for understanding how people appreciate
and yearn to comprehend the origins of literature. When tourists go to
any writer's house, they assume—at the most basic level—that there is
something about the writer's life that connects to their work and that
traces of this connection might be found within the writer's space. Not
everyone who visits literary sites are readers, but they all come to see
the domestic traces of a literary person. These traces are not "naturally
occurring" at house museums. Literary houses must be made into literary
house museums.

At Sam Clemens's houses, each staff has created a plan for how visitors encounter the space and what they will see while they are there. For
instance, at Hannibal, visitors can no longer go in the front door and
tour the house. Since the 1988 restoration of the house, visitors are led
along scaffolding that only allows glimpses into the house. At the Mark
Twain Birthplace State Historic Site, a similar technique separates visitors
from the living space on display. At Hartford, visitors come in the front
door, but are led through the room by a guide, and unless they stay for
another tour, they cannot see the parts of the house reserved for domestic
servants. Each place creates its own map of the space that tourists experience. These maps have changed over time. Even at Quarry Farm, seemingly the least mediated of all these places, scholars are encouraged to use
only a portion of the living space that the Cranes, Clemenses, and the
Langdons would have enjoyed.

Interpretive maps are even more wide ranging at other historic sites
across the United States that celebrate Sam Clemens's wanderings. The
Museum of Appalachia in Clinton, Tennessee claims to have what they
call "the Clemens Family Cabin." This restored cabin is supposedly where
Sam Clemens was conceived before his parents made the trek to Missouri. Meanwhile, the State of California celebrates Clemens with the
Mark Twain–Bret Harte Trail, which itself features about a half-dozen
markers and sites, including a "reconstructed cabin" that commemorates
the writers' three months on Jackass Hill in Tuolumne County, California. Several opera houses and public theaters that were stops along
Clemens's speaking tours celebrate his performances with markers. Mark
Twain State Park and Mark Twain Lake abut the Florida birthplace, Mark
Twain National Forest stretches throughout southern Missouri, and active
archeological digs associated with Clemens are underway in at least two
states.[5] There is a long list of places that want to stake a claim on Clemens.

The proliferation of house museums associated with Clemens *should*
mean that his life has been adequately commemorated and mapped. But

the sheer number of sites vying to be closely associated with him makes it clear that, in the end, Clemens—and maybe all writers—can't be mapped. As much as it seems it is possible to know Clemens at these sites, they are each just a careful, mediated piece of him. Each site arranges its objects, artifacts, and mementos as best it can to evoke the real person who lived in these houses. Ultimately, though, it's up to the visitor to locate Sam Clemens's literary imagination.

# Notes

## Preface

1. See the many volumes of work on Mark Twain and Celebrity, including George William Sanderlin, *Mark Twain: As Others Saw Him* (New York: Coward, McCann & Geoghegan, 1978); Louis J. Budd, *Our Mark Twain: The Making of His Public Personality* (Philadelphia: University of Pennsylvania Press, 1983); Alan Gribben, "The Importance of Mark Twain," *American Quarterly* 37, no.1 (1985); Justin Kaplan, *Mr. Clemens and Mark Twain: A Biography* (New York: Simon and Schuster, 1991); and Karen Lystra, *Dangerous Intimacy: The Untold Story of Mark Twain's Final Years* (Berkeley and Los Angeles: University of California Press, 2006); among many, many others.

2. Faulkner's praise of Clemens was not universal and in this same interview, Faulkner also called Clemens a "hack writer." James Meriweather and Michael Millgate, ed., *Lion in the Garden: Interviews with William Faulkner, 1926–1962* (New York: Random House, 1968), 137.

3. See Linda Haverty Rugg, *Picturing Ourselves: Photography and Autobiography* (Chicago: University of Chicago Press, 1997), 47–48, and Budd, *Our Mark Twain*, 48–83.

4. Sam Clemens had many homes, and at least a few of them have been lost. If these houses still existed and they were museums today, it is likely they would narrate very different stories about Clemens's life. Several more houses, apartment buildings, and hotels where he lived for a short time claim him as well. At least one house where he lived in Greenwich Village from 1904 until 1908 was razed in 1954 despite its association with Clemens and Washington Irving. See "Mark Twain's Former Home Still Remains a Landmark: Famous Fifth Avenue House Will Be Preserved by Present Owner—Property in Same Family for Two Centuries—Irving Stayed There," *New York Times,* August 10, 1924; "Get Twain House Items: N.Y.U. and Greenwich Village Chamber Plan to Use Objects," *New York Times,* May 6, 1954; and coverage of the international effort to preserve the house in James W. Powell, "Mark Twain's Lost House," *Mark Twain Journal* 20 (1980).

5. This often-misunderstood quote from Clemens's 1897 notebook, "I am not an American, I am *the* American," has caused debate among Twain scholars. Misat-

tributed in a number of scholarly works, Clemens was quoting, according to Barbara Schmidt, his friend Frank Fuller and not speaking about himself. The quote was featured prominently on the packaging and promotion of Ken Burns's 2001 documentary, *Mark Twain*. See Schmidt's discussion of the controversy over the quote in "Frank Fuller, The American Revisited," *The Twainian* 58, no. 1 (2002).

6. This simple definition comes from Edward Alexander's chapter, "To Interpret" in Edward P. Alexander, *Museums in Motion: An Introduction to the History and Functions of Museums* (Nashville: American Association for State and Local History, 1979). However, the foundational literature on historical interpretation always begins and ends with Freeman Tilden's *Interpreting Our Heritage: Principles and Practices for Visitor Services in Parks, Museums, and Historic Places* (Chapel Hill: University of North Carolina Press, 1957).

7. See in particular West's chapter, "Gender Politics at the Orchard House Museum," in Patricia West, *Domesticating History: The Political Origins of America's House Museums* (Washington, D.C.: Smithsonian Institution Press, 1999).

8. John Ruskin, *The Seven Lamps of Architecture* (London: Smith, Elder and Co., 1849), 180.

9. Ibid.


## Introduction

1. See Charles Tilden Sempers, "Mark Twain: Living Now in Riverdale—His Old Home in Hartford and the Life He Lived There," *New York Times,* December 7, 1901. Throughout the study, I use Sam Clemens as often as possible to differentiate between the historical person who is commemorated and his pseudonym persona.

2. Although Kenmore in Fredericksburg, Virginia, was probably preserved and restored because of its association with George Washington's sister, Betty Washington Lewis, the house is largely interpreted through her husband, Fielding Lewis, and interprets his contribution to Fredericksburg and the sacrifices he made to aid the American Revolution. Moreover, of course, Washington Lewis herself is largely only famous by her familial association with George Washington.

3. This genre of generic house museum stories (in this case, the explanation of the rope bed that has to be tightened and the pervasiveness of bedbugs) and the explanation that kitchen fires were the most common contributor to house fires and a leading cause of women's deaths (second only to childbirth) are almost unavoidable in most house museums. I heard both stories recently on a tour of the John Chadd house in Chaddsford, Pennsylvania. Such stories are part of the narrative repertoire of house museums of a certain period.

4. It continues to surprise me that historic sites—federally funded, state funded, and privately funded—continue to interpret the history of slavery in the United States with silence. Although Colonial Williamsburg has made a gesture toward interpreting the lives of enslaved peoples in Colonial Virginia, most sites merely have a small display of archeological "evidence." For instance, at Monticello, a site where you would imagine that the coverage in the popular press of Thomas Jeffer-

son's relations with enslaved people—especially Sally Hemings—would have called into relief a meaningful interpretation of slavery, this interpretive change is just being realized. See coverage of recent exhibits on Jefferson and slavery in Edward Rothstein's "Life, Liberty and the Fact of Slavery," *New York Times*, January 26, 2012. For more information on the interpretation of slavery at historic sites, see the collection edited by James Oliver Horton and Lois E. Horton, *Slavery and Public History: The Tough Stuff of American Memory* (New York: New Press, 2006).

5. Because Mount Vernon and the Mount Vernon Ladies Association have been so well funded in recent times, the "ordinary life" displayed there is extreme. Mount Vernon features a lively living farm, including heritage breeds of sheep and horses that can trace their linage to beasts George and Martha would have seen grazing on the estate. Likewise, the outbuildings have been restored and reconstructed in perhaps the greatest detail of any historical house museum in the country. A fully functioning greenhouse was warmed in the winter by an adjoining slave quarters' stove. In its acknowledgment of the lives of enslaved peoples, Mount Vernon is far more developed than any of the other sites mentioned here. Perhaps this is because George freed "his" slaves upon his death; thus, the depiction of lives of enslaved peoples at Mount Vernon serves to tell a flattering story of the first president. Not often added to this story was the fact that Martha Washington held many slaves in her own name; she held enough to easily run the estate without her husband's. George Washington did not press her to free those she claimed. Her children inherited these slaves.

6. See Susan J. Matt, "You Can't Go Home Again: Homesickness and Nostalgia in U.S. History," *Journal of American History* 94, no. 2 (2007): 497, and her more recent in-depth work on this subject, *Homesickness: An American History* (Oxford: Oxford University Press, 2011).

7. Literary house museums have not been immune to the affects of the current recession, which has caused the closing of a number of historic sites and museums. See Tracie Rohzon's "Homes Sell, and History Goes Private," *New York Times*, December 31, 2006. However, the fact that there are still a growing number of sites devoted to authors when other historic house museums are facing dire financial times seems to speak to something special about the allure of the literary site. Some authors' houses are facing hard times. Newspapers again recently reported Edith Wharton's the Mount is facing serious financial shortcomings (in part because of their efforts to purchase Wharton's library), and the Poe House in Baltimore has had its budget slashed by city officials and is currently struggling to find alternative funding. See Clarence Fanto, "Mount Seeks Help," *Berkshire Eagle*, January 8, 2010; Charles McGrath, "Landmark Massachusetts Building Where Wharton Wrote Faces Foreclosure," *New York Times*, February 23, 2008; and Dan Barry, "A Violation of Both the Law and the Spirit," *New York Times*, January 28, 2008. On the Poe House, see Jeffrey Nichols, "Twain House Director: Poe House Can Be Saved," *Baltimore Sun*, February 11, 2011; Kate Taylor, "Fiscal Woe Haunting Baltimore Poe House," *New York Times*, August 7, 2011; Carolyn Kellogg, "Could the Poe Movie Save Edgar Allan Poe's Baltimore House?" *Los Angeles Times*, August 8, 2011; and the odd offer outlined in Chris Kaltenbach's "PETA Offers to Help Keep Poe House Open: Animal-Rights Group Wants to Display a Pro-Vegan Ad at

the Baltimore Museum in Exchange for Financial Help," *Baltimore Sun,* February 14, 2011.

8. Today, perhaps because fewer visitors read Hawthorne's novel, the House of the Seven Gables presents the story of Caroline Emmerton and her efforts alongside the details of the house that connect to the novel. See the museum's Web site: http://www.7gables.org/history_property.shtml. You can still go up the narrow hidden passageway. For an excellent history of interpretation at the site, see Tami Christopher, "The House of the Seven Gables: A House Museum's Adaptation to Changing Societal Expectations since 1910," in *Defining Memory: Local Museums and Constructions of History in America's Changing Communities* (New York: Alta Mira, 2007), 63–76.

9. As the many literary tourists to sites associated with Dan Brown's novels might attest, sometimes literary tourists are not looking for history, they are looking for fiction.

10. The earliest American tourist guide I have found comes from 1853, by various authors, *Homes of American Authors: Comprising Anecdotical, Personal, and Descriptive Sketches.* Susan Marie Bishop's collection and research has confirmed my findings. Her bibliographic work points to a huge increase in publishing on this subject at the turn of the century. This phenomenon is certainly worthy of further study.

11. See, for instance, B. J. Welborn, *Traveling Literary America: A Complete Guide to Literary Landmarks* (Lookout Mountain, TN: Jefferson Press, 2005). Washington, D.C., recently braced for a new round of literary tourists inspired to see the sites associated with Dan Brown's most recent book. Enterprising tour guides and tourism bureaus are already creating resources for Brown fans. Among the many tour guides created for Brown's most recent book, see *Destination DC: The Lost Symbol,* 2009, Washington, D.C. Convention and Tourism Bureau, available at http://beta. washington.org/visiting/experience-dc/the-lost-symbol, October 1, 2009.

12. Nicola J. Watson, *The Literary Tourist: Readers and Places in Romantic and Victorian Britain* (New York: Palgrave Macmillan, 2007), 1.

13. It is interesting to note that Herbert doesn't venture a guess as to the percentages of pilgrims and users that visit any literary site, nor does he see any room between these two categories of tourists. David Herbert, "Literary Places, Tourism and the Heritage Experience," *Annals of Tourism Research* 28, no. 2 (2001): 313–14.

14. Ibid., 327. Herbert's comment on tourists' suspicion about the placement of inauthentic objects in Jane Austen's house had me excited. When I tracked him down to follow up on these results, he let me know that he had retired and thrown out of all of his research data. There are about a half dozen of these studies, including Tammie J. Kaufman and Denver E. Severt, "Heritage Tourism: Historic Preservationist Attitude and the Heritage Site Case Study of William Faulkner's Homeplace," *Tourism Review International* 10, no. 3 (2006); Clare Fawcett and Patricia Cormack, "Guarding Authenticity at Literary Tourism Sites," *Annals of Tourism Research* 28, no. 3 (2001); and David T. Herbert, "Artistic and Literary Places in France as Tourist Attractions," *Tourism Management* 17, no. 2 (1996).

15. For an excellent account of the "problem" with tourism studies' closeness to the tourism industry, see Adrian Franklin and Mike Crang, "The Trouble with

Tourism and Travel Theory," *Tourist Studies* 1, no. 1 (2001).

16. See Ning Wang, "Rethinking Authenticity in Tourism Experience," *Annals of Tourism Research* 26, no. 2 (1999): 349–70, and John H. Falk, "An Identity-Centered Approach to Understanding Museum Learning," *Curator* 49, no. 2 (2006). One important figure in this discussion is Jay Rounds, who helped redesign the interpretive structure of the Hannibal house after 2000. He is still actively involved in the planning process there. See Jay Rounds, "Doing Identity Work in Museums," *Curator* 49, no. 2 (2006).

17. Roy Rosenzweig and David P. Thelen, *The Presence of the Past: Popular Uses of History in American Life* (New York: Columbia University Press, 1998), 15, 105. In Rosenzweig and Thelen's racial and ethnic breakdown of their survey respondents, only Pine Ridge Ogalala residents ranked museums lower than members of their own family. African Americans, Mexican American, and White Americans (their categories) all shared statistically nearly identical responses to history museums and historic sites (Appendix 2, Table 2, p. 235).

18. Ibid., 106.

19. Lawrence Buell, "The Thoreauvian Pilgrimage: The Structure of an American Cult," *American Literature* 61, no. 2 (1989): 175–99, 179, 185. Buell frames his discussion of the sites associated with Thoreau with John Muir's tourist accounts in Concord and Henry James's writing about visiting the city. He also explores early guidebooks to literary Concord and New England and other published and unpublished accounts. Buell is currently part of a campaign to raise funds to restore Henry David Thoreau's birthplace; see http://www.thoreaufarm.org/.

20. Writers like Stephen King might argue that there is a fine line between tourist canonization and stalking. Longfellow was so popular in his time that his family made the public happy by creating a statuary version of the poet available in their yard. They eventually installed an elaborate garden to re-route tourists away from the house.

21. Other considerations of American literary houses include the chapter on the Concord, Massachusetts, house Wayside in Erin Hazard's "The Author's House: Abbotsford and Wayside," *Literary Tourism and Nineteenth-Century Culture,* ed. Nicola Watson (New York: Palgrave Macmillan, 2009). Also from the same collection, see Paul Aaron Westover, "How America 'Inherited' Literary Tourism," *Literary Tourism and Nineteenth-Century Culture,* ed. Nicola Watson (London: Palgrave, 2009). A longer discussion of Shelley Fisher Fishkin's critical travelogues tracing Mark Twain's influences and Diana Fuss's readings of the Emily Dickinson House in Amherst, Massachusetts, is found in chapter 4.

22. Anne Trubek, "The Evidence of Things Unseen: The Sweet Gloom of Writers' House Museums," *The Believer,* October 6, 2006, 23–29, 23. I know Trubek is speaking figuratively here, because, after all, at the Mark Twain Boyhood Home and Museum you can get on a raft placed along the Mississippi River. It is clearly a popular spot in the museum—so popular that the staff has had to place a sign imploring visitors "please do not jump up and down on the raft."

23. Ideally, each site should hire an outside historian or graduate student to create an administrative history of the institution. Administrative histories do not solve all the problems of understanding a site's history, but they do provide staff with an

important sense of the museum's historical work in a community and can explain why things are the way they are, what has worked in the past to engage visitors, and what has been a disaster in the past. They are especially useful documents for historic sites—institutions that should seek to be self-reflective about their own history and their own history-interpreting practices.

24. Ralph Gregory celebrated his 101st birthday September 27, 2010, with the Washington Historical Society in Washington, Missouri, where he still serves as an honorary curator for their museum. For a recent review of his work, see Susan Weich, "Historian, 101, Still Volunteering at Library Named for Him," *St. Louis Post-Dispatch,* March 16, 2011.

25. For a recent collection that uncovers the history of American birthplace commemoration, see Seth C. Bruggeman's *Born in the U.S.A.: Birth, Commemoration, and American Public Memory* (Amherst: University of Massachusetts Press, 2012).

26. See Dwight Pitcaithley, "'A Cosmic Threat': The National Park Service Addresses the Causes of the American Civil War," *Slavery and Public History: The Tough Stuff of American Memory,* ed. James Oliver Horton and Lois E. Horton (New York: New Press, 2006).

27. Those involved with the Center for Mark Twain Studies at Elmira College are careful to distinguish that Quarry Farm is not a museum, but a living house. My discussion considers the house as a *kind of museum* as a matter of comparison to the other sites, but their distinction is an important one that is explored more fully in chapter 4.

## Chapter One

1. Clemens indicates in his biography that the population was one hundred. Mark Twain and Michael J. Kiskis, *Mark Twain's Own Autobiography: The Chapters from the North American Review,* 2nd ed. (Wisconsin Studies in Autobiography, Madison: University of Wisconsin Press, 2009), 112. In 2000, Florida's population was nine, but by the 2010 Census, this remaining population had disappeared. See 2010 U.S. Census Bureau data on Florida village, Missouri, through on-line American FactFinder: http://factfinder2.census.gov/ and http://2010.census.gov/2010census/.

2. See the Abraham Lincoln Birthplace National Historic Site: http://www.nps.gov/abli/ (accessed September 21, 2009).

3. See Frederick Jackson Turner and State Historical Society of Wisconsin, *The Significance of the Frontier in American History* (Madison: State Historical Society of Wisconsin, 1894) and the many editions of and about Turner published between 1920 and 1940. See also Richard Etulain's excellent summary of Turner's influence, *Writing Western History: Essays on Major Western Historians* (Reno: University of Nevada Press, 2002).

4. The bust was removed in 1964 after vandalism became a problem; park officials moved the bust to the shrine site despite vocal protests from local citizens. The bust had suffered a few tumbles off its perch, and officials were concerned that it

might one day end up in the Salt River below. Ralph Gregory, personal interview by author, November 8, 2007.

5. The reconstructed log cabin is not marked in any way, but was built from a number of log structures that were once at the bottom of the Salt River Valley. The logs from these structures were salvaged by the historically minded group, Friends of Florida. Two members hoped to "reconstruct" a number of the cabins on Missouri Department of Natural Resources land in Florida and leased the area where the cabin stands for one hundred years. However, only one cabin was ever built. Tourists often confuse the cabin with the Mark Twain birthplace cabin because it is the only semi-historical looking building around. The Missouri Department of Natural Resources has broken the lease and asked the Friends of Florida to move the cabin, which it claims is inauthentic to the time period and confuses visitors about which cabin is "real." See "Newspaper clippings" file at Missouri Department of Natural Resources, State Park Division, Archives, *Monroe City Lake Gazette,* July 20, 2005.6. Fred Kaplan, *The Singular Mark Twain: A Biography* (New York: Doubleday, 2003), 9–13.

7. Lorenzo J. Greene, Gary R. Kremer, and Antonio Frederick Holland, *Missouri's Black Heritage,* rev. ed. (Columbia: University of Missouri Press, 1993), 25–26.

8. On Florida history and the potential use of the Salt River for navigation, see Frank Lamson, *Statement by F. B. Lamson, Secretary Mark Twain Park Association,* Mark Twain Birthplace State Historic Site Archives (1924). The Mark Twain Birthplace State Historic Site Archives are hereafter referred to as the Birthplace Site Archives.

9. John Huffman, recently retired site administrator at the birthplace, pointed out that a great number of visitors to the birthplace end up coming as a result of a trip to the more popular Mark Twain Boyhood Home and Museum in Hannibal, the subject of chapter 2, or the tourist trap Tom Sawyer's Cave in Hannibal, Missouri, which is about a half hour away by car. John Huffman, discussion with the author, January 7, 2008.

10. Both General Pershing's childhood home and the Mark Twain Birthplace are Missouri State Historic Sites, run by the Missouri Department of Natural Resources.

11. The site was thus marked through 2009, http://www.mostateparks.com/twainpark/map.htm (accessed December 18, 2007). However, Missouri State Parks now have new Web sites, and the site is officially marked on its interactive map as the Mark Twain Birthplace Museum, http://mostateparks.com/map/mark-twain-state-park (accessed August 11, 2011).

12. For information on the national development of state parks, see Ney C. Landrum, *The State Park Movement in America: A Critical Review* (Columbia: University of Missouri Press, 2004).

13. See http://www.mostateparks.com/twainpark.htm (accessed August 14, 2009) and http://www.mvs.usace.army.mil/MarkTwain/ (accessed January 16, 2012).

14. Charles Hammer, "A Home at Last for the Old Twain House," *Kansas City Star,* November 22, 1959.

15. Lawrence Buell has argued that the religious experience of pilgrimage is not lost in literary pilgrimage, though he speaks in particular about rituals performed visiting the site of Henry Thoreau's cabin. Buell's discussion of Victor and Edith

Turner's arguments about the nature of contemporary religious pilgrimage and its connection to tourism are worthy of further exploration. In fact, though shrines are rarely formally dedicated today, we often refer to the houses and places associated with literary figures as shrines. Even scholars do this. See chapter 4 for a discussion of scholars' responses to Quarry Farm as a shrine. See Lawrence Buell, "The Thore-auvian Pilgrimage: The Structure of an American Cult," *American Literature* 61, no. 2 (1989): 179.

16. Such sites in Missouri that celebrate Western expansion include the Jesse James House; the Pioneer Museum in Barry County; the Patee House that cel-ebrates Jesse James and the history of the Pony Express; the Laura Ingalls Wilder Historic Home and Museum in Wright County; Missouri-Town, a hodge-podge of pioneer buildings collected and arranged to simulate a pioneer village in Jack-son County; and Booneville Village, Daniel Boone's family outpost in St. Charles County, among many more, no doubt.

17. On the rocking chair is the caption, "Jane Clemens' Rocking Chair: In Keokuk, Iowa, both Jane Clemens and George Edward Marshall resided at the home of her eldest son, Orion Clemens. To celebrate her birthday, Marshal, a public schoolteacher, took Mrs. Clemens shopping for a gift. Her choice was this reddish-orange rocker. The Thonet Rocker Mrs. Clemens selected was designed and mar-keted by Michael Thonet, a European cabinetmaker. This type, a Thonet Bentwood Rocker, was introduced in 1860." Though the chair came from long after Clemens's birth, it is included in the shrine.

18. In interviews with former site administrators, none takes credit for creating this display, although several commented that they did their best to "keep it up." It is likely that the exhibit was initially created by Ralph Gregory or park staff when the museum opened in 1960.

19. In the museum wing of the shrine are the site offices and reading room where John Huffman generously answered my research requests from their work-ing files. The reading room is well equipped for the traveling Mark Twain scholar and includes the many published editions on Clemens's letters, scholarship, and biographies.

20. A number of individuals in the small towns near Florida became collectors of Mark Twain memorabilia and formed the Mark Twain Research Center. They col-lected first editions as well as items that had belonged to the Clemens family. Over the years these artifacts have made their way into the shrine's permanent collection.

21. The former site administrator John Huffman estimates of visitation numbers for 2007 were 31,371, significantly higher than 2008's at roughly 18,911. John Huffman, e-mail message to author, November 26, 2008. See also the introduction to Seth Bruggeman, *Born in the USA: Birth and Commemoration in American Public Memory,* edited collection (Amherst: University of Massachusetts Press, 2012).

22. Clifton Johnson, *Highways and Byways of the Mississippi Valley* (New York: Macmillan Company, 1906), 170.

23. Ibid., 179.

24. Ibid., 179–80.

25. Mark Twain, "Lincoln Memorial: A Plea by Mark Twain for the Setting Apart of His Birthplace," *New York Times,* January 13, 1907.

26. For a discussion of the role that Lincoln's birthplace played in his election, see Edward Pessen, *The Log Cabin Myth: The Social Backgrounds of the Presidents* (New Haven, CT: Yale University Press, 1984).

27. Italics added by author. Mark Twain, *A Birthplace Worth Saving,* ed. Lincoln Farm Association (New York: Lincoln Farm Association, 1906).

28. Clemens's skepticism about relics is most evident in this often-quoted passage from *Innocents Abroad:* "We find a piece of the true cross in every old church we go into, and some of the nails that held it together . . . . I think we have seen as much as a keg of these nails. Then there is the crown of thorns; they have part of one in Sainte Chapelle, in Paris, and part of one also in Notre Dame. And as for bones of St. Denis, I feel certain we have seen enough of them to duplicate him if necessary." Mark Twain, *The Innocents Abroad; or, The New Pilgrim's Progress* (Hartford, CT: American Publishing Company, 1870), 165. For recent discussions of the historiography of U.S. history and national interests in the commemoration of "historically significant" great men, see William Hogeland, *Inventing American History* (Cambridge: MIT Press, 2009); James W. Cook, Lawrence B. Glickman, and Michael O'Malley, *The Cultural Turn in U.S. History: Past, Present, and Future* (Chicago: University of Chicago Press, 2008); and Ian R. Tyrrell, *Historians in Public: The Practice of American History, 1890–1970* (Chicago: University of Chicago Press, 2005).

29. It is possible that this visit to Stratford shaped his belief that most literary sites have very little to do with the geniuses who are born there. The Stratford birthplace has often been seen as problematic, although essential, in the development of literary tourism in Britain. See Nicola J. Watson, *The Literary Tourist: Readers and Places in Romantic and Victorian Britain* (New York: Palgrave Macmillan, 2007).

30. Olivia Clemens thought she was on her way to "Hempworth." Clemens mentions the surprise in a letter. See Samuel L. Clemens, Letter to Moncure D. Conway. Hartford [Conn.] (UCCL 00821), October 18, 1875. http://www.marktwain-project.org/xtf/view?docId=letters/UCCL00821.xml;style=letter;brand=mtp (accessed August 9, 2009).

31. See Samuel L. Clemens to Charles E. Flower. Hartford [Conn.] (UCCL 01276). October 27, 1875, http://www.marktwainproject.org/xtf/view?docId=letters/UCCL01276.xml;style=letter;brand=mtp (accessed August 9, 2009).

32. The "New Place," Shakespeare's final home in Stratford, and the mulberry tree he planted in the front yard inspired so many on-lookers that the last owner of the residence, the Reverend Francis Gastrell, ripped the tree out and destroyed the house in 1759. The legend goes that the townspeople were so angry that Gastrell had removed the tree that they stoned the house, and the owner razed the house after the damage. Apparently, some thought to salvage the tree and make mementos out of the wood. When Washington Irving traveled to Stratford sometime between 1815 and 1820, he was offered a relic of the tree from a man who claimed to have helped remove it. Washington Irving, *The Sketch-Book of Geoffrey Crayon, Gent.* (New York: G. P. Putnam's Sons, 1888), 354.

33. For information on Shakespeare mulberry relics and fakes, see Folger Shakespeare Library, *Fakes, Forgeries and Facsimiles,* 2004, http://www.folger.edu/html/exhibitions/fakes_forgeries/FFFmulberry.asp (accessed August 14, 2011).

34. Samuel L. Clemens, Letter to the Editor of the *New York Evening Post,* Hartford, Conn., November 23, 1880 (UCCL 12212). http://www.marktwainproject. org/xtf/view?docId=letters/UCCL12212.xml;style=letter;brand=mtp (accessed January 12, 2012).

35. Ibid.

36. I queried the staff at the Mark Twain House in Hartford in August 2008 about the existence of the Shakespeare mulberry on the grounds. Their historic landscape report makes no mention of it. It was likely removed in an effort to "improve" museum grounds and was possibly removed with the construction of the visitors' center in 2002.

37. Some in St. Louis preferred Field's work and the work of Kate Chopin to that of Mark Twain, whom they saw as a mere humorist; see Alexander Nicholas DeMenil, "A Century of Missouri Literature," *Missouri Historical Review* 15, no.1 (1920): 74–126.

38. Little did they or Twain know that at the 1904 fair in St. Louis, relics from Twain's birthplace, in the form of carved canes made from the timbers of the house, were sold as mementos. About the canes, see *Paris Mercury* (Paris, MO), June 22, 1934. About the Paris envoy, see "Mark Twain Unveils Field Memorial Tablet St. Louis, June 7," *Idaho Statesman* (Boise, ID), June 8, 1902.

39. Sam Clemens quoted in "Eugene Field Tablet, Birthplace Memorial Unveiled by Mark Twain," *St. Louis Globe Democrat,* June 7, 1902.

40. About the mishap, see "Note and Comment," *Springfield Daily Republican* (Springfield, MO), June 14, 1902. About the call to replace the dedication plaque, see "St. Louis," *Kansas City Star,* June 12, 1902.

41. Mark Twain, *Autobiography of Mark Twain,* vol. 2, ed Albert Bigelow Paine (New York: Harpers, 1924), 1175.

42. The Abraham Lincoln birthplace cabin was possibly constructed in small part from some timbers that came from the original structure where he was born, but these timbers had already been recycled and were in use in buildings when they were scavenged *to build* the birthplace cabin. Additionally, over the years, the cabin came to trade timbers with, of all structures, the Jefferson Davis birthplace cabin, which had been purchased by the same exhibitioner. Abraham Lincoln and Jefferson Davis were born within a few miles of each other. The cabins were dismantled and reassembled in so many different places that no one knows for sure which timbers were which. See former National Park Service chief historian Dwight Pitcaithley's "Abraham Lincoln's Birthplace Cabin: The Making of an American Icon," *Myth, Memory, and the Making of the American Landscape,* ed. Paul A. Shackel (Gainesville: University Press of Florida, 2001).

43. See Bruggeman, *Born in the USA.*

44. Her birthplace has been celebrated over the years through various means. The county in which it resides is now called Dare County, and in 1937, President Franklin Delano Roosevelt authorized a postage stamp that commemorated the 350th anniversary of Dare's birth. Little is known about Dare other than the fact of her birth.

45. Patricia West, *Domesticating History: The Political Origins of America's House Museums* (Washington, D.C.: Smithsonian Institution Press, 1999), and Mike

Wallace, *Mickey Mouse History and Other Essays on American Memory; Critical Perspectives on the Past* (Philadelphia: Temple University Press, 1996).

46. See Seth C. Bruggeman's *Here, George Washington Was Born: Memory, Material Culture and the Public History of a National Monument* (Athens: University of Georgia Press, 2008). A current effort to build a replica of Washington's childhood home at Ferry Farm is now underway. John Noble Wilford, "Washington's Boyhood Home Is Found," *New York Times,* July 3, 2008.

47. See Barbara Welter, "The Cult of True Womanhood: 1820–1860," *American Quarterly* 18, no. 2 (1966): 151–74, and Linda K. Kerber, "Separate Spheres, Female Worlds, Woman's Place: The Rhetoric of Women's History," *Journal of American History* 75, no. 1 (1988): 9–39.

48. One notable exception to that rule is the John F. Kennedy's birthplace in Brookline, Massachusetts, which has recently recalibrated its historical interpretation to focus primarily on the life of Rose Kennedy. For a description of how the National Park Service has begun to reinterpret JFK's birthplace, see Christine Arato's chapter in *Born in the USA,* and Alexander von Hoffman, *John F. Kennedy's Birthplace: A Presidential Home in History and Memory* (National Park Service, U.S. Department of the Interior, 2004), http://www.nps.gov/history/history/online_books/jofi/birthplace.pdf. (accessed January 16, 2012).

49. Gregory, "Orion Clemens on Mark Twain's Birthplace," 16–18.

50. There are, of course, several exceptions; many times a woman's birthplace may be noted with a plaque—as in the case of Willa Cather's birthplace near Winchester, Virginia, but it is rare to have a house or site preserved to honor the birth of a woman. Exceptions include the Pearl S. Buck birthplace, Laura Ingalls Wilder birthplace (reconstruction), Elizabeth Cady Stanton Birthplace, and Alice Paul birthplace.

51. For a discussion of the American market for guidebooks to British authors' homes, see the introduction to Watson, *The Literary Tourist.*

52. Péter Dávidházi, *The Romantic Cult of Shakespeare: Literary Reception in Anthropological Perspective* (New York: St. Martin's Press, 1998).

53. Watson, *The Literary Tourist.*

54. About the transformation from the practice of visiting writers' graves at places like Poet's Corner in Westminster Abbey and Shelley's and Keats's graves in Rome, see chapter 1, "An Anthology of Corpses" in Watson, *The Literary Tourist.* For an account of the David Garrick's Stratford Jubilee, see Dávidházi, *The Romantic Cult of Shakespeare.*

55. Aaron Santesso, "The Birth of the Birthplace: Bread Street and Literary Tourism before Stratford," *English Literary History* 71 (2004): 385.

56. Historical preservationists interested in how the structure of the Stratford birthplace has changed over time have begun moving in this direction. See Julia Thomas, "Bringing Down the House: Restoring Shakespeare's Birthplace," *Literary Toursim and Nineteenth-Century Culture,* ed. Nicola Watson (London: Palgrave Macmillan, 2009). A combined approach might provide the ability to speculate about these motivations.

57. Santesso, "The Birth of the Birthplace," 378.

58. For James's account of his time in Concord and Salem, see chapter 8 of Henry James, *The American Scene* (London: Richard Clay & Sons, 1907), and

Henry James, "Letter from Henry James," *The Essex Institute Historical Collections* 41 (1904). If he or Santesso were to tour Salem today, I think they would find a very different experience than what James found more than one hundred years ago. Salem today is as kitschy as it comes, with numerous witch houses, museums, and gift shops that celebrate the legacy of the Salem Witch Trials alongside Hawthorne's literary creations.

59. Anne Trubek, *A Skeptic's Guide to Writers' Houses* (Philadelphia: University of Pennsylvania Press, 2011).

60. Because Santesso is interested in Milton, it is easy to see why he believes that Milton's work is so connected to the climate of its creation. Shakespeare scholars might argue likewise. Shakespeare's centrality in the literary canon, the fact that his works are actively and popularly performed all over the world, and that the site of his birth has been turned into a Shakespeare-Disneyland, does not necessarily mean that he is easier to understand.

61. The sophisticated literary tourism that Santesso sees as preferable to the prepackaged tourism that he sees in the Stratford model might be found at Twain's summer retreat in Elmira, New York. This kind of literary tourism requires a scholar's or true enthusiast's devotion to an author. Part of Santesso's argument is that the harder it is to understand an author's work the truer the literary tourism experience. But within this argument he privileges the place of the elite understanding of high literature over the lay understanding and appreciation of popular literature. But he does not offer a version of a devotee's experience at any popular writer's site other than Shakespeare's birthplace. Santesso, "The Birth of the Birthplace," 388.

62. See Anne Trubek's work on the disappointment she finds at literary houses. Anne Trubek, "The Evidence of Things Unseen: The Sweet Gloom of Writers' House Museums," *The Believer,* October 6, 2006. See also, Brock Clarke, *Backstory: A Burning Question: An Arsonist's Guide to Writers' Homes in New England,* 2007, Algonquin, http://arsonistsguide.com/backstory.html. (accessed January 16, 2012).

63. Over time the birthplace might have created a stronger narrative that connects the cabin and the nearby farm of Clemens's uncle and aunt, the Quarleses. Clemens in his autobiographical writing mentions how important summers at their farm were to him growing up, in large part because there he was exposed to the lives of many slaves. The state park now barely alludes to the time that Clemens spent on Quarles's farm in the summer as having an influence through his introduction to Uncle Dan'l. The farm is currently the focus of archeological investigation by its current owner in the hopes that something there might connect to the Clemenses' time with the Quarleses. Perhaps there is another Clemens site in the works. See Brent Engel, "Digs Planned at Farm Twain Enjoyed as a Boy," *Hannibal Courier Post,* September 1, 2009.

64. See Shirley Hoover Biggers, *American Author Houses, Museums, Memorials, and Libraries: A State-by-State Guide* (Jefferson, NC: McFarland, 2000). Laura Ingalls Wilder's birthplace, as already mentioned, is a "replica."

65. Abraham Lincoln's fictitious birthplace was shipped all over the United States; Hawthorne's birthplace and others have been relocated to make them more convenient for tourists; and even Shakespeare's birthplace in Stratford was once threatened with a move when P.T. Barnum planned to relocate the whole building,

stone by stone, to the United States. See chapter 23 in P. T. Barnum, *Struggles and Triumphs: Or, Forty Years' Recollections of P. T. Barnum* (Buffalo: Warren, Johnson and Co., 1872).

66. *Monroe County Appeal* (Paris, MO), October 3, 1890. It is interesting to note that the description of the house that was sold matches the description of the house that is now enshrined in the museum that is part of the Mark Twain State Park, with the exception of the exterior wall chimney. However, it also matches the description of at least one other house that also claimed to have been Clemens's birthplace. I found a transcription of this particular article in the clippings file at the museum; under it, hand written, were the words: "This was not done." This was most likely written by a former site administrator Ralph Gregory. Attribution to Gregory comes from John Huffman. Huffman, discussion with the author.

67. See Joe Burnett, *Paris Mercury,* October 17, 1890.

68. Sam Pollard, *Monroe County Appeal,* June 18, 1897.

69. *Paris Mercury,* June 22, 1934.

70. See Ralph Gregory, *M. A. "Dad" Violette: A Life Sketch* (Florida, MO: 1969), 3. Ralph Gregory (b. 1909) was the first site curator for the birthplace. His efforts to prove that the house was "authentic" led him to write a short biography of Violette.

71. Albert Bigelow Paine, *Mark Twain: A Biography, the Personal and Literary Life of Samuel Langhorne Clemens,* vol. 1 (New York: Harper and Brothers Publishers, 1912), 12.

72. Ibid.

73. There are two or three houses that the family lived in while they were in Florida, according to Clemens's biography and his mother's account. The family lived in the house where he was born only for a few months, and then they moved into a slightly larger structure. There may have been a larger house that John Marshall Clemens built for the family where they lived briefly before relocating to Hannibal, Missouri, when Clemens was three. These houses and their locations are unknown. It is likely that Violette's mother was the same woman whom Clifton Johnson spoke with when he visited Florida. His tour was just one year before Paine's. She provided him with the location of the house that he describes in his 1906 account. The age and description Johnson gives roughly match Mrs. Eliza Damrell (Violette) Scott.

74. *Hannibal Courier Post,* quoted in Gregory, *A Life Sketch,* 3. It may be that when Violette purchased the house the lean-to was still attached or a room had been added. As the birth cabin stands today, it is only a two-room structure.

75. It is likely that he charged rent for the campgrounds and cabins that he developed nearby. He may have occasionally allowed other activities to go on at the cabin. There is an undated photograph in the Birthplace Site Archives of a couple in their wedding clothes standing in front of the birthplace cabin. They reportedly spent their first night as a married couple in the birthplace.

76. Gregory, *A Life Sketch,* 4.

77. Dad Violette, Letter to the Editor of *Missouri Life,* Debra McAlear Gluck (Chesterfield, MO: Birthplace Site Archives, History File, 1986).

78. Armstrong, "Fulfilling a Vision: A Letter to the Missouri Department of Natural Resources," *Hannibal Courier Post,* June 5, 1995.

79. Frank Lamson, *Statement by F. B. Lamson, Secretary Mark Twain Park Association,* Birthplace Site Archives, 1924, 1.

80. Armstrong, "Fulfilling a Vision."

81. After her death, a few of the letters that Dad Violette had written to her and to her father made it back into the collections at the state historic site.

82. "Historical Notes and Comments: Mark Twain Memorial Park Association," *Missouri Historical Review* 18, no. 2 (1924): 288–90.

83. This organization, with the Women's Federated Club, did much work to make their plan appealing to the governor as he founded the Missouri State Park System. I have not been able to find any record of this organization or its involvement with the Mark Twain Memorial Park Association. I assume it is an umbrella organization of many of the women's clubs in the Moberly and Florida area.

84. Lamson, *Statement,* 2.

85. "Historical Notes and Comments," *Missouri Historical Review,* 290.

86. See "Evolution of the System (Missouri State Parks)," Missouri Department of Natural Resources, Division of Parks, Recreation, and Historic Preservation Archives, 1991. I have dated this source from a Department of Natural Resources history of the Missouri State Parks, through internal information, to 1991. Heather Rudy, DNR Archivist, shared this document.

87. See Gov. Arthur Hyde, Hyde Papers, 7, Gubernatorial, State Parks, 1923–1924, F. 689–692, (University of Missouri Western History and Manuscripts Collection).

88. *Performa Decree of Incorporation of Mark Twain Memorial Park Association,* February 28, 1924.

89. Dad Violette, Letter to Frank B. Lamson, Florida [Missouri], 1927. Mark Twain Birthplace State Historic Site Archives, Ruth Lamson File. If the registration book to which Violette refers survives, it is not at the Birthplace Site Archives. It may be somewhere deep in the archives of the Missouri Department of Natural Resources but was not found during my time in the archives. I believe that Violette kept this book from the time he purchased the house. His numbers seem fantastic given the current visitation at the site.

90. The track of land that the association had purchased was not the original site of the cabin, nor was it in the core of downtown Florida. It purchased a one-hundred-acre stretch that made up the top of a bluff overlooking the Salt River Valley.

91. "Settles Controversy About Twain Home," *Enterprise,* October 24, 1929.

92. Ibid. Claims that John Clemens built this birth house conflict with evidence that establishes that Violette's cabin was the family's first residence in Missouri. In these accounts, Jane Lampton Clemens gives birth to Samuel Clemens shortly after the family arrived from Tennessee, and the Clemens family settled in the Violette cabin briefly and then John Marshall Clemens built a larger house for the family. The evidence that is later seen as incontrovertible by Ralph Gregory and others comes from Orion Clemens's letter about the birth house. See Ralph Gregory, "Orion Clemens on Mark Twain's Birthplace," *Mark Twain Journal* 20, no. 2 (1980).

93. "Settles Controversy About Twain Home."

94. Gregory, *A Life Sketch.*

95. Florida was, by this time, an all-white village. C. E. Hamilton (Owner of General Store), Letter, August 26, 1939, signed by W. L. Crigler, R. H. Hamilton,

R. E. Rouse (Banker), C. H. Hamilton, E. O. P. Heidler, John B. White, A. W. Bousman, John Massey (Farmer), J. W. Keith, Moss Hamilton, George Muanda, J. B. Johnson, John F. Blue, R. S. Roberts, Ed Buffington (Telephone Operator), J. L. Clairy, R. D. Norman, George Littrell, James Keith, A. L. Littrell, Dan P. Violette, etc. Copies of petition can be found at the Birthplace Site Archives and in the Archives of the Missouri Department of Natural Resources in Jefferson City. I first came across it in the archive at the reading room. Portions of the text had been edited for a poster exhibit on CCC Company 1743 at the birthplace.

96. Ibid.

97. Dan Violette was integral in the planning of the Mark Twain Centennial activities in Hannibal in 1935 as a leader of the Centennial Commission. See the committee listing in the Mark Twain Boyhood Home and Museum archives or the Kansas City Public Library's Missouri Valley Special Collections, Mark Twain Centennial Committee, *Mark Twain Centennial Announcement Dinner and Broadcast,* ed. Hon. George A. Mahan and Daniel Violette (Hannibal: Program and Menu, Mark Twain Hotel, 1935).

98. John Cunning, "CCC Company 1743: The Thunderbirds," *Preservation Issues* 1 (1996), http://law.wustl.edu/staff/taylor/preserv/v6n1/cccco.htm (accessed January 16, 2012).

99. "The Park Problem," *Monroe County Appeal,* October 12, 1939.

100. "Will Not Let Them Go into Park Town," *Monroe County Appeal,* October 26, 1939.

101. It is worth noting that all of the towns that had black populations or allowed the CCC enrollees to visit are in much better shape today than Florida. Whether this has anything to do with Florida's ban and sundown "laws" would require more research.

102. Interview with Unnamed Company 1743 Enrollee, Birthplace Site Archives, Florida, Missouri, 1997. The cassette tapes of these interviews, including the unnamed enrollee quoted here and Ernest Dickerson, are likely held in the Birthplace Site Archives. I was not able to listen to these interviews in their entirety and have taken these outtakes from longer transcriptions held there.

103. Ernest Dickerson, interview by Connie Ritter, January 7, 1997. Birthplace Site Archives, Florida, Missouri.

104. Cunning, "CCC Company 1743." The company itself was the subject of Missouri State Park research in the 1990s. The park system performed the research to prepare nominations of its CCC-built structures for the National Register of Historic Places, so they themselves could be the object of preservation.

105. *The Twainian* was started by George Hiram Brownell and the Mark Twain Society of Chicago as a publication that dealt with all things Twain. It was the place where many of Clemens's letters first saw publication and a clearinghouse for earliest scholarly considerations of Twain. After Davis took over the publication and acquired the archives that Brownell collected, he sought avidly to find a home for them where he could control access. Many of these materials now reside in the research room at the Mark Twain Birthplace State Historic Site.

106. It is not entirely clear what caused the state to allocate resources to build the museum/shrine. It is likely that this plan (although not this particular building

design) had been in the works since at least the time of the CCC development of the park. It took almost twenty years for the state to make its shrine in Florida.

107. Stan Fast, telephone interview by author, November 20, 2007.

108. John Cunning's "CCC Company 1743: The Thunderbirds" was incredibly helpful in understanding this part of the park's history. His article was the result of research on CCC work across the state of Missouri so that the state might nominate the CCC buildings to the National Register.

109. John Huffman, former site administrator, discussed his decision to omit the names with me as I went through the documents in the reading room at the birthplace.

110. State resources at small sites like the birthplace, which over its lifetime has only had one or two full-time employees, are not generous. John Huffman assured me that he would have liked to have kept both displays up but he needed the poster board and that the repurposing of the exhibit probably had little to do with its content.

111. See the Missouri Department of Natural Resources Archives, Missouri State Park Board, "Museum Prospectus for Mark Twain Birthplace Memorial Shrine, Mark Twain State Park" (Jefferson City: 1961); Nancy Honerkamp, "Notes on Interpretation: Mark Twain Shrine State Historic Site" (Jefferson City: 1979); Daniel Holt, "Museum Assessment Program Grant: Mark Twain Birthplace" (Jefferson City: 1985). Some of these plans, especially Honerkamp's, carefully made the argument for the inclusion of African American history at the birthplace.

112. Stan Fast, telephone interview. It is possible that these houses are the cabin currently enclosed at the shrine. Careful examination revealed that the house was falling apart and might have been rebuilt into the structure there today (sans the distinct second chimney). Another image shows what might be the same house with a lean-to kitchen in the back and a small front porch. There are other images of the birthplace in circulation as well.

113. Signs are now slightly better than they once were, but as my visit reveals, the birthplace is only labeled as "historic site" on the official map of the state park that surrounds it. For an account of the various complaints about signage over the years, see William C. Holmes, "Memo: To: Jack Hilton, Regional Supervisor, Region 1, Subject: Signs for Mark Twain Birthplace" (Missouri Department of Natural Resources, State Park Division, Archives, File: Signs, 1980). See also Ann Nickell, "Memo: To: Frank Wesley, Subject: Road Signs at Mark Twain" (Missouri Department of Natural Resources, State Park Division, Archives, File: Signs, 1995).

114. Ralph Gregory, interview by author

115. Gregory, "Orion Clemens on Mark Twain's Birthplace," 16–18.

116. Stan Fast, Memo to Samuel J. Wegner, Assistant Supervisor Region 1: Birthplace Cabin Authenticity (Florida, MO: Mark Twain Birthplace State Historic Site, Missouri Department of Natural Resources, Historic Preservation Program, March 4, 1983), 1.

117. Ibid. Fast performed his analysis on the "backside" of the cabin, because he believed this side of the house would yield more information about the original structure. Since it had not faced the street and did not serve as a backdrop for tourists and their photographs, it would probably have received less attention and "restoration."

118. Italics author's. Fast, Memo, 3.

119. Fast, telephone interview. In my interview with Stan Fast, I revealed that I had interviewed Gregory and that I had read Fast's 1983 memo. This may have contributed to his description of Dad Violette and his wording here, which does not assert that the cabin is the birthplace but does indicate it might have some connection to Clemens. Perhaps the cabin is merely one of the many "old houses" that "Mark Twain looked at and played in" as a child.

120. Huffman, discussion.

121. Fast, telephone interview.

122. In 1999, the Mark Twain Birthplace State Historic Site saw 99,239 visitors; 66,344 in 2000; 65,697 in 2001; 59,803 in 2002; 56,036 in 2003; 38,635 in 2004; 32,113 in 2005; 40,322 in 2006; 29,369 in 2007; and 38,461 in 2008. Overall attendance to Missouri State Parks has dropped from a high in 1999 of more than 18 million annual visitors to less than 15 million in 2008. See overall attendance figures at the Missouri State Parks Web site's attendance data page: http://www.mostateparks.com/attendance/index.html.

## Chapter Two

1. Clemens makes this claim in his autobiography. See Mark Twain, *Autobiography of Mark Twain,* ed. Albert Bigelow Paine, vol. 2 (New York: Harpers, 1924), 174. It is also interesting to note that at other times he claimed another childhood friend, "Frank F.," also served as inspiration for Huckleberry Finn using almost the same language to describe both. See Mark Twain and Michael J. Kiskis, *Mark Twain's Own Autobiography: The Chapters from the North American Review* (Madison: University of Wisconsin Press, 1990), 191.

2. Clifton Johnson, *Highways and Byways of the Mississippi Valley* (New York: Macmillan Company, 1906), 160.

3. Albert Bigelow Paine, *Mark Twain: A Biography, the Personal and Literary Life of Samuel Langhorne Clemens,* vol. 3 (New York: Harper and Brothers, 1912), 1166–71. By the 1890s, Hannibal had become the "fourth-largest lumber center in America" and had twelve lumber mills. In Hannibal, by 1904, "there were four banks, three shoe factories, a newly opened public library, the largest Portland cement plant in the world, twelve cigar factories, two breweries, one hundred twelve factories, [and] a street-car system." See Ron Powers, *White Town Drowsing* (Boston: Atlantic Monthly Press, 1986), 14–15. A number of other books recount Hannibal's history. The many volumes produced by Roberta and J. Hurley Hagood, including *The Story of Hannibal* (1976), *Hannibal Too: Historic Sketches of Hannibal and Its Neighbors* (1986), and *Hannibal Yesterdays: Historic Stories of Events, People, Landmarks, and Happenings in and near Hannibal* (1992), were very useful in this research. J. Hurley Hagood served for a time as the president of the Mark Twain Home Foundation Board. For an early and brief history of the city of Hannibal and Marion County, see R. I. Holcombe, *History of Marion County, Missouri* (1884; reprint, Hannibal, MO: Marion County Historical Society, 1979).

4. Johnson, *Highways and Byways of the Mississippi Valley,* 161.

5. Ibid., 160–82.

6. See http://www.marktwainmuseum.org/ (accessed January 16, 2012).

7. Jay Rounds, telephone interview by author, July 9, 2008.

8. Many of Clemens's works were autobiographical. He encouraged a connection between his past and his writing. For work of Clemens and his biography, please see the introduction in Twain and Kiskis, *Mark Twain's Own Autobiography.*

9. The site of the house, long thought to have been rented by the Blankenship family, is around the corner from the boyhood home. Because Sam Clemens mentioned Blankenship as a possible source for Huckleberry Finn, locals came to refer to the structure as the "Huck Finn house," until it was razed in 1911. A replica of a portion of this house was constructed on the original site in 2006. See Henry Sweets, "Dedication of the Huckleberry Finn House," *The Fence Painter* 27, no. 4 (2007)

10. Johnson, *Highways and Byways of the Mississippi Valley,* 162–64. According to a 1928 source the "hoochie coochie," "[is] the famous Turkish muscle dance. Barred from nearly all carnivals of the better class." See Percy White, "More About the Language of the Lot," *American Speech* 3, no. 5 (1928): 414. According to another source, "The Chicago World Fair of 1893 gave the widest possible publicity to the new Negro dances . . . the cakewalk, the pasamala, the hoochie koochie, the bully dance and the bombershay" and the dance became similarly popular at the St. Louis World's Fair in 1904. *The Oxford English Dictionary,* s.v. "hoochy-koochy," University of Kansas Libraries: http://dictionary.oed.com.ezproxy2.library.ku.edu/ (accessed October 7, 2008).

11. *Hannibal Courier Post,* June 11, 1911, quoted on the Hannibal Free Public Library's Web site: http://digital.hannibal.lib.mo.us/B0805.htm.

12. As late as 1911, the year that Nellie Smith died, the Huck Finn house was demolished. That same year some Missourians felt that "the place of birth or other places connected with such natives of Missouri as Mark Twain and Eugene Field ought to be suitably marked." See F. A. Sampson, "Scenic and Historic Places in Missouri," *Missouri Historical Review* 11, no. 1 (1912): 147. However, visitors to Hannibal had no trouble finding Clemens's boyhood home. Not all of Johnson's favorite spots were yet "suitably marked."

13. Johnson, *Highways and Byways of the Mississippi Valley,* 162.

14. Paine, *Mark Twain: A Biography,* 1166–71.

15. Mahan quoted in Franklin R. Poage, "Mark Twain Memorials in Hannibal," *Missouri Historical Review* 20, no. 1 (1925): 80.

16. Gregg Andrews writes about Mahan's New South tendencies in his book on Atlas Cement, *City of Dust.* In it, he argues that Mahan "wore many hats . . . and when it came time to putting his own spin on the legacy of Mark Twain, the lines between amateur historian, corporate attorney, and New South promoter at times blurred." Andrews also pointed out that Atlas Cement used Tom Sawyer in an early advertising campaign as a way to cash in on Hannibal's literary history. Gregg Andrews, *City of Dust: A Cement Company in the Land of Tom Sawyer* (Columbia: University of Missouri Press, 1996), 294, 296. On the New South and advertising, see Karen Cox, *Dreaming of Dixie: How the South Was Created in American Popular*

*Culture* (Chapel Hill: University of North Carolina Press, 2011). For the first meaningful history of the New South, see C. Vann Woodward, *Origins of the New South,
1877–1913* (Baton Rouge: Louisiana State University Press, 1951). For a discussion
of myth-making as part of the work of rewriting history in the south, see Paul M.
Gaston, *The New South Creed: A Study in Southern Myth-Making* (New York: Vintage
Books, 1973), and J. William Harris, *The New South: New Histories, Rewriting Histories*
(New York: Routledge, 2008).

17. Andrews, *City of Dust,* 291–94.

18. "Rush Troops to Check Riot; Militia Sent to Ilasco, Mo., Where 1,500 Strik-
ers Threaten Plant," *New York Times,* May 17, 1910.

19. Atlas Portland Cement Company even deployed Mark Twain's image in their
advertising campaigns. See Andrews, *City of Dust,* 300–301.

20. Powers, *White Town Drowsing,* 74.

21. Alexander Nicholas DeMenil, "A Century of Missouri Literature," *Missouri
Historical Review* 15, no. 1 (1920): 74–126, 96–97. In the words of Alexander Nicholas DeMenil in his summary, "A Century of Missouri Literature" in the *Missouri
Historical Review,* "it had always seemed to me impossible that a writer who violated
nearly all the canons of literary art, and whose themes where [*sic*] so thoroughly
commonplace, should become so extensively known and so widely popular as Mark
Twain has become."

22. Brooks's book was one of the first critical studies to take a look at Clemens's
work through the lens of psychology. He found Clemens to be a "natural" artist
thwarted by, among many other obstacles, his domineering pioneer mother. See Van
Wyck Brooks, *The Ordeal of Mark Twain* (New York: E. P. Dutton & Company, 1920),
28–44. Brooks also blamed Clemens's extravagant way of life on his wife, Olivia
Langdon. This view of Clemens did not go unchallenged, but Brooks's critical views
left a long shadow on biographical, psychological, and psychoanalytical readings of
Clemens's work.

23. C. J. Armstrong quoted in Sweets, "The Sculpture's Lessons: Examination of
Tom & Huck," 1. Henry Sweets, "The Sculpture's Lessons: Examination of Tom &
Huck," *The Fence Painter* 2, no. 1 (1982): 1, 3.

24. Andrews's interpretation of Mahan's rhetoric indicates that Mahan did his
best to make Clemens's words match his capitalist motives. *Hannibal Courier Post*
quoted in Andrews, *City of Dust,* 294.

25. George A. Mahan's life was in some ways similar to the life of Sam Clemens.
He, like Clemens, was born outside of Hannibal on a small farm. His parents came
to Missouri from a slaveholding state and were themselves slaveholding farmers
in Marion County, Missouri. See Terrell Dempsey, *Searching for Jim: Slavery in Sam
Clemens's World* (Columbia: University of Missouri Press, 2003), 173–74, J. Hurley
Hagood, Roberta Roland Hagood, Thomas H. Bacon, and C. P. Greene, *Mirror
of Hannibal,* rev. ed. (Hannibal, MO: Hannibal Free Public Library, 1990 [1905]),
367. Although sixteen years younger than Clemens, Mahan, too, left Hannibal for
greater things. Mahan studied law at Washington and Lee University and received
his diploma from Robert E. Lee himself, who was in 1870 still acting president of
the university. After his travels, Mahan returned to Hannibal to practice law. He
married Ida Dulany, the daughter of a local lumber baron, in 1883 and became a

prominent citizen in Hannibal. He was director of the Hannibal National Bank, director of the Hannibal Mutual Loan and Building Association, and president of the Hannibal Chamber of Commerce. In 1887, he was elected to the Missouri State Legislature. He also was a trustee and officer at the Missouri State Historical Society from 1910 until his death in 1936. See Hagood et al., *Mirror of Hannibal,* 367.

26. Dempsey, *Searching for Jim,* xi. In 2001, the City of Hannibal agreed to donate the sign to a local history organization, but found it missing from its storage site. That the sign used the spelling "Niggar" rather than "Nigger" here, I think, indicates the Missouri Historical Society or Mahan's attempt to be suitably historical, by fashioning an older "colonial-sounding" version of the offensive word.

27. The depiction of Jim in *Tom Sawyer* is quite different from the more developed character that Clemens created in *Huck Finn.*

28. Still today at Mount Vernon the tour guides explain that George Washington was conflicted about the practice of slavery and freed his slaves upon his death. But as we know, he only freed his own slaves, while Martha owned enough to keep Mt. Vernon well staffed. See Jennifer L. Eichstedt and Stephen Small, *Representations of Slavery: Race and Ideology in Southern Plantation Museums* (Washington, DC: Smithsonian Institution Press, 2002), and James Oliver Horton and Lois E. Horton, *Slavery and Public History: The Tough Stuff of American Memory* (New York: New Press, Distributed by Norton, 2006).

29. Terrell Dempsey asserts that, "the word is not part of Jim's name in the novel *Huck Finn.* In Hannibal, however, that's how he was known—because that's how all black people were known until very recently." Dempsey, *Searching for Jim,* xi. I should point out that this use of "Nigger" Jim was not limited to Hannibal. In Hartford, Connecticut, where Sam Clemens's adult home is located, preservationists also referred to "Nigger" Jim in the 1930s. A program for a Centennial theater event in Hartford, Connecticut, lists a cast of characters, which include "Nigger Jim," and several productions well into the fifties include Jim played by a white actor in blackface. Hannibal is not alone in its racism or in its depiction of Jim. See the program for the "Pageant of Letters in Hartford" performed at the Town and Country Club on June 17 and 18, 1932, in the *Mark Twain Memorial Scrapbook, 1930–1935* in the institutional records of Mark Twain House and Museum in Hartford, Connecticut.

30. Mark Twain Centennial Committee, *Mark Twain Centennial Announcement Dinner and Broadcast: Program and Menu, Mark Twain Hotel,* ed. Hon. George A. Mahan and Daniel Violette (Hannibal, MO: 1935), 2.

31. See chapter 1 for an account of Dan Violette's role in the petition to keep the "Colored" CCC Company 1743 out of Mark Twain State Park and Florida, Missouri. Dan Violette's father, M. A. "Dad" Violette was the primary instigator in the effort to preserve Sam Clemens's birthplace in Florida.

32. Lloyd Stark quoted in Hagood and Hagood, *Hannibal Yesterdays,* 193.

33. Today the museum is closed New Year's Day, Easter, Thanksgiving, and Christmas.

34. Franklin R. Poage, "Mark Twain Memorials in Hannibal," *Missouri Historical Review* 20, no. 1 (1925): 80–81.

35. Author's emphasis. Donald McKay, "On the Vanishing Trail of Tom Sawyer," *New York Times,* October 27, 1929, 1.

36. Ibid.

37. Ibid. Sid, in *The Adventures of Tom Sawyer,* is Tom's younger half-brother. When Sam Clemens lived in the house, it is likely that he first shared his room with his older brother, Orion, and then later with his younger brother Henry, and perhaps sometimes with both. Here McKay seems to be confusing biography and fiction, something the city and the caretaker probably encouraged.

38. Ibid.

39. By 1929, a good portion of Hannibal's black population had decided to move elsewhere, either north to Chicago and Detroit or across the Mississippi River to towns that were known to be less racist than Hannibal. According to other later accounts, there were at least 3,000 African Americans living in Hannibal in 1946, but this may have also been a result of northern migration. See John A. Winkler, *Mark Twain's Hannibal: Guide and Biography* (Hannibal, MO: Becky Thatcher Book Shop, 1946). Gregg Andrews discusses out-migration of Hannibal's black population between 1900 and 1910 in chapter 1 of his book, *City of Dust,* 9–10.

40. Nicola Watson has argued that "authenticity and uniqueness [at a literary site is] only achieved through the reproduction and dissemination of its likeness." See Watson, *The Literary Tourist,* 63. As the house made its way onto postcards and became illustrated as Tom Sawyer's house over and over again, it is possible that the house came to be more authentically "Tom Sawyer's house," because it was so immediately recognizable through its proliferation in print. Though images of Sam Clemens in front of the house sold as postcards in great numbers, even they couldn't outsell the millions of illustrated editions of the very popular novel.

41. The commission transformed the annual Hannibal Fall Festival into the Mark Twain Fall Festival. Other celebrations included public weddings, quilt shows, and an arts and crafts show. In October 1935, the Burlington Railroad aided by Nina Gabrilowitsch, Sam Clemens's only grandchild, and local winners of the Tom, Huck, and Becky contests, christened the Mark Twain Zephyr in Hannibal. The first all stainless-steel Burlington train had cars named after characters from Clemens's books. The dedication attracted Missouri governor Guy Park and senator Harry S. Truman. See J. Hurley Hagood and Roberta Roland Hagood, *Hannibal Too: Historic Sketches of Hannibal and Its Neighbors,* 1st ed. (Marceline, MO: Walsworth Pub. Co., 1986), 285–90.

42. See HABS documents HABS MO, 64-HANIB, 8 at the Library of Congress. Photos are attributed to Alexander or Paul Piaget.

43. WPA work at places such as the boyhood home came about as a result of the 1935 Historic Sites Act, which was administered through the National Park Services (NPS). The NPS established the Branch of Historic Sites and Buildings to help preserve historic buildings in both private and public hands. See Wallace, *Mickey Mouse History,* 184–85.

44. Although the national register for historic structures did not yet exist in 1937, HABS, a relief program to employ out-of-work architects, cataloged important American architecture in all its forms and styles through photography and detailed survey drawings. Part of the New Deal focus on America included the careful documentation of historic structures. For a discussion of the history of HABS, see John A. Burns, Historic American Buildings Survey/Historic American Engineering

Record and Historic American Landscapes Survey, *Recording Historic Structures,* 2nd ed. (Hoboken, NJ: John Wiley & Sons, 2004). For a classic discussion of the 1930s documentary impulse, see William Stott, *Documentary Expression and Thirties America* (Chicago: University of Chicago Press, 1986).

45. F. T. Russell, Letter to Mrs. Doris L. Hassell, Mark Twain Boyhood Home Archive: Vertical File, "Mark Twain Museum, History of," July 14, 1952, 1.

46. In addition, the WPA mobilized local women and schoolchildren who collected rags and made elaborate rugs so the floors of the house would not be bare.

47. George Washington's birthplace saw its numbers sink from 60,000 visitors in 1940 to 15,000 in 1941. By 1942, only 8,000 visitors toured the park. Seth Bruggeman points out that immediately after the war visitor numbers quadrupled. Within a few years, most national parks were seeing record numbers of newly mobile postwar consumers. See Bruggeman, *Here, George Washington Was Born,* 117–19.

48. The caretakers at the boyhood home usually made most of their living by running a small souvenir business out of the house and later the museum. With the onset of World War II, the caretakers were unable to find and purchase souvenirs to sell at the house, and with increased visitation they were not able to keep them in stock for long.

49. Morris Anderson and Mark Twain Municipal Board, "Letter: To Honorable Mayor and City Coucil of the City of Hannibal," Hannibal: Mark Twain Boyhood Home and Museum Archives, March 5, 1945, vol. Vertical File "Mark Twain Museum, History of."

50. Sarah Marshall Mahan, George and Ida Mahan's daughter-in-law, purchased the land and removed the old buildings there. She planted a rose garden there dedicated to the memory of her husband.

51. For a summary of the various museum properties and how they came to be under the care of the Mark Twain Boyhood Home and Museum, see Mark Twain Museum, *Research: Museum History,* 2006, Mark Twain Boyhood Home and Museum. Available: http://www.marktwainmuseum.org/content/research/museum_history.php (accessed July 15, 2007).

52. See http://www.marktwainmuseum.org/content/research/museum_history.php (accessed July 28, 2008). Some have not recognized the John M. Clemens Justice of the Peace Office as having any historical connection with John M. Clemens or the Clemens family. See the Mark Twain Forum Archives, e-mail by Terrell Dempsey, "Re: Mickey Mouse," *Mark Twain Forum* https://listserv.yorku.ca/cgi-bin/wa?A2=ind0202&L=TWAIN-L&P=R909&I=-3, February 24, 2002 (accessed January 16, 2012).

53. Dr. and Mrs. Orville Grant let the Clemens family live in the small apartment behind the drugstore. This is where John Marshall Clemens died and the family was able to move back into their home at 208 Hill Street only through the financial assistance of a family member from St. Louis.

54. For an excellent and nuanced discussion of the postwar forces that led to the demolition of historic sites across the United States, please see the chapter "Preserving the Past" in Mike Wallace, *Mickey Mouse History,* 177–221.

55. "During his presidency, [Winkler] personally supervised the restoration of the Pilaster House and the moving and placing of the Law Office in the Mark Twain

Historical area. He provided the funds for furnishing and restoration of the Becky Thatcher Home and the book store on the first floor . . . Mr. Winkler, in cooperation with Charles Walker, was responsible for searching and securing furniture for the Mark Twain Boyhood Home, Pilaster House, and Law Office . . . At a National Trust for Historical Preservation [meeting] held in St Louis in 1958, Winkler was presented a silver cup by the organization, 'for his work in connection with Historic Preservation of Mark Twain related buildings in Hannibal.'" Quote from J. Hurley Hagood and Roberta Roland Hagood, *Hannibal Yesterdays: Historic Stories of Events, People, Landmarks, and Happenings in and near Hannibal,* 1st ed. (Marceline, MO: Jostens, 1992), 196.

56. Emphasis in original. George McCue, "Missouri Mecca, 125,000 Visited Mark Twain Home in Hannibal Last Year," *St. Louis Post Dispatch,* January 18, 1953.

57. Ibid.

58. This was lent to the museum by Clara Clemens Gabrilowitsch. When she died, most of the artifacts she had let the museum borrow became the property of the museum. See Winkler, *Mark Twain's Hannibal.*

59. It seems that this particular item has been of great interest to literary pilgrims over the years. See Tom Weilt, "Paying a Visit to the Boyhood Home of Mark Twain in Hannibal, Mo.," *New York Times,* May 4, 1980.

60. John A. Winkler, *Mark Twain's Hannibal: Guide and Biography* (Hannibal, MO: Becky Thatcher Book Shop, 1946), 9.

61. Ibid., 5.

62. Ibid.

63. Interest in and tourism to sites of where the history of slavery is particularly poignant is something that current work on slavery and tourism in the Unites States has just begun to study. See sociological account by Eichstedt and Small, *Representations of Slavery.* See also the practical guide to current issues in the field by Horton and Horton, *Slavery and Public History.* A comprehensive account of the history of slavery tourism in the United States has not yet been written.

64. The new museum building located at 120 North Main Street, two blocks down from the boyhood home, came to the museum as a donation from the Home Board's chairman Herb Parham with matching gifts from Monsanto, the company where he was a longtime employee. The Becky Thatcher House, long owned by John Winkler, son-in-law to Dulany Mahan, and operated as a gift shop for tourists over several decades, was finally purchased by the museum in 2001. The property on which the newly built replica of "Huck Finn's House" was donated to the museum in 2001. See Web site (http://www.marktwainmuseum.org/index.php/research/museum-history) for a complete list of historic properties and their acquisition.

65. Twain, *The Innocents Abroad,* 175–77. On November 2, 1967, Winkler made the final payment for the mannequins for the law office. The total for the last law office mannequin payment was $976.25. The scene that the city last paid for was described on the invoice as, "Red-haired Sam Clemens with expression of horror looking at figure of man who had been stabbed in breast and whose body had been carried into room and laid on floor unbeknownst to Sam." Jerry Roth Associates created the figures especially for the museum. They were installed on November 2, 1967. The one-page invoice was found in the "Mark Twain Museum, History of"

vertical file of the Mark Twain Boyhood Home and Museum Archive. Winkler paid for these, and perhaps for all of the figures, himself.

66. What is left of these displays are slated for removal as the Mark Twain Boyhood Home and Museum has marked the Becky Thatcher House, the Justice of the Peace Office, and Grant's drugstore for structural preservation and new interpretative plans.

67. Mary Poletti, "Mark Twain Museum Closes Former Drugstore, Hopes to Undertake Complete Renovation," *Quincy Herald Whig,* June 14, 2011.

68. The year 1990 was the last time any of the exhibits in the upstairs of Grant's drugstore were refurbished. The Jane Clemens Neighbors paid to have new clothing made for the mannequins. See Henry Sweets, "New Garments for Pilaster House," *The Fence Painter* 10, no. 1 (1990).

69. George Gable Weight, "'Huck' and 'Tom' and 'Mark' in Hannibal, Mo.," *New York Times,* July 31, 1960.

70. Charles Bridgham Hosmer, *Presence of the Past: A History of the Preservation Movement in the United States before Williamsburg* (New York: Putnam, 1965), 866–73.

71. This is the subject of chapter 3.

72. One of Hannibal's first histories was commissioned in anticipation of the bicentennial and came out in 1976. See J. Hurley Hagood and Roberta Roland Hagood, *The Story of Hannibal* (Hannibal, MO: Hannibal Bicentennial Commission, 1976).

73. Henry Sweets, discussion with author, August 2, 2007.

74. Sweets was the first trained historian to be on staff at the museum. His training as a historian should have exposed him to historiography that dealt with the new social history and movements to include working-class, women, non-white historical subjects in the broad strokes of U.S. history.

75. Wilson H. Faude, telephone interview by author, November 13, 2008.

76. Henry Sweets, "Mark Twain Home and Museum," *Journal of the West* 19, no. 1 (1980): 76.

77. Mark Twain Home Board, *Statement of Purpose* (Hannibal, MO: Mark Twain Home Foundation, 1987).

78. Regina Faden, telephone interview by author, July 8, 2008.

79. Powers, *White Town Drowsing,* 105.

80. Ibid. Ron Powers also wrote other books about his hometown, including the 2001 account, *Tom and Huck Don't Live Here Anymore: Childhood and Murder in the Heart of America.* He coauthored *Flags of Our Fathers* (2002) with James Bradley, and cowrote portions of the Clint Eastwood feature film of the same name. His reflections on his childhood in Hannibal have provided leads for much of the research for this chapter.

81. Powers, *White Town Drowsing,* 58.

82. This theme park scheme is worthy of a chapter in itself. Thankfully, Ron Powers has written a thorough and biting account of its planning and ultimate failure in his *White Town Drowsing.* Here are some of the highlights. In the theme park the "defining glory of that entire project—indeed, its justification for existing—would lie in that 150-acre array of ingenious arcades, attraction, and period-pieces curiosities designed to re-create the mood of Mark Twain's

era in American life," 128–29. "There would be a courthouse and a hanging tree, where mock trials and hangings would entertain the pilgrims. There would be an active nondenominational church suitable for actual tourist weddings and christenings, there would be a Judge Thatcher's Barbecue (named in honor of Becky Thatcher's father in *The Adventures of Tom Sawyer;* Becky herself would be commemorated by a Strawberry 'n' Cream Shop). There would be a Huck's Sandwich Shanty, not to mention Tom's Ship Shop, there would be a stagecoach depot and an Aunt Polly's Vegetable Garden (food services would include such vegetables as watermelon, apples, and peaches), a Tom 'n' Huck's fishing hole, a primitive-weapons display, and a Halley's Comet mine shaft and planetarium. There would be a haunted riverboat and a shooting gallery video arcade" (129). Powers, *White Town Drowsing.*

83. Marjorie Benders quoted in Powers, *White Town Drowsing,* 111.

84. Powers, *White Town Drowsing,* 142.

85. Ibid., 68.

86. Henry Sweets, "Viewing Gallery Project Underway at Boyhood Home," *The Fence Painter* 4, no. 4 (1984/1985): 1–2.

87. This kind of restoration work, on a much grander scale, had already been completed at Mark Twain's Hartford Home, which will be discussed in the next chapter. The Hartford house was one of the largest projects of its kind, because of the elaborate refurbishment of Gilded Age details. The restoration of the Hartford house (1955–1978) may have set very high standards for the production at Hannibal. But the boyhood home faced very different restoration problems from Hartford. There is almost no documentation of the Hannibal house from the period of its occupation by the Clemens family—no photos, no architectural drawings, or correspondence about the building of the structure and the materials used, and no catalogue of furnishings. These items all helped the Mark Twain Memorial and Library Commission in Hartford determine restoration principles. Other small historic sites in the United States were beginning to see historical archeology as a useful pursuit, not only to uncover details for in-depth restorations, but because artifacts and the process of change itself attracted tourists.

88. Powers, *White Town Drowsing,* 213–14.

89. See Henry Sweets, "Archaeological Findings," *The Fence Painter* 5, no. 1 (1985). For an account of Richard Guyette's dendrochronology report, see Henry Sweets, "Update on Mark Twain Boyhood Home Restoration Research," *The Fence Painter* 8, no. 2 (1988).

90. Albert Bigelow Paine, *Mark Twain: A Biography,* vol. 3 (New York: Harper and Brothers, 1912), 1168.

91. Cotton had been part of the project from the beginning. He devised the viewing platform solution for the boyhood home so it could stay open during the sesquicentennial celebrations. In 1988, he was rehired to complete the historic restoration. See the discussion of the viewing platform in Henry Sweets, "Viewing Gallery Project Underway at Boyhood Home," *The Fence Painter* 4, no. 4 (1984/1985). See also, Henry Sweets, "Mark Twain Boyhood Home Restoration Raises Questions," *The Fence Painter* 8, no. 1 (1988).

92. Sweets, discussion.

93. Henry Sweets, "Boyhood Home Uncovered," *The Fence Painter* 11, no. 1 (1991)

94. Sweets, discussion.

95. Shelley Fisher Fishkin, *Lighting out for the Territory: Reflections on Mark Twain and American Culture* (New York: Oxford University Press, 1996), 25–26.

96. The new museum and its renovation and exhibition design was largely funded by Herb Parham and his employer Monsanto. Henry Sweets, discussion with author, August 2, 2007.

97. See Henry Sweets, "Tom and Becky Are Fifty," *The Fence Painter* 25, no. 3 (2005). The contest still goes on today, although the categories on which contestants may be judged has been expanded a tad. In 2006, the museum and the city added a Huck Finn contest to their slate of Mark Twain summer activities. The winner receives a new bicycle and "was open to area boys and girls ages 8–12." Henry Sweets, "Huck Finn Festival a Hot Time," *The Fence Painter* 27, no. 5 (2007).

98. Fishkin, *Lighting out for the Territory,* 13–67.

99. Ibid., 30.

100. I understand Fishkin's expectations. I had only read *The Adventures of Huckleberry Finn* while in a college honors English class and had little to no exposure to Twain's writing before. My English course followed not long after the release of Fishkin's book and the mainstream interpretive shift to seeing *Huck Finn* as a breakthrough text in both technique—through the dialect voice of Huck—and as a novel that responded critically to the racism during the period in which it was written (1885).

101. For an excellent discussion of this turn, see the first chapter of Claudia Stokes, *Writers in Retrospect: The Rise of American Literary History, 1875–1910* (Chapel Hill: University of North Carolina Press, 2006).

102. As of January 2008, the shops in Hannibal still sold racist figurines and salt and pepper shakers and all kinds of regalia from both sides of the Civil War, but I have not noticed a single bull whip any time I have visited Hannibal.

103. Fishkin, *Lighting out for the Territory,* 20.

104. Ibid., 19.

105. Ibid., 24.

106. It is interesting to note that Fishkin looks for the authentic Hannibal of Clemens's time, too. Much like some of the tourists' accounts we have seen before, she seeks a connection to him by wading into the waters of the Mississippi River. There she tried to imagine the city's landing crawling with freedmen working the boats, much as illustrator Donald McKay did nearly fifty years before.

107. Faye Bleigh quoted in Fishkin, *Lighting out for the Territory,* 34–35.

108. Dempsey, *Searching for Jim.*

109. Terrell Dempsey, telephone interview by author, July 12, 2008.

110. Tom Quirk, Public Remarks, Mark Twain Boyhood Home and Museums, Hannibal, Missouri, June 16, 2007.

111. Dempsey, telephone interview.

112. The building the Mark Twain Home Foundation acquired for a new museum was a massive old department store two blocks away from the boyhood home. The foundation board and Henry Sweets began the process of outlining exactly what they wanted in the museum space, which was to be devoted to Sam

Clemens's writing rather than his biography. To help them brainstorm the museum foundation brought in a panel of Mark Twain scholars.

113. Mark Twain Home Foundation, *Master Plan for Site Use, Interpretation and Exhibitions, Revised and Updated* (Hannibal, MO: Mark Twain Museum, 2006), 5.

114. Rounds, telephone interview. Unfortunately, I have not accessed the raw data that these studies collected, but instead have only the summarized reports included in the master plan form. Mark Twain Home Foundation, *Master Plan for Site Use, Interpretation and Exhibitions, Revised and Updated* (Hannibal, MO: Mark Twain Museum, 2006).

115. Rounds, telephone interview.

116. Ibid.

117. Ibid.

118. Ibid.

119. Mark Twain Home Foundation, *Master Plan for Site Use, Interpretation and Exhibitions,* and Rounds, interview.

120. Mark Twain Home Foundation, *Master Plan for Site Use, Interpretation and Exhibitions.*

121. Ibid.

122. "Mark Twain Museum Seeks to Add $10 Million to Edowment," *Associated Press,* July 8, 2009. Though the museum had begun raising funds for the renovation of the Becky Thatcher House several years ago, this summer with the departure of Regina Faden at Historic St. Mary's City, Maryland, the new director Cindy Lovell rejuvenated the campaign. See "Mark Twain Museum Seeks to Add $10 Million to Endowment" and Cindy Lovell, "Looking for a Few Tom Sawyers," *Hannibal Courier Post,* July 22, 2009.

123. Betsy Taylor, "Mo. Museum Works to Save Becky Thatcher House," *Associated Press,* August 1, 2008.

124. Faden, telephone interview.

125. See Regina Faden, "Museums and Race: Living up to the Public Trust," *Museums and Social Issues: A Journal of Reflective Discourse* 2, no. 1 (2007) and "Presenting Mark Twain: Keeping the Edge Sharp," *Mark Twain Annual* 6, no. 1 (2008).

126. See Roy Rosenzweig and David P. Thelen, *The Presence of the Past: Popular Uses of History in American Life* (New York: Columbia University Press, 1998).

127. Henry Sweets, "Dedication of the Huckleberry Finn House," *The Fence Painter* 27, no. 4 (2007): 1.

128. Henry Sweets, e-mail correspondence with the author, July 15, 2011.

## Chapter Three

1. She was disappointed that Clemens and his family were concerned with the material trappings of his age. Most readers who encounter Twain, know only the stories of Tom Sawyer and Huck Finn and sometimes assume that the crafter of these tales must have always lived among such settings. You can see why the boyhood home in Hannibal has been such a success over the years. It confirms some of the visitors' strongest assumptions about Clemens.

2. The house was designed by architect Edward Tuckerman Potter (b. 1831). See Sarah Bradford Landau, *Edward T. and William A. Potter: American Victorian Architects,* Outstanding Dissertations in the Fine Arts (New York: Garland, 1979). Potter was known largely for his ecclesiastical architecture. The Clemens house may be all that remains of Potter's domestic architecture (he had also designed the now lost George and Lily Warner house nearby). Edward Potter designed many of Lehigh University's original buildings and laid out the campus design in the 1850s. He built numerous Episcopal churches throughout New York, Connecticut, and Florida. He was early on influenced by Richard Upjohn, the architect most responsible for the Gothic Revival in the United States, and Potter was a member of Upjohn's firm before he branched out on his own. Most of the surviving churches that Potter designed share many of the same elements as the Clemens house. The buildings have elaborate brickwork and colorful slate tile roof designs. It is important to note that the Clemens house, though largely designed by Potter, was based on Olivia Clemens's sketches. She indicated where she wanted certain rooms based on the grounds. For a brief account of Olivia Langdon Clemens's design ideas for the Hartford house, see Susan K. Harris, *The Courtship of Olivia Langdon and Mark Twain,* Cambridge Studies in American Literature and Culture (New York: Cambridge University Press, 1996), 170–71.

3. See chapter 2 for a brief discussion of Rockwell's illustrations based on Clemens's boyhood home in Hannibal, Missouri.

4. Second only to Mystic Seaport, which is a reconstructed seaport and village.

5. You have two options at the ticket counter, to tour the house or to also tour the servants' quarters on a separate tour.

6. There are exhibits in the visitors' center, some permanent, some visiting. Two permanent exhibits exist: one on Louis Comfort Tiffany and one on printing that seems to be geared for children.

7. There are a few pieces that stand out as simple, including a desk that belonged to Clemens's mother in the dining room and the furniture in the girls' rooms.

8. The two windows were also designed to commemorate the construction of the house and engraved with a design that integrates objects associated with Clemens, including pipes, steins, a bottle of champagne, pool cues, and a central letter "C" with the date of the house's completion, 1874. See the HABS photos at the Library of Congress to find details of these windows.

9. I asked staff at the Mark Twain House and Museum why they had a separate tour for this part of the house. Their answers all revealed it was a practical decision. As it is, a tour through the main part of the house takes between forty-five minutes to an hour. Most visitors cannot comfortably add on another forty-five minutes for an in-depth tour of the servants' quarters. In addition, the servants' quarters include the kitchen and other smaller service areas of the house that accommodate fewer visitors in the space per tour; only ten to twelve visitors can make their way through these spaces efficiently, whereas eighteen normally make their way through the main house. The kitchen and servants' quarters were restored at a slightly later date, so they were not historically part of the main tour. To be fair, the guides do work in stories about George Griffin and the carriage driver and his family into the main tour. It does seem that staff has tried to integrate the

upstairs/downstairs divide in the house. Patti Philippon, discussion with author, July 12, 2011.

10. Bill Brown, *A Sense of Things: The Object Matter of American Literature* (Chicago: University of Chicago Press, 2003), 21.

11. Charles Hopkins Clark, "The Charter Oak City," *Scribner's Monthly*, 1876, 2. See Kerry Driscoll, "Mark Twain's Music Box: Livy, Cosmopolitanism, and the Commodity Aesthetic," *Cosmopolitan Twain*, ed. Ann M. Ryan and Joseph B. McCullough (Columbia: University of Missouri Press, 2008).

12. "The Preposterous New House That Mark Twain Built: Hartford Letter to the Springfield Union," *Daily Rocky Mountain News,* October 25, 1873. This particular account was reprinted in newspapers across the United States including the Little Rock, Arkansas, *Daily Republican, Daily Evening News* in San Francisco, *Georgia Weekly Telegraph, Georgia Journal and Messenger,* and mostly likely many other local papers.

13. *Hartford Daily Times,* March 23, 1874.

14. "Mark Twain's House," *Advertiser,* January 30, 1874. This review in particular echoes or foreshadows decades of critical work on Mark Twain and the "American" nature of his rhetorical styling.

15. Mark Twain, Harriet Elinor Smith, Benjamin Griffin, Victor Fischer, Michael B. Frank, Sharon K. Goetz, Leslie Diane Myrick, and Bancroft Library, *Autobiography of Mark Twain* (Berkeley and Los Angeles: University of California Press, 2010), 247.

16. "Sam Clemens to Olivia Langdon Clemens, 3 July 1874," Hartford, Conn. (UCCL 01105), 2002, 2007. http://www.marktwainproject.org/xtf/view?docId=letters/UCCL01105.xml;style=letter;brand=mtp (accessed January 24, 2012).

17. Although the house was not considered a monstrosity by the Clemenses' educated near neighbors, it is clear that other educated people in the area found the house gauche. The lasting perception of the house as ugly contributed to the difficulty that Katharine Seymour Day had preserving it.

18. "John Calvin's Bust in Mark Twain's House," *Boston Daily Advertiser,* November 8, 1876.

19. Isabella Hooker quoted in Driscoll, "Mark Twain's Music Box," 145.

20. "Mark Twain at Home," *The American Socialist: Devoted to the Enlargement and Perfection of Home,* January 11, 1877.

21. See Driscoll's review of other Nook Farm homes, including Charles Dudley Warner's house in Driscoll, "Mark Twain's Music Box," 148.

22. Driscoll argues the trip was certainly not only about outfitting their house, but also about ensuring that Clemens had the appropriate worldly education made necessary by his status. It was on this trip Clemens attempted to learn German. Her overarching argument is that this was to ensure that the Clemenses had all the necessary cosmopolitan qualities to feel comfortable in their Hartford circle and beyond. Driscoll uses the music box that Olivia Clemens picked out in Geneva for Sam Clemens's birthday as vehicle to discuss the Clemenses anxiety about class, culture, and sophistication. The Mark Twain House & Museum acquired a music box, through a gift from a neighbor, approximating the original's design and age to complete the house. The museum staff had the music box restored to working

4

order, but no longer plays it for visitors. Patti Philippon, discussion with author, July 12, 2011.

23. The Clemenses had even brought back with them to Hartford a sapling from "the Shakespeare Mulberry." See chapter 1 for a longer discussion of the Shakespeare mulberry. It had been a literary tourist memento for decades and had the status equal to that of the "true cross" with certain pilgrims to Stratford. Likewise, William Willard, a Hartford resident, carved elaborate memorial canes from a tree that came down on the Clemens house grounds. The Mark Twain House and Museum has a small collection of these canes in their archives. Each cane celebrates Twain and his literature but also is inscribed with personal messages for the cane's original recipient. Although these canes were not sold as tourism mementos, they have had a lively second life among Twain collectors and collectors of outsider art.

24. Watson, *The Literary Tourist,* 9.

25. See Ann Rigney, "Abbotsford: Dislocation and Cultural Remembrance," *Writers' Houses and the Making of Memory,* ed. Harald Hendrix (New York: Routledge, 2008). Washington Irving's writings on Abbotsford and Scott contributed to Abbotsford's popularity among American tourists (See Washington Irving, William Lukens Shoemaker, Robert Lowell, and William Harris Arnold, *Abbotsford and Newstead Abbey: The Crayon Miscellany* (Philadelphia: Carey, Lea & Blanchard, 1835).

26. Ostego Hall was lost to fire in 1853.

27. See Erin Hazard, "The Author's House: Abbotsford and Wayside," in *Literary Tourism and Nineteenth-Century Culture,* ed. Nicola Watson (New York: Palgrave Macmillan, 2009), 63–72, 68.

28. Powers, *Mark Twain: A Life,* 337. One of the Abbotsford editions was given to Olivia Langdon Clemens's mother and the other made it onto their shelves in Hartford.

29. Clemens quoted in George Parsons Lathrop, "A Model State Capital," *Harper's Magazine,* October 1885, 731.

30. Kerry Driscoll points out that the Clemenses' European trip to collect these items was actually a cost-cutting measure. Similar goods in the United States would have been prohibitively expensive for the Clemenses.

31. Lathrop, "A Model State Capital," 715–34. Lathrop was himself a poet and accomplished writer and most likely regularly was acquainted with Clemens. Lathrop was also married to Nathaniel Hawthorne's daughter, Rose, and thus is acquainted with several literary households. Interestingly, Nathaniel Hawthorne visited Abbotsford twice and was not inspired to remake his own home, but rather he became more certain than ever to keep his privacy and solace in his home at Wayside in Concord. See Hazard, "The Author's House: Abbotsford and Wayside."

32. Parsons, "A Model State Capital," 731–32.

33. Ibid., 731.

34. For early American literary tour guidebooks, see *Homes of American Authors: Comprising Anecdotical, Personal, and Descriptive Sketches, by Various Writers* (New York: G. P. Putnam and Co., 1853), Richard Henry Stoddard, *Poets' Homes. Pen and Pencil Sketches of American Poets and Their Homes* (Boston: Lothrop and Company, 1877); Arthur Gilman, *Poets' Homes. Pen and Pencil Sketches of American Poets and Their Homes,* 2nd ed. (Boston: Lothrop, 1879); and Richard Henry Stoddard, *The Homes*

*and Haunts of Our Elder Poets* (New York: D. Appleton and Company, 1881). Bacon's 1902 edition is the first guide where I have found the Hartford house listed.

35. Nicola Watson has argued that the first real literary tourist destination outside of the graves of writers was, of course, Shakespeare's birthplace in Stratford, which gained popularity with Richard Garrick's 1769 celebration the Shakespeare Jubilee. But even this elaborate celebration did not cement the birthplace in the minds of English men and women as much as seeing images of Shakespeare's birthplace reproduced in print. She argued its canonical tourist status "was only achieved through the reproduction and dissemination of its likeness." She goes on to say that an "engraving in the *Gentleman's Magazine* . . . linked the Birthplace and the Shakespeare you might read at home together within print culture." Much like the images that circulated in *Harper's* and elsewhere, it is likely that visitors had a sense of the Twain house before they got there. Watson, *The Literary Tourist,* 63.

36. Edwin M. Bacon, *Literary Pilgrimages in New England: To the Homes of Famous Makers of American Literature and among Their Haunts and the Scenes of Their Writings* (New York: Silver, Burdett and Company, 1902), 473.

37. It is likely that staff at the house may have facilitated a tour in the Clemenses' absence.

38. Bacon, *Literary Pilgrimages in New England,* 474.

39. Harald Hendrix, "Writers' Houses as Media of Expression and Remembrance: From Self-Fashioning to Cultural Memory," in *Writers' Houses and the Making of Memory,* ed. Harald Hendrix (New York: Routledge, 2007), 1–14.

40. See Sam and Olivia Clemens's correspondence on the house in the Mark Twain Papers.

41. The Clemens girls often used the house as a stage for performances, including occasionally their father's work. Powers, *Mark Twain: A Life,* 500.

42. On cost of living, see Clark, "The Charter Oak City," 2.

43. "Samuel Clemens to F. G. Whitmore, Roverdale, [April 5, 1903]," Mark Twain House and Museum Archive. Each word underlined was emphatically underscored twice by Clemens. A thousand dollars a month was a significant amount of money to spend on maintaining a house he did not live in.

44. Walter Schwinn, "The House That Mark Built" (Hartford, CT: Mark Twain House and Museum Archives, n.d.), 210–12.

45. Emile Henry Gauvreau, *My Last Million Readers* (New York: E. P. Dutton & Co., 1941), 79.

46. It is interesting to note that Willie O. Burr lived next-door to the Twain and Stowe houses on the corner of Farmington Avenue and Forest Street in what would someday come to be called the Chamberlin-Burr Day House, which is now the headquarters for the Harriet Beecher Stowe Center. Burr was the editor and owner of the *Hartford Daily Times,* the *Hartford Courant's* main competitor. There is little evidence that Burr was concerned with the preservation of the Twain house, though his paper did report on the preservation efforts. He, however, unlike Gauvreau, did not make a public plea that the house be saved even though it shared a yard with him. See the Stowe Center's Web site for information on the Chamberlin-Burr Day House. http://www.harrietbeecherstowecenter.org/visit/dayhouse.shtml (accessed June 14, 2009).

47. Gauvreau, *My Last Million Readers,* 80–82.

48. See among others Bob Tedeschi, "Writers Unite to Keep Twain House Afloat," *New York Times,* September 21, 2008, and Julia M. Klein, "Mark Twain Museum Is in Deep Water," the *Wall Street Journal,* September 18, 2008. It is interesting that both authors use the common boat on water metaphor in their article titles, since so many have believed the house was designed after a steamboat.

49. Day's mother, Alice Beecher Hooker Day, had been a close friend of Olivia Langdon Clemens during her years in Hartford, and though Day's sights were set on Stowe's legacy, the Clemens's legacy in Hartford was intertwined. At least two branches of the Beecher-extended family settled in Hartford. The Clemenses came to the neighborhood later, but they came in part because of their familiarity and closeness with the Beecher family members who lived in Elmira, New York. There, where Olivia Langdon had been raised, her family attended Thomas Beecher's church. Isabella Beecher Hooker (Day's grandmother) and Thomas Beecher were the children of Lyman Beecher and his second wife, Harriet Porter; whereas Henry Ward Beecher, Harriet Beecher Stowe, and Catherine Beecher were all children of Lyman Beecher with his first wife, Roxana Foote.

50. Katharine Day was the daughter of Alice Beecher Hooker Day and the granddaughter of Isabella Beecher Hooker, the feminist founder of New England Women's Suffrage Association and free-love advocate. See Allison Sneider, *Suffragists in an Imperial Age: U.S. Expansion and the Woman Question, 1870–1929* (New York: Oxford University Press, 2008), 41. See also Katharine Seymour Day, "Diary, 1896 May 30–August 29, Diary [Incomplete]," *Katharine Seymour Day Collection* (Hartford, CT: Harriet Beecher Stowe Center, 1896).

51. See Walter Schwinn, "The House That Mark Built," 253–54, and Dawn C. Adiletta, "Katharine Seymour Day, 1870–1964: Painter—Gardener—Activist" (Hartford, CT: Harriet Beecher Stowe Center, 2001). Day studied psychology, then a new field, and philosophy at Radcliffe and history and political science at Berkeley (University of California); she also studied anthropology with Frank Boas at Columbia University in New York. It seemed that in her forties, wherever she went, she enrolled in college classes. She also took classes at the Sorbonne. In 1936, at age sixty-six, Day completed a master's degree in English at Trinity College in Hartford. Her thesis, "Mark Twain's First Years in Hartford and Personal Memories of the Clemens Family," Trinity College, 1936, provided much of the initial background research on Sam Clemens's life in Hartford. Katharine Seymour Day is well worth an extensive biography. Her mother, Alice Day, resided in the Clemens's Hartford house for a few months in 1895 when her own house was still occupied after a trip to Europe. It is possible that Katharine Seymour Day visited there with her and certainly knew the house well. See Resa Willis, *Mark and Livy: The Love Story of Mark Twain and the Woman Who Almost Tamed Him* (New York: Routledge, 2003), 220–21.

52. For a discussion of American Ladies Historical Associations, the first place to start is with Ann Pamela Cunningham and the other women she inspired to join the Mount Vernon Ladies Association. See West, *Domesticating History.* See also Caroline E. Janney, *Burying the Dead but Not the Past: Ladies' Memorial Associations and the Lost Cause* (Chapel Hill: University of North Carolina Press, 2008) for an extended historical context. For a discussion of women's costumed teas at sanitary fairs (the

precursor in some ways to ladies' historical associations), see Karal Ann Marling, *George Washington Slept Here: Colonial Revivals and American Culture, 1876–1986* (Cambridge, MA: Harvard University Press, 1988), 76.

53. Katharine Seymour Day, "To Alice (Hooker) Day." Harriet Beecher Stowe Center: Katharine Seymour Day Collection, 1926 [no date], 2. It seems she was at least as interested in collecting material by *all* the Beechers as she was in Harriet Beecher Stowe. Though, of course, it is likely that she thought of Stowe primarily as a Beecher.

54. Ibid. Likely Mrs. Slade intended to contact Dr. Ida Langdon, professor of literature at Elmira College.

55. Clara Langdon, "Letter to the Editor," *Hartford Courant,* May 17, 1928. As far as I can tell, Clara Langdon was not related to Olivia Langdon Clemens.

56. See Mary Shipman's handwritten notes about her time on the board of trustees at the Mark Twain House and Museum Archives. Here she described how Victorian architecture "positively revolted most people" in Hartford and how "they disliked the style of architecture so much that they couldn't believe that it had any historic value." Mary Shipman, Manuscript (Hartford, CT: Mark Twain House and Museum Archives, n.d.), 5.

57. The mortgage amount varies in the notes of the association and in how it is reported in the press. It is clear that the mortgage was at least this much; it may well have been more. They seem to have raised a total of $101,093.35 by June 1929 according to a note included in the earliest Scrapbook in the Archives of the Mark Twain House and Museum from 1919 to 1929.

58. Connecticut State Assembly, *Charter (April 29, 1929) Substitute for House Bill No. 574, 224. An Act Incorporating the Mark Twain Library and Commission* (Hartford, 1929).

59. Schwinn, "The House That Mark Built." Having tenants helped the commission stay afloat, and tenants occasionally saved the house from disaster, as was the case when a storm damaged the roof and caused a massive flood in 1943. See Mark Twain Memorial & Library Commission, "Report of the House Committee, Minutes of the Trustees' Meeting of the Mark Twain Library and Memorial Commission" (Hartford, CT: Mark Twain House and Museum Archives, October 28, 1943).

60. Despite her feminist roots, Day seems to have believed that the Mark Twain Memorial and Library Commission should be presided over by a man. She may have believed that male leadership gave the organization a more professional standing in the community and distinguished it from sentimental ladies' organizations.

61. There may have been 1 three-thousand-dollar bequest from the estate of a former board member during Day's tenure specifically to be used on the principle. In 1932, after the stock market crash, the bank that held their mortgage closed its doors and their debt moved to a new bank as they still struggled to make their payments. At one point, the cash-strapped board was forced to take on another loan to make major repairs to the house and took on a note from one of the board members for five thousand dollars.

62. Some of the fund-raising events that Day organized included engaging Winston Churchill to speak. Day sold a block of tickets in hopes of raising funds for the house on January 31, 1932; see Katharine Seymour Day, "Miss Day's Notes on the

Mark Twain House" (Hartford: Mark Twain House and Museum Archives, 1954). By all accounts the Churchill's lecture, "The Destiny of English Speaking People," was a success, but after all was said and done, the Mark Twain Museum and Library Commission brought in only $350.70. See Mark Twain Memorial and Library Commission, "Minutes of the Trustees' Meeting" (Hartford, CT: Mark Twain House and Museum Archives, February 16, 1932).

Day also believed that any "educational" program might be used to bring in much-needed funds for the memorial. In 1933, she engaged Professor Edward Humphrey from Trinity College to run a series of seminars at the house for which a commission charged an admission. The topics he covered ranged from "Hitler's Third Reich: Glorified Intolerance" to "Paul Valery and French Intellectual Supremacy." Humphrey put together a second lecture series for 1934. A flier for his seminar series in the fall of 1933 can be found in the archives at the Mark Twain House and Museum see "An Author's House a Pleasant Evening with Thomas Hardy," *Inter Ocean,* March 20, 1892.

63. For a discussion of the importance of community pageants at the turn of the century and their professional production in the 1930s, see David Glassberg, *American Historical Pageantry: The Uses of Tradition in the Early Twentieth Century* (Chapel Hill: University of North Carolina Press, 1990). Glassberg argues that by the 1930s the country's collective rage for pageantry was largely over, and the production of community pageants had become so professionalized that the experiential celebration was lost for most participants (248). Charlotte Perkins Gilman lived nearby in Norwich, Connecticut and was on hand for a number of Day's fund-raising events, despite her aversion to the glorification of traditional ideas of home that constrained women's roles. See "Introductory" in Charlotte Perkins Gilman, *The Home: Its Work and Influence* (New York: Charlton Company, 1910).

64. *Pageant of Letters in Hartford* was produced and arranged by Miss Inez Temple and performed at the Town and Country Club on June 17 and 18, 1932. A program from the event, along with photographs of the cast in costume can be found in the *Mark Twain Memorial: M.T.M. Scrapbook, 1930–1935* at the Mark Twain House and Museum Archive.

65. See coverage of this particular event in "'Living Book Reviews' Get Presentation: Tableaus Given at Mark Twain Memorial Garden Party with Aid of Branch Library," *Hartford Courant,* June 8, 1939. See also its coverage in "Books Come to Life in Presentations at Twain's House," *Hartford Times,* June 8, 1939. For photographs of the event, including Day and Holcome in costume, see the Mark Twain House and Museum Archives, Mark Twain Memorial and Library Commission, *M.T.M. Scrapbook, 1935–1954* (Hartford, CT: Mark Twain House and Museum Archives). Sarah Wheeler's Living Book Reviews were popular at other venues as well. See "Book Lovers See 'Living Reviews'; Tableaux Depicting Poems Are Part of Literary Tea at R. S. Reynold's Home," *New York Times,* September 25, 1937.

66. Inez Temple was singled out in 1921 for the honor of writing and producing the pageant for the annual meeting of the Sons and Daughters of the American Revolution that was held in Hartford. Her pageant, "The Spiritual Interchange of Nations," met great reviews and was thought to have done "great work" toward educating "new Americans" and the "foreign women of Hartford" about American

history and the United States' relationships with other nations. See *Daughters of the American Revolution Magazine* 55, no. 9 (1921): 349. Temple's plays were eventually published in Inez Temple, *Pageants Past,* ed. Ruth Wyllys (Hartford, CT: Hartford Chapter of the Daughters of the American Revolution, 1940).

67. Clemens's admiration of minstrel performance has made him the subject of many contemporary studies of blackface and minstrelsy and its cultural meaning in the United States. Eric Lott, in *Love and Theft: Blackface Minstrelsy and the American Working Class* (New York: Oxford University Press, 1993), points out that black-face was not simple. As much as blackface was a racist performance of offensive stereotypes, it was also a vehicle where these images could be deployed to critique the status quo, and often included critiques of local and national politics of white supremacy. See, in particular, the first chapter of *Love and Theft* for Lott's discussion of Twain and minstrelsy and chapter 8 for his discussion of *Uncle Tom's Cabin* in blackface. Day may have been inspired by the many performances of *Uncle Tom's Cabin* that circulated in her youth as part of the minstrel circuit.

68. Laurence Vail Coleman, *Historic House Museums* (Washington, D.C.: American Association of Museums, 1933), 18. For a brief history of the American Association of Museums, see Ellen Hick's "The AAM after 72 Years," *Museum News* (May/June 1978): 44–48. For a discussion of Coleman's contribution to the professionalization of museums, see Ronald F. Lee, *The Origin and Evolution of the National Military Park Idea* (Washington, D.C.: National Park Service, 1973), http://www.nps.gov/history/history/online_books/history_military/nmpidea2.htm (accessed April 8, 2009).

69. Coleman, *Historic House Museums,* 17–21. Coleman was not just visiting because he was interested in Sam Clemens; he, as director of the American Museum Association at the Smithsonian, let the staff there know that he "offered to publish items of interest about the Mark Twain Memorial in the association magazine." See Mark Twain Memorial and Library Commission, "Minutes of the Trustees' Meeting" (Hartford, CT: Mark Twain House and Museum Archives, October 19, 1932). His work at the house was to legitimate their efforts (and his own) and to connect them to the larger house museum movement in the country. There is no doubt that his status required that he get a special tour from Katharine Day herself.

70. Coleman, *Historic House Museums,* 20. Emphasis in the original.

71. While living in the Stowe house, Day planted "colonial-revival style gardens" and saved the Early Republic period "Wadsworth stable." Day worked with other local preservationists to have it moved from downtown Hartford to nearby Lebanon, Connecticut. For an account of Day's effort to preserve the Wadsworth stable (circa 1820) and her other efforts in Hartford urban planning and preservation, see Adiletta, "Katharine Seymour Day, 1870–1964" 1–2. See Wallace, *Mickey Mouse History.*

72. Coleman, *Historic House Museums,* 21. The colonial revival has been investigated by a number of important scholars, and I will not delve too greatly into its trajectory here. See as an introduction, Alan Axelrod and Henry Francis du Pont Winterthur Museum, *The Colonial Revival in America,* 1st ed. (New York: Norton, 1985). See also, Marling, *George Washington Slept Here.*

73. Day also preserved what is now called the "Day house" at the corner of

Farmington Avenue and Forest Street—what was then called the Chamberlin-Burr house. This house now holds the archives for the Harriet Beecher Stowe collection and is where the Stowe Center holds events and has its headquarters. It is filled with items that Day collected during her very long life and artifacts, manuscripts, and letters that the center has collected since her death. The Stowe Center is a first-class research center, just as Day had hoped. As a result of her endowment and the careful management of the collection, the Stowe Center is in excellent financial shape in comparison to its neighbor. The Stowe Center director, Katherine Kane, has made overtures to the Mark Twain House and Museum over the last two years, offering "leadership" during its difficult times.

74. Catharine E. Beecher and Harriet Beecher Stowe, *The American Woman's Home* (New Brunswick, NJ: Rutgers University Press, 2004). Day many years later reflected upon her work preserving her family's legacy in Hartford. Day asserted that "good ancestry" had guided her. Day quoted in Arman Hatsian, "Katharine S. Day Turns 90," *Hartford Courant,* May 8, 1960, 4. Day was well aware of her own ancestral legacy in Hartford; after all, she was a direct descendant of John Hooker, Hartford's founder. She was also a Beecher, a Seymour, and a Day. Each of these families made their way into volumes outlining Hartford and Connecticut history. Glenn Weaver described Day's family history in his 1982 history of Hartford. Weaver explains the social order of early Hartford, thus, at the top of the eighteenth-century social structure were what he called the "better sort," and which in Connecticut were known as "the Standing Order." These citizens made up 5 to 10 percent of the population and were largely Congregationalists, large landowners, and important merchants. Weaver elaborates that "among these families were the Allyns, the Bunces, the Goodwins, the Hayneses, the Olmsteads, the Pitkins, the Seymours, and the Wadsworths." Glenn Weaver and Connecticut Historical Society, *Hartford: An Illustrated History of Connecticut's Capital,* 1st ed. (Woodland Hills, CA: Windsor Publications, 1982), 35.

75. Of course, Gillman is famous for her own radical domestic literature and progressive feminist housing designs, such as the kitchen-less house. See Gilman, *The Home: Its Work and Influence* (New York: Charlton Company, 1910). See also Dolores Hayden's expert analysis of Gilman's ideas. Dolores Hayden, *The Grand Domestic Revolution: A History of Feminist Designs for American Homes* (Boston: MIT Press, 1982).

76. The only other house museum in operation at the time that was overtly connected with a woman writer was the Orchard house, which told the stories of both Bronson and Louisa May Alcott. For a discussion of the conflicts over whom to celebrate at the Orchard house, see West, *Domesticating History.*

77. Hatsian, "Katharine S. Day Turns 90," 4.

78. See Schwinn, "The House That Mark Built," 261. Schwinn died before he was able to complete the manuscript. Although his focus is primarily on the house while it belonged to the Clemenses, his last chapters were especially useful in outlining a sense of the institutional history of the museum and set me on the track of many useful sources for this chapter. Schwinn was the president of the Mark Twain Memorial and Library Commission in 1952 and had to give up his position to work in Poland for the Foreign Service. He rejoined the Mark Twain Memo-

rial in 1964 as a trustee and then again as president in 1965 for a short period. He remained committed to the Twain house throughout his life. His manuscript is the most comprehensive account of changes in the house. For more information on Schwinn, see the Library of Congress's collection of interviews on the Foreign Service, Walter Schwinn, *Interview with David Courtwright,* ed. Foreign Service History Center of the George Washington University (Hartford, CT: Library of Congress, 1987), http://international.loc.gov/service/mss/mssmisc/mfdip/2005%20txt%20 files/2004sch15.txt (accessed October 2, 2009).

79. Mark Twain's house in Hartford would not have been preserved if it were not for the efforts of Katharine Seymour Day. Almost all of what was once Nook Farm is gone today. George and Lily Warner's house is gone, as is the childhood house that Katharine Hepburn grew up in. No other effort to preserve the neighborhood stood the test of postwar development in Hartford. In 1959, the last surviving Nook Farm houses, other than the Day house, the Stowe house, and Mark Twain's home were torn down to make room for a new public high school. Thirty years later, the high school is already so pressured for space that it is built up to the very edge of its property lines abutting the land belonging to the Mark Twain House and Museum.

80. It is impossible to know if she was inspired to restore the Stowe house by the restoration efforts already in the works at the Clemens house, or if she had always planned to endow the restoration of the house upon her death. The Stowe house's more modest design and decoration made it a much easier house to restore. Staff at the house used Stowe's own domestic advice literature as a guide for some of the decorations throughout. Visitors can see ideas from *The American Woman's Home* worked out in the parlor where staff has wrapped ivy around draperies and window treatments just as the Beecher sisters advise in their book. See Catharine Esther Beecher and Harriet Beecher Stowe's *The American Woman's Home.*

81. Weaver and Connecticut Historical Society, *Hartford: An Illustrated History of Connecticut's Capital,* 93.

82. See Susan D. Pennybacker, "The Life and Death of Joseph Watson," *Twain's World: Essays on Hartford's Cultural Heritage,* ed. Larry Bloom (Hartford, CT: Hartford Courant, 1999).

83. Weaver and Connecticut Historical Society, *Hartford: An Illustrated History of Connecticut's Capital,* 126. Hartford was hardly a place of racial and ethnic harmony throughout the long period that Day lived there. Nothing in the notes from meetings in 1934 indicate any notice of the "near race riot" that Weaver describes. Hartford could sorely use a comprehensive history that includes a balanced approach to its historical narrative; Weaver's is hardly adequate and often offensive.

84. A Mr. Coope and Mr. Joseph Frank Snecinski are mentioned by name in the minutes of the Mark Twain Museum and Library Commission. Mr. Coope seems to have been the primary agent assigned to the organization of the papers of the commission. My efforts in the archives of the Mark Twain House and Museum were, in part, aided by his diligent work creating a chronological scrapbook from Day's various and sundry collections of clippings. The members of the Mark Twain Memorial and Library Commission kept in touch with both men as they joined the armed forces and fought in WWII. See specifically Mark Twain Memorial and Library Commission meeting notes from May 19, 1938, and May 16, 1940.

85. The bed has been the subject of recent scholarship. See Bill Brown's introduction in his *A Sense of Things.*

86. Day quoted in Roger Dove, "Many Problems Threaten Twain-Stowe-Burr 'Literary Corner,'" *Hartford Courant,* February 14, 1954.

87. See Mark Twain Memorial and Library Commission, "Minutes of the Trustees' Meeting" (Hartford, CT: Mark Twain House and Museum Archives, February 18, 1954), at the Mark Twain House and Museum Archives. Day was now eighty-four and she was concerned that she should no longer manage the commission.

88. Ibid.

89. See the unpublished notes of Mary Shipman held in the archives of the Mark Twain House and Museum in Hartford, Shipman, "Ms."

90. See Mark Twain Library and Memorial Commission, "June 24, 1954 Minutes of the Trustees' Meeting" (Hartford, CT: Mark Twain House and Museum Archives, 1954).

91. Katharine Seymour Day, Letter to Mr. Ronald Neame, C/O Untied Artists, July 17, 1954. In 1954, using the word "shrine" to describe a historic house or memorial was not unheard of. Six years later, in Florida, Missouri, when they dedicated the new museum space surrounding the Mark Twain birthplace cabin, the State of Missouri built into the limestone above the entrance the words: "Mark Twain Shrine"—not Mark Twain birthplace and not Mark Twain Cabin. The word "shrine" would be enough to indicate to travelers that they had arrived. Walden Pond was called a literary shrine in 1957 in the *New York Times.* Between 1930 and 1964 (when Day died) the *New York Times* refers to U.S. literary shrines at Walden Pond, the site of Jack London's house, Hawthorne's birthplace, the House of the Seven Gables, the Alcott house, Mark Twain's house in Hartford, Thomas Wolfe's house, Mark Twain's house on 5th Avenue, and Whitman's Camden house. Nonliterary mentions of American shrines include a bevy of Catholic shrines, a site devoted to Theodore Roosevelt, the Truman birthplace, shrines for Marines, a shrine for the bill of rights, a shrine for freedom of the press, a freedom shrine at Arlington cemetery, shrines for Revolutionary War battlefields, Woodlawn (the house that George Washington gave to his adopted daughter, Nellie Custis), a national shrine to Jewish Americans killed in war, a shrine to the U.S.S. *Texas,* a shrine at the home of James Buchanan, the home of sculptor Walter Russell, Chief Justice John Jay's house, and many, many more. A shrine in the mid-twentieth century, other than a site for religious pilgrimage and reflection, was clearly a place for reflecting upon heroic deeds and national pride. Almost all nonreligious sites were devoted to men and their deeds. The large majority of these nonreligious shrines were not altars or other public monuments, but houses opened to the public as museums.

92. See Shipman, "Ms."

93. The transition from rental house to full museum was a very slow one, which happened over years rather than months. Although the trustees were able to "claim" rooms as they became unoccupied, some of the residents had to eventually be moved by formal request of the board.

94. The library moved out in May 1956. See Mark Twain Library and Memorial Commission, "Minutes of the Trustees' Meeting" (Hartford, CT: Mark Twain House and Museum Archives, October 4, 1956).

95. "Why Do the People Neglect a Memorial?" *Hartford Courant,* 1955.

96. Norman Holmes Pearson, like Katharine Seymour Day, is certainly deserving of a biography. His influence in modern poetry is nearly unfathomable. The details of his life come from three overlapping secondary sources, H. D., Norman Holmes Pearson, and Donna Krolik Hollenberg, *Between History and Poetry: The Letters of H. D. and Norman Holmes Pearson* (Iowa City: University of Iowa Press, 1997); Robin W. Winks, *Cloak and Gown: Scholars in the Secret War, 1939–1961,* 2nd ed. (New Haven, CT: Yale University Press, 1996); and Donald Clifford Gallup, *Pigeons on the Granite: Memories of a Yale Librarian* (New Haven, CT: Beinecke Rare Book and Manuscript Library, Yale University, 1988). Pearson, though a secondary subject in these books, requires greater research and further exploration to understand his contribution to American literary memory.

97. His interest in the house as a literary text well predated Harald Hendrix's insights in the architecture of the literary imagination.

98. Wilson H. Faude, telephone interview by author, November 13, 2008. Faude seemed to give Sam Clemens primary credit in the style and decisions in the house in many of his statements in our interview.

99. Wilson H. Faude, *The Renaissance of Mark Twain's House: Handbook for Restoration* (Larchmont, NY: Queens House, 1978), 2.

100. Pearson sent a note to the meeting instructing the board in this matter. See Mark Twain Library and Memorial Commission, "Minutes of the Trustees' Meeting" (Hartford, CT: Mark Twain House and Museum Archives, April 18, 1960).

101. Pearson's literary approach was very focused in biography, but in his approach to the house, he is nearly New Critical in his thinking. Despite his advocacy for the restoration process, it is almost as though those involved believe that the house would tell them all they need to know about it through "close-reading." For an example of Person's critical literary approach, see his analysis of Hawthorne's use of the "past" in *The House of the Seven Gables,* which he perceives as "regenerative." See Norman Holmes Pearson, "Hawthorne's Usable Truth," *Hawthorne's Usable Truth and Other Papers Presented at the Fiftieth Anniversary of the New York Lambda Chapter, Phi Beta Kappa* (Canton, NY: St. Lawrence University, 1949), 7.

102. Faude, telephone interview.

103. Staff at the other Clemens sites have done historical research to determine the likely furnishings and interiors, but little actual documentation exists about what was in either home. Significantly, the Hartford house came about later in Clemens's life, when he and Olivia were actively writing to each other and friends about the objects they acquired, about the cost of constructing the house, and eventually their engagement of Tiffany and Associated Artists to redecorate in 1881. Though the Hartford house staff wishes for more complete inventories and photographic records, they have a great deal to work from compared with most historic house museums.

104. The specimens they collected from various points in the restoration of the house are still part of the permanent collection in the archives.

105. Mark Twain Library and Memorial Commission, "Minutes of the Trustees' Meeting" (Hartford, CT: Mark Twain House and Museum Archives, April 27, 1955). Emphasis author's. Although the house was restored in time for its centenary,

"Susie's room" and a few others were not entirely finished. This ended up taking place after the official one-hundred-year birthday party that the trustees held for the house museum. Additionally, in true scholarly fashion, the interpretation of the historic details uncovered at the house has been constantly reinterpreted as research continues. Board members were particularly keen on new histories of the Victorian era and new biographies and scholarship on Sam Clemens. Additionally, several staff members became involved in actively contributing to Mark Twain scholarship, as no one knew more about Sam Clemens's personal domestic life than the board members involved in the research at the house in Hartford. See Faude's *The Renaissance of Mark Twain's House* for information on the 1974 celebration and outstanding restoration plans.

106. Ibid.

107. Leslie Hanscome, "Mark Twain: A Yearning for Yesterday," *Newsweek,* May 2, 1960, 52.

108. "Tiffany's Twain Door," *Hartford Times,* February 11, 1958. In 1970, the Mark Twain House and museum held its own Louis Comfort Tiffany Show using their extensive collection. See scrapbook for 1958 for program at the Mark Twain House and Museum Archives.

109. In 1957, the National Trust through substantial gifts from the Lily Foundation, Mellon family, and the DuPont family was finally able to work toward aid to nationally significant historic structures. Importantly the National Trust also reinvigorated the Historic American Building Survey. Their efforts, aligned with institutions like the Mark Twain House and Colonial Williamsburg, began to re-professionalize the field of historic preservation, which had fallen to the wayside after the initial New Deal efforts came to a halt with the beginning of World War II. See Wallace, *Mickey Mouse History,* 186–87.

110. Since there had been an addition to the servants' wing of the house when they redecorated, restoring the house entirely to its pre-Associated Artists era seemed somewhat impractical.

111. Although it is historically proper, and even Twainian, to refer to the period as the Gilded Age, practitioners involved with the house and the general public still call the period "Victorian" rather than Gilded Age.

112. Unfortunately, none of these interviews seem to exist in written or recorded form today and can only be assumed from the documents that came out of Stone's careful research. My own research into these times was hampered by access to surviving members of the restoration crew. Pearson died young and Stone had lost much of his memory about the work he did for the house. Hal Holbrook is modest about contributing to efforts at the house, but records there show he was of great help with fund raising and that he provided connections for researchers with key informants. He began working with trustees at the house in 1954 or 1955, as his own research into Mark Twain was developing. Hal Holbrook, communication with author, December 1, 2008.

113. Faude, *The Renaissance of Mark Twain's House,* 61.

114. Interestingly, most house museums are just beginning to think about their houses as dynamic spaces that have more than one "right" interpretive arrangement.

115. Frederick Anderson, "Introduction" in Edith Colgate Salsbury, *Susy and*

*Mark Twain: Family Dialogues* (New York: Harper and Row, 1965), xvii.

116. For newer work on Mark Twain and domesticity, see Harris, *The Courtship of Olivia Langdon and Mark Twain;* Leland Krauth, *Proper Mark Twain* (Athens: University of Georgia Press, 1999); Michael J. Kiskis, "Mark Twain and the Tradition of Literary Domesticity," *Constructing of Mark Twain: New Directions in Scholarship,* ed. Laura E. Skandera Trombley (Columbia: University of Missouri Press, 2001); and Victor Doyno, "Samuel Clemens as Family Man and Father," *Constructing of Mark Twain: New Directions in Scholarship,* ed. Laura E. Skandera Trombley (Columbia: University of Missouri Press, 2001).

117. Emphasis author's, "[Clemens to Joseph H. Twichell, January 19, 1897 · London, England], (UCCL 05169)." In Mark Twain Project Online. Berkeley and Los Angeles: University of California Press, 2007.

118. It was a bad time to sell a house such as the Clemens house, as has been noted in the introduction to this chapter; moreover, the country was recovering from the financial panic of 1893, and few could pay what the house cost the Clemenses to build. They sold the house at great loss. Olivia Clemens wrote details to Sam Clemens about the specific items she wanted from the house so that they could be sent on to their townhouse in New York. She never set foot in the house after Susy died.

119. There were several biographers of Twain who argued essentially the same thing. But unlike Van Wyck Brooks, who popularized the argument that Olivia Clemens badly influenced and censored Clemens's writing, Salsbury was the first to popularize that Clemens's writing was at times a family affair, a process mediated by family responsibilities and aided by having a household of creative children that Clemens used as sounding boards. See Brooks, The *Ordeal of Mark Twain* and Salsbury, *Susy and Mark Twain.*

120. "Newsletter of the Mark Twain Library and Memorial Commission," 1, no. 4 (November 1956). Some items that the board could not purchase or secure for the museum were studied as evidence for their eventual acquirement or reproduction.

121. "Newsletter of the Mark Twain Library and Memorial Commission," 2, no. 1 (April 1957). Emphasis mine.

122. "Twain's Old Home Destoyed by Fire: Stormfield, at Redding, Conn., Burns—Present Owners Flee for Lives," *New York Times,* July 26, 1923.

123. "Minutes of the Executive Committee of the Mark Twain Library and Memorial Commission" (Hartford, CT: Mark Twain House and Museum Archives, July 19, 1957).

124. Mary Shipman's picks for new board members did not necessarily know one another as they were each chosen for the particular skills and assets that they could bring with them to the house. Over the years they became fast friends as well as strategically diversified support for the house.

125. The frog-jumping contest was especially popular with local children. Reports each year of the event received full-page coverage in the Hartford newspapers. Local children started training their frogs early. There was terrible outrage when in the 1980s under extreme pressure from animal activists and zoologists that pointed out that these frogs were not cared for in appropriate manner, the contest was shut down. See the scrapbook for clippings coverage of the contest and its demise.

126. See Mark Twain Library and Memorial Commission, "Minutes of the Trustees' Meeting" (Hartford, CT: Mark Twain House and Museum Archives, April 16, 1962).

127. Faude, telephone interview.

128. For these numbers, see the Mark Twain Library and Memorial Commission, "Minutes of the Trustees' Meeting" (Hartford, CT: Mark Twain House and Museum Archives, October 27, 1957), and Tony Davenport, "Mark Twain's Fantastic House," *New York Herald,* February 23, 1958.

129. See "Mark Twain Memorial Scrapbook, 1961, 1962, 1963" (Hartford, CT: Mark Twain House and Museum Archives, 1963). See Mark Twain Library and Memorial Commission, "Minutes of the Trustees' Meeting" (Hartford, CT: Mark Twain House and Museum Archives, May 14, 1964).

130. Candice Bushnell quoted in John Dowd, "Clemens Home World Mecca," *Hartford Times,* February 10, 1962. Although Candice Bushnell, a trustee and temporary director at the museum, indicated that all "types" came to visit the house, she did not specifically indicate that all "races" came to the house. School groups did visit the Twain house from Hartford and beyond. Most Hartford public schools, including the one next-door to the Twain house, had by the middle of the 1960s a majority black population.

131. See, for instance, Charles E. Claffey, "Twain's Bizarre Home Survives as Memorial," *Boston Daily Globe,* January 16, 1960; Marjorie Mills, "Spring's Really in the Air," *Boston Sunday Herald,* February 28, 1960; and Leslie Hanscome, "Mark Twain: A Yearning for Yesterday," *Newsweek,* May 2, 1960. The Twain house even makes it onto the weekend television news. See "Twain Museum on C.B.S. Saturday," *Hartford Times,* March 8, 1963. Sam Clemens's popularity seems to have soared in the Soviet Union during the cold war. When the Clemens house on 5th Avenue and 9th Street in Manhattan was razed, Soviets protested and wrote angry letters to American newspapers. For an interesting account of this house and the controversies surrounding its demolition, see Powell, "Mark Twain's Lost House."

132. For numbers on 1967 visitation, see Edmund Pinto, "The House That Mark Twain Built," *New England Homestead,* 1968.

133. Wallace, *Mickey Mouse History,* 179.

134. See Ethan Carr, *Mission 66: Modernism and the National Park Dilemma* (Amherst: University of Massachusetts Press, 2007).

135. The free day idea seems to have come in response to a letter to the editor in the *Hartford Courant,* in which a local resident complained that she was not able to afford the price of the museum but felt that she had a right to see the house nonetheless. For an account of the reinstated open house days in response to the cost of the museum ticket price, see Gordon D. Duggan, "Letter to the Editor of the Times," *Hartford Times,* April 15, 1972.

136. Mark Twain House and Museum, "History of the Institution," http://www.marktwainhouse.org/about/history.shtml (accessed September 23, 2006).

137. "Proposed Site Is Part of City's Rich Heritage," *Hartford Courant,* September 26, 1956.

138. Stacey Close, "Fire in the Bones: Hartford's N.A.A.C.P., Civil Rights and Militancy, 1943–1969," *Journal of Negro History* 86, no. 3 (2001): 228–63, 238.

139. During these years, Hartford's total population dropped because of white flight to the suburbs. Though unfortunately placed to the members of the museum board and advocates of the Nook Farm historic district, it was an ideal place to locate a high school. The Nook Farm neighborhood preserved a little bucolic area of the city, which was close to the center of downtown Hartford, but removed enough to shelter young people from some of the turmoil of inner-city life.

140. These riots lasted on and off for over a month and left much of Hartford's black and Puerto Rican neighborhoods and several of its branch libraries decimated. By 1969, Hartford had a population of more than 20,000 residents of Puerto Rican descent. See Jose Cruz, "A Decade of Change: Puerto Rican Politics in Hartford, Connecticut, 1969–1979," *Journal of American Ethnic History* 16, no. 3 (1997). These riots in 1969 were preceded by a number of smaller riots in Hartford that involved the Hartford black community, its ethnic white communities, its Italian immigrant community, and the nearly all-white police force. See Close, "Fire in the Bones." Little has been written on the history of Hartford's black residents. See the on-going Hartford Black History Project online: http://www.hartford-hwp.com/ HBHP/index.html (accessed July 9, 2011).

141. For an excellent, and now classic, discussion of urban industrial decay and "racialized urban poverty," see Thomas J. Sugrue, *The Origins of the Urban Crisis: Race and Inequality in Postwar Detroit: With a New Preface by the Author,* A Princeton Classic Edition, 1st Princeton Classic ed. (Princeton, NJ: Princeton University Press, 2005).

142. Steve Courtney, "Rich in So Many Ways," *Twain's World: Essays on Hartford's Cultural Heritage,* ed. Larry Bloom (Hartford, CT: Hartford Courant, 1999).

143. Ibid., 65.

144. See Donna Ann Harris, *New Solutions for House Museums: Ensuring the Long-Term Preservation of America's Historic Houses* (Lanham, MD: Altamira Press, 2007), and Gail Lee Dubrow and Jennifer B. Goodman, eds., *Restoring Women's History through Historic Preservation* (Baltimore: Johns Hopkins University Press, 2003).

145. For an extended discussion of the "radical" shift in public history, see chapter 1 in Cathy Stanton, *The Lowell Experiment: Public History in a Postindustrial City* (Amherst: University of Massachusetts Press, 2006), 7. For a discussion of the New Social History experiment at Colonial Williamsburg, see the classic Richard Handler and Eric Gable, *The New History in an Old Museum: Creating the Past at Colonial Williamsburg* (Durham, NC: Duke University Press, 1997), 223–24.

146. Hal Holbrook, Letter to Polly Peck, June 1974. Mark Twain House and Museum Archives, Hartford, Connecticut.

147. Grace Martin, "The Dreamer Who's Become a Doer," *West Hartford News,* November 11, 1976.

148. Bill Faude started volunteering at the house with his mother when he was a teenager. His volunteer work developed into summer employment while he was home from boarding school and then college, and thus he was there in the 1960s when the trustees were swept up in the full romance of their hunt for Twain furnishings and documents. The board often mentioned Faude's travels, college career, and time in military service in their quarterly newsletter. It was clear that the authors of the newsletter watched his progress closely. That Salsbury essentially chose him as her successor in research on the house is fitting. Where she did exacting research, his

was even more so because he had her meticulous and thoughtful work as a starting point. Wilson H. Faude, telephone interview.

149. See Wilson H. Faude, "Associated Artists and the American Renaissance in the Decoartive Arts," *Winterthur Portfolio* 10, no. 1 (1975), and Wilson H. Faude, "Candace Wheeler, Textile Designer," *The Magazine Antiques* 112, no. 2 (1977). Faude's research may have saved all that is left of Candace Wheeler's designs. Through his research on the Twain house wallpapers, he was able to acquire and preserve the last remaining scraps and sketches of her work through her heirs. Without his influence, it is likely that this research would not have been done and her work lost. His research contributes to the growing body of scholarship that takes women's nineteenth-century contributions to decorative arts seriously. A current Wheeler "exhibit" at the Mark Twain House and Museum (Fall 2008) outraged Faude. The museum staff recreated two separately hand-tinted versions of a Wheeler wallpaper and asked visitors to "vote" with cash donations for which one would be installed in the downstairs guest bedroom. While I cannot fault a museum for trying to make money any way it can as it was struggling with imminent closure, Faude objected to its vulgar method of making the decision about the wallpaper. It did not meet his "perfect" guidelines for how the house should be restored. Faude, telephone interview.

150. "Twain Memorial Acquires Unique Tiffany Furniture," *Hartford Courant,* January 1, 1977.

151. This was compounded by the fact that so many people in Hartford were not interested in holding on to their family's various Victorian items and saw the house museum as a perfect repository. The staff had so many valuable gifts coming in that it was difficult not to accept excellent pieces from well-meaning donors.

152. Eleanor Charles, "Visitors' Center to Be Built at Mark Twain House," *New York Times,* January 20, 2002, 9.

153. Patti Philippon quoted in Mark Twain House and Museum, "What's New," http://www.marktwainhouse.org/visitor/whats_new.php (accessed July 2008).

154. Each new exhibit does not necessarily raise funds in itself, but the press surrounding the exhibit often does. Patti Philippon, discussion with author, October 2008.

155. Nearly every major newspaper in the country ran a story of the museum's peril in 2008. In a fund-raising effort that made no excuses for its financial blunder with the new visitors' center, the museum seems to have regained its footing, nearly cut its staff in half, and gained new direction for their interpretation efforts. See Klein, "Mark Twain Museum Is in Deep Water"; Tedeschi, "Writers Unite to Keep Twain House Afloat"; and Debra Bogstie, "Mark Twain's House Savings Are No Laughing Matter," *NBC Connecticut,* August 11, 2009. http://www.nbcconnecticut. com/news/local-beat/Mark-Twain-52908192.html (accessed January 24, 2012).

156. At its peak the museum employed forty-nine people, but by 2008, when it went public with its financial troubles after a valiant attempt to recover financially through cost-saving measures, the staff was reduced to fifteen people. Today the museum is on the mend and has hired three new staff members. Although stretched thin, their programming is more vibrant than ever before.

157. See Tanya Barrientos, "Houses, Histories and the Future," Spring 2008, Pew

Charitable Trust, *Trust Magazine*, Available: http://www.pewtrusts.org/our_work_report_detail.aspx?id=38618&category=426 (accessed March 1, 2009); Marian Godfrey and Barbara Silberman, "A Model for Historic House Museums," Spring 2008, Pew Charitable Trust, *Trust Magazine*, Available: http://www.pewtrusts.org/our_work_report_detail.aspx?id=38618&category=426 (accessed March 1, 2009); Donna Ann Harris, *New Solutions for House Museums: Ensuring the Long-Term Preservation of America's Historic Houses* (Lanham, MD: Altamira Press, 2007); and especially Gerald George, "Historic House Museum Malaise: A Conference Considers What's Wrong," *Historic House Conference; Association for State and Local History*, 2002, http://www.aaslh.org/images/hhouseart.pdf (accessed August 23, 2007).

## Chapter Four

1. See "Idea of Shutting Fire-Truck Plant Saddens Elmira," *New York Times*, February 10, 1985; Thomas Lueck, "Declining Elmira Buoyed by Plant Reopening," *New York Times*, June 2, 1985; Robert Boorstin, "Profiting from the Aura of Twain," *New York Times*, June 26, 1987; Randolph Picht, "New Industries Breathe Life into New York Town," *Wichita Eagle*, September 13, 1987; Associated Press, "Depressed City Bolts Back to Prosperity—New Attitude Fires up Elmira, N.Y.," *Chicago Tribune*, August 18, 1987; and Dana Milbank, "Its Claim to Twain Brings Elmira, N.Y., Fortune and Fame: Author Visited His in-Laws, Became Favorite Son; Hannibal, Mo., Cries Foul," *Wall Street Journal*, August 16, 1991.

2. Potter designed the study with a similar chimney that split to allow windows on all eight sides of the building. Eventually this decorative element was renovated, because two miniature chimneys did not allow the smoke to leave the room sufficiently.

3. Gayle Earley, telephone interview, January 30, 2008.

4. Irene Langdon, discussion with the author, January 25, 2008.

5. Bryan Reddick, personal interview, January 17, 2008. Cowles Hall, built in 1855, was one of the college's first buildings and is also octagonal in design.

6. Most notably, after Susan Crane's death in 1924, there were many renovations to the house. The most obvious was a two-story addition that now serves as the study for scholars while they are there. These 1920s renovations are also responsible for most of the conveniences at the house and for the exterior look of the house. Jervis Langdon Sr. covered the exterior in stucco in the "Tudor-revival" style of the day. See Lorraine Welling Lanmon, "Quarry Farm: A Study of the 'Picturesque,'" *Quarry Farm Papers*, ed. Darryl Baskin (Elmira, NY: Elmira College Center for Mark Twain Studies, 1991), 13.

7. The center provides a small stipend to defray travel costs and also stocks the kitchen on behalf of the fellows, so they can dine at Quarry Farm and keep focused on their scholarship.

8. Scholars add to the archive by their very presence there. The things they leave behind might include personal items, but almost always include their comments in the guest book, their publications in the collection, and quite often their financial contributions to the center.

9. This volume itself began as a dissertation that obviously benefited from time at Quarry Farm and the resources made available through Elmira College's Center for Mark Twain Studies.

10. The recent *Dear Friends* newsletter from the center lists fifty-two monographs as a result of research time spent at Quarry Farm, but could not possibly include all of the articles and dissertations that have come about through research and writing facilitated by residency at the site. "Dear Friends: Anniversay Edition," ed. Elmira College Center for Mark Twain Studies: An Occassoinal Newsletter for its Friends (Elmira, NY: 2008).

11. See Jervis Langdon, Elmira College, Chemung County Historical Society and National Trust for Historic Preservation, *Four (4)—Party Agreement Regarding Quarry Farm, Elmira, N.Y., December 31, 1982* (Elmira, NY: 1982), copy held at the Mark Twain Archive, Gannett-Tripp Library, Elmira College.

12. Langdon, discussion with author.

13. For press coverage of Sam Clemens's time in Elmira, see "Interview with Mark Twain in His Mountain Studio in Chemung—Remarkable Declarations: A Remarkable Statement for a Literary Man," *Hartford Daily Courant,* August 30, 1876; "Mark Twain's Summer Home: A Visit to His House and Study in the Suburbs of Elmira," *New York Times,* September 10, 1882; "A Misunderstood Man," *Chicago Daily Tribune,* November 7, 1882; Edwin J. Park, "A Day with Mark Twain: The Genial Humorist at His Summer Home," *Chicago Daily Tribune,* September 19, 1886; and "Mark Twain: He Plays as Umpire at Game of Base-Ball at Elmira," *Los Angeles Times,* July 16, 1887.

14. First published in a Turkish newspaper, it eventually found readers in the *New York Herald* and has since been collected and redistributed by Twain and Kipling scholars alike. Rudyard Kipling, "Rudyard Kipling on Mark Twain," *New York Herald,* August 17, 1890.

15. Photogravure is the process through which photographs or other images where transferred into mechanized engravings for the likes of publications like *Harper's Magazine.* Today, the *Wall Street Journal* continues this style of illustration.

16. Rudyard Kipling, "Rudyard Kipling on Mark Twain."

17. During their first years there, and even when Kipling visited, getting to Elmira was a longer journey than most wanted to make for a summer getaway. Jervis Langdon Jr. called upon his railroad expertise and researched the trip from Hartford to Elmira. The trip took two days and the last leg, from Manhattan to Elmira, took more than ten hours during most of the years that the Clemenses spent their summers there. Eventually, rail service did improve. Kipling complains of arriving in the middle of the night having come all the way from Hartford. See Jervis Langdon, "Feature," *Dear Friends* 22 (1991).

18. Kipling, "Rudyard Kipling on Mark Twain," 5.

19. Lanmon indicates the Downing illustration of "Design X, Bracketed Cottage, with Veranda," figures 42 and 43 in *Architecture of Country Houses* (New York, 1850) as possible models and points out that it was likely that Susan Crane was aware of Downing's popular house design books. Lorraine Welling Lanmon, *Quarry Farm: A Study of the "Picturesque,"* ed. Darryl Baskin. Quarry Farm Papers (Elmira, NY: Elmira College Center for Mark Twain Studies, 1991), 5–7.

20. Kipling, "Rudyard Kipling on Mark Twain," 5.

21. See *Four (4)—Party Agreement*.

22. Elmira College's relationship to the Langdons and Clemenses predates commemoration. Jervis Langdon, Olivia Langdon's father, was one of the founding trustees for the college in 1855. Olivia attended the college (which was then called the Elmira Female College) as a day student, and eventually Jean Clemens, Sam and Olivia Clemens's youngest daughter, attended the college briefly. Mark Woodhouse, personal interview, January 31, 2008.

23. Joan V. Lindquist, "A Room of His Own," *Mark Twain Journal* 21, no. 3 (1983): 40.

24. Current center director Barbara Snedecor is in the process of updating the volume for republication. For a brief history of the Mark Twain Society, see Herbert Wisbey and Robert Jerome, "Editor's Note," *Mark Twain Society Bulletin* 10, no. 2 (1987): 2.

25. Herb Wisbey's scholarly interest was American religious history. He served as a member of the board for the Chemung County Historical Society, which made him a perfect choice to look after Quarry Farm in the early years of the center. See Bill Triechler, "Herberty A. Wisbey, Jr., April 20, 1919–March 17, 2000," *Crooked Lake Review* (2000), Obituary, http://www.crookedlakereview.com/authors/wisbey.html (accessed September 19, 2009).

26. A number of people that I talked to while visiting Quarry Farm, including Mark Woodhouse, University and Mark Twain Archive archivist at Gannett-Tripp Library, and Bryan Reddick, mentioned Quarry Farm's role in raising the stature of the college under President Meier's term. Meier became president of the college in 1987 and is its second-longest serving president. Byran Reddick, personal interview by author, and Mark Woodhouse, personal interview.

27. See "Idea of Shutting Fire-Truck Plant Saddens Elmira" and Milbank, "Its Claim to Twain Brings Elmira, N.Y., Fortune and Fame."

28. Alan Gribben, *Mark Twain's Library: A Reconstruction* (Boston: G. K. Hall, 1980).

29. Alan Gribben, personal interview by author, February 29, 2008.

30. See "Announcements: The Elmira College Center for Mark Twain Studies at Quarry Farm," *American Literature* 59, no. 1 (1987); "Announcements: Quarry Farm Fellowships," *American Literature* 63, no. 1 (1991); and "Commentary," *Nineteenth-Century Literature* 43, no. 4 (1989). To the great sadness of many Twain scholars who had come to Quarry Farm under Baskin's directorship, Baskin died suddenly of a heart attack in 1992 before he could see the second international conference come to fruition. Assistant director Gretchen Sharlow became acting director as she headed up the center's first international conference. She became the center's director not long after. Sharlow's work at the center had been essential to center's growth even before she became director. Under her stewardship programming expanded and the center grew in national prominence with Twain scholars and the local community. After Sharlow's retirement in 2002, and the brief directorship of Jane McCone, Barbara Snedecor became director in 2004. Snedecor has continued the programs that have inspired so much loyalty from Twain scholars and local Twain fans over the years. Gretchen Sharlow, personal interview, January 29, 2008. For a brief summary of the center's history, see "Dear Friends: Anniversay Edition," 1–3.

For an account of Jane McCone's tenure at the center, see Mary Clarkin, "Museum's Director Resigns: McCone Found to Have a History of Job-Hopping, Questionable Resumes," *Hutchinson News,* March 9, 2006.

31. Harold Bush, Shelley Fisher Fishkin, and Maria Zuppello quoted in "Dear Friends: Anniversay Edition," 5, 7, 13.

32. Harold Bush, quoted in "Dear Friends: Anniversay Edition," 5.

33. Emphasis author's. Connie Anne Kirk quoted in "Dear Friends: Anniversay Edition," 9.

34. Nicola J. Watson, *The Literary Tourist,* 1.

35. David Herbert, "Literary Places, Tourism and the Heritage Experience," *Annals of Tourism Research* 28, no. 2 (2001): 313.

36. Fishkin and others have noted Jervis Langdon's important work in the Underground Railroad. He contributed to Frederick Douglas's escape. See Shelley Fisher Fishkin, *Lighting out for the Territory: Reflections on Mark Twain and American Culture* (New York: Oxford University Press, 1996), 80.

37. Fishkin's account was written for a popular audience. Her personal interactions and readings of Twain have led at least one scholar to point out that Sam Clemens has inspired many who study him to believe that they have a personal, autobiographical connection to him. Some scholars' works have crossed over into advocacy of Mark Twain. See Harold Bush, "Our Mark Twain? Or, Some Thoughts on the 'Autobiographical Critic,'" *New England Quarterly* 73, no. 1 (2000).

38. See the discussion of Santesso in chapter 1. Aaron Santesso, "The Birth of the Birthplace: Bread Street and Literary Tourism before Stratford," *English Literary History* 71 (2004): 377–403.

39. Emphasis in original. Mary Boewe, *Quarry Farm Guest Book,* October 11, 1996.

40. Jan Younger, *Quarry Farm Guest Book,* June 15, 1999.

41. Scott McLean, *Quarry Farm Guest Book,* July 20, 1994.

42. Susan K. Harris quoted in "Dear Friends: Anniversary Edition."

43. Jan McIntire-Strasburg, *Quarry Farm Guest Book,* October 22, 1999.

44. Budd, "Dear Friends: Anniversary Edition," 5.

45. Emphasis mine. Diana Fuss, *The Sense of an Interior: Four Writers and the Rooms That Shaped Them* (New York: Routledge, 2004), 5.

46. Ibid., vii.

47. Ibid., 43–57.

48. Fishkin, *Lighting out for the Territory,* 77–79. It is important to note that Fishkin is decidedly less excited to be close to Twain's things when she is in Hannibal and most excited when she feels she is closest to the Twain that she admires in Elmira.

49. Harald Hendrix, *Writers' Houses and the Making of Memory* (New York: Routledge, 2007), 1.

50. Ibid.

51. See "Wish List," *Dear Friends* (Elmira College Center for Mark Twain Studies: An Occasional Newsletter for Its Friends, 1988), 7.

52. Jim Leonard, "Re: Unbroken Indeed." *Email to Mark Twain Forum,* August 11, 2009.

53. See Mark Twain Forum discussion archives (Twain-L) from August 2009

for a fuller picture of conference events. https://listserv.yorku.ca/cgi-bin/
wa?A1=ind0908&L=twain-l (accessed January 28, 2012).

54. Alan Gribben, Letter to Darryl Baskin, August 4, 1987, copy held at the
Gannett-Tripp Library, Archives and Special Collections, Elmira College.

55. Ibid.

56. Jervis Langdon Sr. had been a supporter of the festivities in Hannibal and
contributed items to the city's temporary museum.

57. Laurence Vail Coleman, *Historic House Museums,* 20–21.

## Epilogue

1. Edward Rothstein, "Forget What You Know of Twain, Then Delight in Your
Rediscovery," *New York Times,* September 17, 2010.

2. Dell Upton, *Architecture in the United States* (New York: Oxford University
Press, 1998), 17.

3. For instance, at a Willa Cather roadside marker, Loewen faults the State of
Nebraska for not indicating that Cather was a lesbian. This fact above all other
possible descriptive omissions of Cather as a literary stylist makes him irate. James
Loewen, *Lies across America: What Our Historic Sites Get Wrong* (New York: Simon and
Schuster, 2007), 342.

4. The new Mark Twain library branch is working hard to meet the needs of the
neighborhood's changing population, by offering support for a growing Spanish-
speaking segment of the community and new refugees from Myanmar and Bhutan.
The library even serves a free lunch to students who participate in its summer reading program. For more information on the current Mark Twain Branch, see http://
www.hplct.org/locations-hours/mark-twain.

5. See "Archaeologists Investigate Mark Twain's Virginia City," *Nevada Appeal,*
July 22, 2009, and Engel, "Digs Planned at Farm Twain Enjoyed as a Boy," *Hannibal
Courier Post,* September 1, 2009.

# Bibliography

Adiletta, Dawn C. "Katharine Seymour Day, 1870–1964: Painter—Gardener—Activist." Hartford, CT: Harriet Beecher Stowe Center, 2001.

Alexander, Edward P. *Museums in Motion: An Introduction to the History and Functions of Museums.* Nashville: American Association for State and Local History, 1979.

Anderson, Frederick. "Introduction." *Susy and Mark Twain: Family Dialogues.* Ed. Edith Salsbury. New York: Harper and Row, 1965.

Andrews, Gregg. *City of Dust: A Cement Company in the Land of Tom Sawyer.* Columbia: University of Missouri Press, 1996.

Axelrod, Alan, and Henry Francis du Pont Winterthur Museum. *The Colonial Revival in America.* 1st ed. New York: Norton, 1985.

Bacon, Edwin M. *Literary Pilgrimages in New England: To the Homes of Famous Makers of American Literature and among Their Haunts and the Scenes of Their Writings.* New York: Silver, Burdett and Company, 1902.

Barnum, P. T. *Struggles and Triumphs: Or, Forty Years' Recollections of P. T. Barnum.* Buffalo, NY: Warren, Johnson and Co., 1872.

Beecher, Catharine Esther, and Harriet Beecher Stowe. *The American Woman's Home.* Ed. Nicole Tonkovich. New Brunswick, NJ: Rutgers University Press, 2002 reprint (1869).

Biggers, Shirley Hoover. *American Author Houses, Museums, Memorials, and Libraries: A State-by-State Guide.* Jefferson, NC: McFarland, 2000.

Board, Missouri State Park. *Museum Prospectus for Mark Twain Birthplace Memorial Shrine, Mark Twain State Park.* Jefferson City, Missouri, 1961.

Brooks, Van Wyck. *The Ordeal of Mark Twain.* New York: E. P. Dutton & Company, 1920.

Brown, Bill. *A Sense of Things: The Object Matter of American Literature.* Chicago: University of Chicago Press, 2003.

Bruggeman, Seth C. *Here, George Washington Was Born: Memory, Material Culture and the Public History of a National Monument.* Athens: University of Georgia Press, 2008.

Budd, Louis J. *Our Mark Twain: The Making of His Public Personality.* Philadelphia: University of Pennsylvania Press, 1983.

Buell, Lawrence. "The Thoreauvian Pilgrimage: The Structure of an American Cult." *American Literature* 61, no. 2 (1989): 175–99.

Burns, John A., Historic American Buildings Survey/Historic American Engineering Record, and Historic American Landscapes Survey. *Recording Historic Structures.* 2nd ed. Hoboken, NJ: John Wiley & Sons, 2004.

Burton, Cynthia, and Ann Romines. "Saving Willa Cather's Birthplace." *Willa Cather Pioneer Memorial Newsletter* 50, no. 2 (2006): 43–44.

Bush, Harold. "Our Mark Twain? Or, Some Thoughts on The 'Autobiographical Critic.'" *New England Quarterly* 73, no. 1 (2000): 100–121.

Carr, Ethan. *Mission 66: Modernism and the National Park Dilemma.* Amherst: University of Massachusetts Press, 2007.

Clemens, Clara. *My Father, Mark Twain.* New York: Harpers and Brothers, 1931.

Close, Stacey. "Fire in the Bones: Hartford's N.A.A.C.P., Civil Rights and Militancy, 1943–1969." *Journal of Negro History* 86, no. 3 (2001): 228–63.

Coleman, Laurence Vail. *Historic House Museums.* Washington, DC: The American Association of Museums, 1933.

Cook, James W., Lawrence B. Glickman, and Michael O'Malley. *The Cultural Turn in U.S. History: Past, Present, and Future.* Chicago: University of Chicago Press, 2008.

Courtney, Steve. "Rich in So Many Ways." *Twain's World: Essays on Hartford's Cultural Heritage.* Ed. Larry Bloom. Hartford, CT: Hartford Courant, 1999. 60–73.

Cruz, Jose. "A Decade of Change: Puerto Rican Politics in Hartford, Connecticut, 1969–1979." *Journal of American Ethnic History* 16, no. 3 (1997): 45–80.

Cunning, John. "CCC Company 1743: The Thunderbirds." *Preservation Issues* 6, no. 1 (1996). http://www.umsl.edu/~libweb/blackstudies/cccco.htm (accessed December 9, 2007).

Dávidházi, Péter. *The Romantic Cult of Shakespeare: Literary Reception in Anthropological Perspective.* Romanticism in Perspective. New York: St. Martin's Press, 1998.

DeMenil, Alexander Nicholas. "A Century of Missouri Literature." *Missouri Historical Review* 15, no. 1 (1920): 74–126.

Dempsey, Terrell. *Searching for Jim: Slavery in Sam Clemens's World.* Columbia: University of Missouri Press, 2003.

Doyno, Victor. "Samuel Clemens as Family Man and Father." *Constructing of Mark Twain: New Directions in Scholarship.* Ed. Laura E. Skandera Trombley. Columbia: University of Missouri Press, 2001. 28–49.

Driscoll, Kerry. "Mark Twain's Music Box: Livy, Cosmopolitanism, and the Commodity Aesthetic." *Cosmopolitan Twain.* Ed. Ann M. Ryan and Joseph B. McCullough. Columbia: University of Missouri Press, 2008. 140–86.

Dubrow, Gail Lee, and Jennifer B. Goodman, eds. *Restoring Women's History through Historic Preservation.* Baltimore: Johns Hopkins University Press, 2003.

Eco, Umberto. *Travels in Hyper Reality: Essays.* 1st ed. San Diego: Harcourt Brace Jovanovich, 1986.

Eichstedt, Jennifer L., and Stephen Small. *Representations of Slavery: Race and Ideology in Southern Plantation Museums.* Washington, DC: Smithsonian Institution Press, 2002.

Etulain, Richard W. *Writing Western History: Essays on Major Western Historians.* Reno: University of Nevada Press, 2002.

"Evolution of the System (Missouri State Parks)." Missouri Department of Natural Resources, Division of Parks, Recreation, and Historic Preservation Archives, 1991. 1–40.

Faden, Regina. "Presenting Mark Twain: Keeping the Edge Sharp." *Mark Twain Annual* 6, no. 1 (2008): 23–30.

———. "Museums and Race: Living up to the Public Trust." *Museums and Social Issues: A Journal of Reflective Discourse* 2, no. 1 (2007): 77–88.

Falk, John H. "An Indentity-Centered Approach to Understanding Museum Learning." *Curator* 49, no. 2 (2006): 151–66.

Fast, Stan. *Memo to Samuel J. Wegner, Assistant Supervisor Region 1: Birthplace Cabin Authenticity.* Florida, MO: Mark Twain Birthplace State Historic Site, Missouri Department of Natural Resources, Historic Preservation Program, March 4, 1983.

Faude, Wilson H. "Associated Artists and the American Renaissance in the Decoartive Arts." *Winterthur Portfolio* 10, no. 1 (1975).

———. "Candace Wheeler, Textile Designer." *The Magazine Antiques* 112, no. 2 (1977).

———. *The Renaissance of Mark Twain's House: Handbook for Restoration.* Larchmont, NY: Queens House, 1978.

Faulkner, William. *Lion in the Garden: Interviews with William Faulkner 1926–1962.* Ed. James Meriweather and Michael Millgate. New York: Random House, 1968.

Fawcett, Clare, and Patricia Cormack. "Guarding Authenticity at Literary Tourism Sites." *Annals of Tourism Research* 28, no. 3 (2001): 686–704.

Fishkin, Shelley Fisher. *Lighting out for the Territory: Reflections on Mark Twain and American Culture.* New York: Oxford University Press, 1996.

Franklin, Adrian, and Mike Crang. "The Trouble with Tourism and Travel Theory?" *Tourist Studies* 1, no. 1 (2001): 5–22.

Fuss, Diana. *The Sense of an Interior: Four Writers and the Rooms That Shaped Them.* New York: Routledge, 2004.

Gallup, Donald Clifford. *Pigeons on the Granite: Memories of a Yale Librarian.* New Haven, CT: Beinecke Rare Book & Manuscript Library, Yale University, 1988.

Gauvreau, Emile Henry. *My Last Million Readers.* New York: E. P. Dutton & Co., Inc., 1941.

George, Gerald. "Historic House Museum Malaise: A Conference Considers What's Wrong." *Historic House Conference; Association for State and Local History* (2002): 5 pp. http://www.aaslh.org/images/hhouseart.pdf (accessed August 23, 2007).

Gilman, Arthur. *Poets' Homes. Pen and Pencil Sketches of American Poets and Their Homes.* [2nd series]. Boston: D. Lothrop, 1879.

Gilman, Charlotte Perkins. *The Home: Its Work and Influence.* New York: Charlton Company, 1910.

Glassberg, David. *American Historical Pageantry: The Uses of Tradition in the Early Twentieth Century.* Chapel Hill: University of North Carolina Press, 1990.

Godfrey, Marian, and Barbara Silberman. "A Model for Historic House Museums." Philadelphia, 2008. *What to do with these Old Houses?* Spring: Pew Charitable Trust, *Trust Magazine.* http://www.pewtrusts.org/our_work_report_detail.aspx?id=38618 (accessed January 29, 2012).

Gregory, Ralph. *M. A. "Dad" Violette: A Life Sketch.* Florida, MO, 1969.

———. "Orion Clemens on Mark Twain's Birthplace." *Mark Twain Journal* 20, no. 2 (1980): 16–18.

Gribben, Alan. "The Importance of Mark Twain." *American Quarterly* 37, no. 1 (1985): 30–49.

———. *Mark Twain's Library: A Reconstruction.* Boston: G. K. Hall, 1980.

H. D., Norman Holmes Pearson, and Donna Krolik Hollenberg. *Between History & Poetry: The Letters of H.D. and Norman Holmes Pearson.* Iowa City: University of Iowa Press, 1997.

Hagood, J. Hurley, and Roberta Roland Hagood. *Hannibal Yesterday: Historic Stories of Events, People, Landmarks, and Happenings in and near Hannibal.* 1st ed. Marceline, MO: Jostens, 1992.

———. *Hannibal, Too: Historic Sketches of Hannibal and Its Neighbors.* 1st ed. Marceline, MO: Walsworth Pub. Co., 1986.

———. *The Story of Hannibal.* Hannibal, MO: Hannibal Bicentennial

Commission, 1976.

———, et al. *Mirror of Hannibal*. Rev. ed. [Hannibal, MO (200 S. Fifth St., Hannibal 63401): Hannibal Free Public Library, 1990 (1905).

Hammer, Charles. "A Home at Last for the Old Twain House." *Kansas City Star,* November 22, 1959.

Handler, Richard, and Eric Gable. *The New History in an Old Museum: Creating the Past at Colonial Williamsburg*. Durham, NC: Duke University Press, 1997.

Harris, Donna Ann. *New Solutions for House Museums: Ensuring the Long-Term Preservation of America's Historic Houses*. Lanham, MD: Altamira Press, 2007.

Harris, Susan K. *The Courtship of Olivia Langdon and Mark Twain*. Cambridge Studies in American Literature and Culture. New York: Cambridge University Press, 1996.

Hayden, Dolores. *The Grand Domestic Revolution: A History of Feminist Designs for American Homes*. Boston: MIT Press, 1982.

Hazard, Erin. "The Author's House: Abbotsford and Wayside." *Literary Tourism and Nineteenth-Century Culture*. Ed. Nicola Watson. New York: Palgrave Macmillan, 2009. 63–72.

Hendrix, Harald. "Writers' Houses as Media of Expression and Remembrance: From Self-Fashioning to Cultural Memory." *Writers' Houses and the Making of Memory*. Ed. Harald Hendrix. New York Routledge, 2007. 1–14.

Herbert, David T. "Artistic and Literary Places in France as Tourist Attractions." *Tourism Management* 17, no. 2 (1996): 77–85.

"Historical Notes and Comments: Mark Twain Memorial Park Association." *Missouri Historical Review* 18, no. 2 (1924): 288–90.

Hogeland, William. *Inventing American History*. Cambridge, MA: MIT Press, 2009.

Holcombe, R. I. *History of Marion County, Missouri*. Hannibal, MO: Marion County Historical Society, 1979, reprint (original 1884).

*Homes of American Authors; Comprising Anecdotical, Personal, and Descriptive Sketches, by Various Writers*. New York: G. P. Putnam and Co., 1853.

Horton, James Oliver, and Lois E. Horton. *Slavery and Public History: The Tough Stuff of American Memory*. New York: New Press, Distributed by Norton, 2006.

Hosmer, Charles Bridgham. *Preservation Comes of Age: From Williamsburg to the National Trust, 1926–1949*. Vol. 2. Charlottesville: Preservation Press, National Trust for Historic Preservation, University Press of Virginia, 1981.

Irving, Washington. *The Sketch-Book of Geoffrey Crayon, Gent*. Author's rev. ed. New York: G. P. Putnam's Sons, 1888.

————, et al. *Abbotsford and Newstead Abbey.* The Crayon Miscellany. Philadelphia: Carey, Lea & Blanchard, 1835.

James, Henry. *The American Scene.* London: Richard Clay & Sons, 1907.

Janney, Caroline E. *Burying the Dead but Not the Past: Ladies' Memorial Associations and the Lost Cause.* Civil War America. Chapel Hill: University of North Carolina Press, 2008.

Johnson, Clifton. *Highways and Byways of the Mississippi Valley.* New York: Macmillan Company, 1906.

Kaplan, Justin. *Mr. Clemens and Mark Twain: A Biography.* New York: Simon and Schuster, 1991.

Kaufman, Tammie J., and Denver E. Severt. "Heritage Tourism: Historic Preservationist Attitude and the Heritage Site—a Case Study of William Faulkner's Homeplace." *Tourism Review International* 10, no. 3 (2006): 181–88.

Kerber, Linda K. "Separate Spheres, Female Worlds, Woman's Place: The Rhetoric of Women's History." *Journal of American History* 75, no. 1 (1988): 9–39.

Kipling, Rudyard. "Rudyard Kipling on Mark Twain." *New York Herald,* August 17, 1890.

Kirshenblatt-Gimblett, Barbara. *Destination Culture: Tourism, Museums, and Heritage.* Berkeley and Los Angeles: University of California Press, 1998.

Kiskis, Michael J. "Mark Twain and the Tradition of Literary Domesticity." *Constructing of Mark Twain: New Directions in Scholarship.* Ed. Laura E. Skandera Trombley. Columbia: University of Missouri Press, 2001. 13–27.

Krauth, Leland. *Proper Mark Twain.* Athens: University of Georgia Press, 1999.

Lamson, Frank. *Statement by F. B. Lamson, Secretary Mark Twain Park Association.* Mark Twain Birthplace State Historic Site, 1924.

Landau, Sarah Bradford. *Edward T. and William A. Potter: American Victorian Architects.* Outstanding Dissertations in the Fine Arts. New York: Garland, 1979.

Landrum, Ney C. *The State Park Movement in America: A Critical Review.* Columbia: University of Missouri Press, 2004.

Lanmon, Lorraine Welling. *Quarry Farm: A Study of the "Picturesque."* Quarry Farm Papers. Ed. Darryl Baskin. Elmira, NY: Elmira College Center for Mark Twain Studies, 1991.

Lindquist, Joan V. "A Room of His Own." *Mark Twain Journal* 21, no. 3 (1983).

Loewen, James W. *Lies across America: What Our Historic Sites Get Wrong.* New York: Simon and Schuster, 2007.

Lott, Eric. *Love and Theft: Blackface Minstrelsy and the American Working Class.* Race and American Culture. New York: Oxford University Press, 1993.

Lystra, Karen. *Dangerous Intimacy: The Untold Story of Mark Twain's Final Years.* Berkeley and Los Angeles: University of California Press, 2006.

Magelssen, Scott. *Living History Museums: Undoing History through Performance.* Lanham, MD: Scarecrow Press, 2007.

Marling, Karal Ann. *George Washington Slept Here: Colonial Revivals and American Culture, 1876–1986.* Cambridge, MA: Harvard University Press, 1988.

Nickell, Ann. "Memo: To: Frank Wesley, Subject: Road Signs at Mark Twain." Missouri Department of Natural Resources, State Park Division, Archives, File: Signs, 1995.

Paine, Albert Bigelow. *Mark Twain: A Biography, the Personal and Literary Life of Samuel Langhorne Clemens.* Vol. 3. New York: Harper and Brothers, 1912.

Pearson, Norman Holmes. "Hawthorne's Usable Truth." *Hawthorne's Usable Truth and Other Papers Presented at the Fiftieth Anniversary of the New York Lambda Chapter, Phi Beta Kappa.* Canton, NY: St. Lawrence University, 1949.

Pennybacker, Susan D. "The Life and Death of Joseph Watson." *Twain's World: Essays on Hartford's Cultural Heritage.* Ed. Larry Bloom. Hartford, CT: Hartford Courant, 1999. 87–104.

Pessen, Edward. *The Log Cabin Myth: The Social Backgrounds of the Presidents.* New Haven, CT: Yale University Press, 1984.

Pinto, Edmund. "The House That Mark Twain Built." *New England Homestead* (1968).

Pitcaithley, Dwight. "Abraham Lincoln's Birthplace Cabin: The Making of an American Icon." *Myth, Memory, and the Making of the American Landscape.* Ed. Paul A. Shackel. Gainesville: University Press of Florida, 2001. 240–54.

———. "'A Cosmic Threat': The National Park Service Addresses the Causes of the American Civil War." *Slavery and Public History: The Tough Stuff of American Memory.* Ed. James Oliver Horton and Lois E. Horton. New York: New Press, 2006. 169–86.

Poage, Franklin R. "Mark Twain Memorials in Hannibal." *Missouri Historical Review* 20, no. 1 (1925): 79–84.

Powell, James W. "Mark Twain's Lost House." *Mark Twain Journal* 20, no. 2 (1980): 13–16.

Powers, Ron. *Mark Twain: A Life.* New York: Free Press, 2005.

———. *White Town Drowsing.* Boston: Atlantic Monthly Press, 1986.

Reisinger, Yvette, and Carol J. Steiner. "Reconceptualizing Object Authenticity." *Annals of Tourism Research* 33, no. 1 (2006): 65–86.

Rigney, Ann. "Abbotsford: Dislocation and Cultural Remembrance." *Writers' Houses and the Making of Memory.* Ed. Harald Hendrix. New York: Routledge, 2008. 75–91.

Rosenzweig, Roy, and David P. Thelen. *The Presence of the Past: Popular Uses of History in American Life.* New York: Columbia University Press, 1998.

Rounds, Jay. "Doing Identity Work in Museums." *Curator* 49, no. 2 (2006): 133–50.

Rugg, Linda Haverty. *Picturing Ourselves: Photography and Autobiography.* Chicago: University of Chicago Press, 1997.

Ruskin, John. *The Seven Lamps of Architecture.* London: Smith, Elder and Co., 1849.

Russell, F. T. "To Mrs. Doris L. Hassell." Mark Twain Boyhood Home Archive: Vertical File "Mark Twain Museum, History of," July 14, 1952, 3.

Salsbury, Edith Colgate. *Susy and Mark Twain: Family Dialogues.* New York: Harper and Row, 1965.

Sampson, F. A. "Scenic and Historic Places in Missouri." *Missouri Historical Review* 11, no. 1 (1912).

Sanderlin, George William. *Mark Twain: As Others Saw Him.* New York: Coward, McCann & Geoghegan, 1978.

Santesso, Aaron. "The Birth of the Birthplace: Bread Street and Literary Tourism before Stratford." *English Literary History* 71 (2004): 377–403.

Schmidt, Barbara. "Frank Fuller, the American Revisited." *The Twainian* 58, no. 1 (2002).

Schwinn, Walter. "The House That Mark Built." Hartford, CT: Mark Twain House and Museum Archives, n.d.

Sneider, Allison. *Suffragists in an Imperial Age: U.S. Expansion and the Woman Question, 1870–1929.* New York: Oxford University Press, 2008.

Stanton, Cathy. *The Lowell Experiment: Public History in a Postindustrial City.* Amherst: University of Massachusetts Press, 2006.

[Stoddard, Richard Henry]. *The Homes and Haunts of Our Elder Poets.* New York: D. Appleton and Company, 1881.

Stoddard, Richard Henry. *Poets' Homes. Pen and Pencil Sketches of American Poets and Their Homes.* Boston: D. Lothrop and Company, 1877.

Stokes, Claudia. *Writers in Retrospect: The Rise of American Literary History, 1875–1910.* Chapel Hill: University of North Carolina Press, 2006.

Stott, William. *Documentary Expression and Thirties America.* Chicago: University of Chicago Press, 1986.

Sugrue, Thomas J. *The Origins of the Urban Crisis: Race and Inequality in Postwar Detroit: With a New Preface by the Author.* A Princeton Classic Edition. 1st Princeton Classic ed. Princeton, NJ: Princeton University Press, 2005.

Sweets, Henry. "Mark Twain Home and Museum." *Journal of the West* 19, no. 1 (1980): 74–77.

Temple, Inez. *Pageants Past.* Ed. Ruth Wyllys. Hartford, CT: Hartford Chapter of the Daughters of the American Revolution, 1940.

Thomas, Julia. "Bringing Down the House: Restoring Shakespeare's Birthplace." *Literary Toursim and Nineteenth-Century Culture.* Ed. Nicola Watson. London: Palgrave Macmillan, 2009. 73–83.

Tilden, Freeman. *Interpreting Our Heritage; Principles and Practices for Visitor Services in Parks, Museums, and Historic Places.* Chapel Hill: University of North Carolina Press, 1957.

Trubek, Anne. "The Evidence of Things Unseen: The Sweet Gloom of Writers' House Museums." *The Believer,* October 6, 2006: 23–29.

Turner, Frederick Jackson. *The Frontier in American History.* New York: H. Holt and Company, 1920.

———, and State Historical Society of Wisconsin. *The Significance of the Frontier in American History.* Madison: State Historical Society of Wisconsin, 1894.

Twain, Mark. *Autobiography of Mark Twain.* Ed. Albert Bigelow Paine. Vol. 2. New York: Harpers, 1924.

———. *A Birthplace Worth Saving.* Ed. Lincoln Farm Association. New York: Lincoln Farm Association, 1906.

———. *The Innocents Abroad; or, the New Pilgrim's Progress.* Hartford, CT: American Publishing Company, 1870.

———. "A Lincoln Memorial: A Plea by Mark Twain for the Setting Apart of His Birthplace." *New York Times,* January 13, 1907, Sunday ed.:, 8.

———, and Michael J. Kiskis. *Mark Twain's Own Autobiography: The Chapters from the* North American Review. Wisconsin Studies in American Autobiography. Madison: University of Wisconsin Press, 1990.

———, and Charles Neider. *The Autobiography of Mark Twain.* New York: HarperCollins, 2000.

Tyrrell, Ian R. *Historians in Public: The Practice of American History, 1890–1970.* Chicago: University of Chicago Press, 2005.

Upton, Dell. *Architecture in the United States.* New York: Oxford University Press, 1998.

Wallace, Mike. *Mickey Mouse History and Other Essays on American Memory.* Critical Perspectives on the Past. Philadelphia: Temple University Press, 1996.

Walters, Joanna. "Washington DC and Its Freemasons Braced for New Dan Brown Book." London. *The Observer,* September 13, 2099. www.guardian.co.uk/books/2009/sep/13/the-lost-symbol-dan-brown (accessed January 29, 2012).

Wang, Ning. "Rethinking Authenticity in Tourism Experience." *Annals of Tourism Research* 26, no. 2 (1999): 349–70.

Watson, Nicola J. *The Literary Tourist: Readers and Places in Romantic and Victorian Britain.* New York: Palgrave Macmillan, 2007.

Weaver, Glenn, and Connecticut Historical Society. *Hartford: An Illustrated History of Connecticut's Capital.* 1st ed. Woodland Hills, CA: Windsor Publications, 1982.

Welter, Barbara. "The Cult of True Womanhood: 1820–1860." *American Quarterly* 18, no. 2 (1966): 151–74.

West, Patricia. *Domesticating History: The Political Origins of America's House Museums.* Washington, DC: Smithsonian Institution Press, 1999.

Westover, Paul Aaron. "How America 'Inherited' Literary Tourism." *Literary Tourism and Nineteenth-Century Culture.* Ed. Nicola Watson. London: Palgrave, 2009. 184–95.

Willis, Resa. *Mark and Livy: The Love Story of Mark Twain and the Woman Who Almost Tamed Him.* New York: Routledge, 2003.

Winkler, John A. *Mark Twain's Hannibal: Guide and Biography.* Hannibal, MO: Becky Thatcher Book Shop, 1946.

Winks, Robin W. *Cloak & Gown: Scholars in the Secret War, 1939–1961.* 2nd ed. New Haven, CT: Yale University Press, 1996.

# Index

*References to both Sam Clemens and Mark Twain are listed under Mark Twain. Mark Twain is abbreviated as MT. References to Twain's homes are listed primarily under birthplace home (Florida), boyhood home (Hannibal), adult home (Hartford), and summer home (Elmira). Page numbers in bold refer to illustrations in the text.*